655 - 3758

CANDIDATES '88

CANDIDATES '88

Marvin Kalb
Hendrik Hertzberg

Joan Shorenstein Barone Center on
the Press, Politics, and Public Policy
John F. Kennedy School of Government

AH *Auburn House Publishing Company*
Dover, Massachusetts

Library of Congress Cataloging in Publication Data

Candidates '88.

  Includes index.
    1. Presidents—United States—Election—1988.
  2. Presidential candidates—United States—Interviews.
  3. United States—Politics and government—1981–
  I. Kalb, Marvin L.   II. Hertzberg, Hendrik.
  E880.C366   1988   973.927'092'2   [B]   88-16603
  ISBN 0-86569-186-X

Printed in the United States of America

*To the memory of
Joan Shorenstein Barone,
a friend and colleague of warmth
and integrity.*

CONTENTS

ACKNOWLEDGMENTS

For a book, the obligatory list of acknowledgments can be long; for a book that was once a 12-hour television series the list can seem endless. But without the help of many dedicated people neither the series nor the book would have been possible. So here goes:

My thanks to Dean Graham Allison of the John F. Kennedy School of Government for his support, encouragement, and endless cheer, and to all of the others who helped: Dick Thornburgh, director of the Institute of Politics; Dave Runkel; Joe McCarthy; Heather Campion; Jennifer Jordan; Cathy McLaughlin; Bayley Mason; Geralyn White; Carol Sawyer; Steve Singer; Allison Sweeney; Lt. Larry Murphy of the Harvard Police; Jenny Raiser; Sue Wunderlee; Sheila Sheridan; Maryellen Fitzgerald; Naomi Notman; Maura Barrios; Mary Magnuson; and Bill Parent—and to my faculty colleagues who joined in the programs.

A separate note of gratitude is extended to Nancy Palmer, my administrative assistant and program executive, who was "present at the creation" of the project, providing at all times a mix of support, editorial assistance and toughness, encouragement in those inevitable moments of discouragement, patience, and intelligent guidance. She kept her eye on the sparrow's fall.

To my new friends at the New York Stock Exchange Foundation, thanks for all your help: Chairman John J. Phelan, Peter D. Moore, Richard Torrenzano, Greg Furman, Bill DeMeo, and Bob Zito.

To William Ruder and Arnold Hiatt, bless you.

To Walter Shorenstein, as always a friend and supporter.

To the good and creative people of the Public Broadcasting Service, led by Bruce Christensen and his able programming chief, Suzanne Weil, and to those at Boston station WGBH, who rolled up their sleeves and did the work with a consistent professionalism and personal warmth that made me wonder why I didn't get to work with them sooner: Steve Atlas, Aida Moreno, Geoffrey Little, Victoria Devlin, David Atwood, and Clara Bingham, who did the research for me week after week with clarity, diligence, and intelligence.

To John Harney and Eugene Bailey of Auburn House, who undertook the responsibility of publication with their customary efficiency.

To Hendrik Hertzberg, for his editorial suggestions and the graceful way he uses a blue pencil.

Finally, as always, to my wife, Madeleine, and my brother, Bernard, for their unfailing support, good cheer, editorial guidance, and judgment, again my hat off to them. How lucky can I be?

March 28, 1988   MARVIN KALB
                                                          Cambridge, Massachusetts

INTRODUCTION

by Marvin Kalb

"Candidates '88" was born in the dean's office at Harvard's John F. Kennedy School of Government on June 1, 1987. Present were the dean, Graham Allison, and a couple of fresh recruits: former Governor Dick Thornburgh of Pennsylvania, newly installed as director of the Institute of Politics; and myself. It was my first day on the job. I had left NBC News after a 30-year career in network broadcasting to return to Harvard, where, long ago, I had been a graduate student in Russian history. My new titles took almost as long to recite as the average network news story: Edward R. Murrow Professor of Press and Public Policy and Director of the Joan Shorenstein Barone Center on the Press, Politics, and Public Policy. You might say I'd gone from "Meet the Press" to "Ponder the Press."

The agenda in Dean Allison's office was the 1988 presidential campaign. The question was: How might the Kennedy School participate in the great national political ritual that was already beginning to get under way? We ran through some possibilities. A series of seminars, maybe mixing political operatives with academic observers? Not bad, but whatever we ended up doing ought really to involve the players: the candidates themselves. Well, then, how about a series of speeches by the candidates? The Harvard venue might stimulate them—or their speechwriters—to come up with something more substantive than the usual campaign platitudes. But one thing the candidates had plenty of was opportunities to make speeches. Surely Harvard could be more imaginative than that.

Debates? No, I said quickly. No debates. It was true that Harvard had sponsored a couple of them four years earlier, and they had gone pretty well. But 1988 was shaping up as the year of the Great Debate Overload. Dozens were already scheduled, and scheduling still more would add little to the store of public knowledge. In any case, I had serious questions about the form. My mind wandered back to the 1984 campaign. "Where's the beef?" Walter Mondale had asked Gary Hart—the one incandescent moment that everybody remembered. And why was it incandescent? Because it illuminated the issues with special sharpness? No, because it was pithy, memorable, and uncomplicated—a quote not from Tocqueville or Madison, but from a little old lady in a hamburger commercial. It was marketable, it was on television, and it sold.

But somehow it lacked the ring of history. Mondale and Hart had hardly been reincarnations of Lincoln and Douglas; nor had their encounters had much in common with the mid-19th century debates that pitted Calhoun and Clay against Webster, when substance mixed gracefully with style. This wasn't their fault, of course. The fact was that debates in the mid-20th century, brought to you live and in living color on network television, had become the prisoners of the mentality of the ten-second "bite." And with the mob of candidates already announced or preparing to announce, the "bite" problem was sure to be even worse this time around. Even a two-hour-long debate would afford each candidate only a few minutes of time, and the opportunities for follow-up, for any kind of sustained development of a point, would be close to nil.

If we had the option, I thought, it would be wise to resist the temptation to stage yet another debate and instead to resurrect the old-fashioned interview: a couple of chairs, a candidate, and a reporter. And, I suggested further, why not do the interview in front of an audience of students and faculty and allow them to ask questions, too? Dean Allison agreed, and Governor Thornburgh made it unanimous. We had ourselves an idea—if not yet a project.

The next question was where to go with the idea. My first thought, naturally, was one of the commercial networks, since their reach and their resources are incomparable. There was a time when it might have happened. On the CBS of Ed Murrow and Fred Friendly, 25 years earlier, such interviews had been common. In 1962, for example, I had done an hour-long one-on-one with Igor Tamm, a prominent Soviet physicist. But those were the days when the top line in network news departments was not yet the bottom line, when ratings were not yet the yardstick of successful TV journalism. There was, in my judgment, no way that the commercial networks would touch the idea—a judgment quickly confirmed by a few calls to New York and Washington.

There remained PBS, the Public Broadcasting Service. I called

Suzanne Weil, a bright and energetic programming executive at PBS, and she bought the proposal. She informed me that Ricki Green in Washington and Steve Atlas in Boston were coproducing PBS's campaign coverage. "Candidates '88"—the title seemed a natural from the very beginning—would fall under their jurisdiction.

A call to Atlas began an education in the—to me—mysterious new world of public broadcasting. Unlike the commercial networks, PBS was a network in name only. Once upon a time, there had been something called NET, National Educational Television, which, though chronically strapped for funds, had many of the attributes of a true network. It could produce programs, preempt time, make decisions—and make them stick. Under the Nixon administration, however, the system had been revamped and decentralized. The revamping had two goals. One was to encourage local initiative—and that was a grand success, with benefits flowing to viewers in many localities. The other goal was to prevent and reverse the emergence of a strong national noncommercial network—and that, alas, had succeeded as well (though programs such as the MacNeil/Lehrer NewsHour, fortunately, had moved in to fill some of the vacuum). PBS, NET's successor, had a devoted national following. But at the production level, it was more like a shifting consortium of ad-hoc arrangements than a real network. Each station was autonomous, so each could carry the program or not as it wished. Each had to be persuaded. "Candidates '88" was not a hard sell, but it took time to call the programming chiefs of the top 30 stations, inform them of our proposal, and gain their approval—especially when quite a few were doing the sensible thing and vacationing on a beach or a mountaintop retreat. It was, after all, summertime. Only mad dogs and Englishmen, candidates and Kalb were out in the midday sun.

But squeezing out "Spanish One" or "Cooking Two" or a rerun of "I, Claudius" on an otherwise sleepy Sunday afternoon schedule was only part of the problem. Public broadcasting, ironically, means private sponsorship. A commercial network can produce a program now and sell advertising time on it later; but on public TV, even though there are no commercial interruptions, the show does not go on without "first, a word from our sponsor." After long talks with Atlas, WGBH in Boston had decided to produce the series. But there remained the little matter of the approximately $40,000 it would cost to produce and transmit each one-hour broadcast from the Forum of the Kennedy School to the 310 stations that comprise the PBS network. Who was going to pay? The frantic search for a sponsor began. Atlas at first was certain that Harvard could just discretely nod in the direction of one of its many wealthy alumni, and the required $480,000 would simply materialize in the morning mail. I was equally certain that WGBH, home base of such illustrious programs as "Masterpiece Theater," "Frontline," "Nova," and "Mystery," could press the right buttons and produce a half-million dollars. Atlas brutally disabused me of my illusions about WGBH's financial clout. The responsibility was Harvard's. There were many calls to offices, beaches, and retreats, and many discouraging moments of silence and ambiguity. There was also a deadline. If we didn't get the money by mid-September, there wouldn't be enough time for the PBS stations to pencil in and publicize "Candidates '88," which was scheduled to start on Sunday, November 1, 1987. Nor did we yet have commitments from the candidates. Jennifer Jordan of the Institute of Politics was in the midst of the herculean job of finding the right people in the candidates' offices and nailing each candidate into a Sunday slot. I helped when Jordan ran into roadblocks. But the calendar looked disconcertingly empty of commitments as the clock ticked towards September 15, 1987. These were the days when even Nancy Palmer, my administrative assistant who also served as coproducer, director, expediter, and eternal flame of optimism, was getting discouraged.

Then Geralyn White, a resourceful 25-year-old graduate of Harvard College who was helping Dean Allison with a variety of fund-raising responsibilities, had an inspiration. She got through to Bill Ruder of Ruder and Finn, the New York public relations firm, and Ruder had his own inspiration: He would check with the New York Stock Exchange Foundation. He checked, and Peter Moore, the senior vice president, thought that it was a splendid project and, yes, the New York Stock Exchange would sponsor the series. Bingo! Now all we needed to do was get the candidates, no minor detail, on a series called "Candidates '88."

We decided to push for Jesse Jackson for the November 1 curtain-raiser. There were several good reasons. He was at the time the leading Democrat in the polls. Gary Hart, the previous front-runner, had withdrawn in early May, after the *Miami Herald* reported that he had spent the weekend in Washington with a model—a deed of such towering recklessness that his financial resources dried up, his campaign crumbled, and he retreated to the mountains of Colorado (for seven months, anyway). Senator Joseph Biden of Delaware, another prominent Democrat, had also just withdrawn after it was disclosed that he had lifted whole sentences from a campaign speech by British Labor Party leader Neil Kinnock and had misrepresented his academic achievements at Syracuse Law School. A snippet of C-Span videotape had provided the proof, and Biden, on the eve of opening and chairing Judiciary Committee hearings on the nomination of Judge Robert Bork to the Supreme Court, concluded that it was the better part of valor to fold up his presidential tent for 1988 and try again another year. So Jackson seemed the logical choice. There was another reason, too: He was a good television performer. In this age of imagery, when reality emerges out of a rectangular box, usually made in Japan, South Korea, or Taiwan, that meant we would have a good "show," and—who knows?—maybe even respectable ratings.

We had also considered Vice President George Bush as the lead guest. Indeed, we had made numerous efforts, contacting his campaign manager, Lee Atwater, and writing a number of letters to the candidate and those around him. But though their responses were uniformly polite, they were also ambiguous, soaked in suggestions that he was "busy" and "tired" and that he needed more time to consider our initial letter of invitation, which had gone out to the vice president, as it had gone out to all of the other candidates of the two major political parties, in late June. Ultimately, by mid-September, the persistent ambiguities from the vice president's chambers compelled us to move decisively towards Jackson, and we pulled out all the stops.

The Jesse Jackson in 1988 was not the Jesse Jackson of 1984. The clergyman from Chicago and the Carolinas had softened his image and broadened his message, but, like Bush and a number of the other candidates, he wanted to keep his options loose. Our key intermediary proved to be Ann Lewis, a smart, liberal Democratic party activist who was one of Jackson's closest advisers, and her word was pure gold. She returned calls, she delivered on her promises, and she produced Jackson for November 1, 1987.

Slowly our calendar of Sundays began to be populated with commitments. Ideally, we would have preferred a Republican to follow a Democrat, and so on, but campaign schedules are slithery things. We maintained a posture of maximum flexibility—and a change here, a change there, and we were in good shape. Republican Delaware Governor Pete du Pont appeared on November 8, 1987, then, in order, Republican Alexander Haig on November 15, Democrat Richard Gephardt on November 22, Democrat Michael Dukakis on November 29, Democrat Paul Simon on December 6, Republican Pat Robertson on December 13, Democrat Albert Gore on December 20, Republican Jack Kemp on December 27, a resurfaced Gary Hart on January 3, 1988 after a penciled-in George

Bush finally said no, Democrat Bruce Babbitt on January 10, and Republican Bob Dole in January 17.

The Bush decision to forego an appearance on "Candidates '88" is worth looking at, not only because it made headlines but also because it was instructive about the man and his campaign.

From no other candidate was it so difficult to get a decision. It was easy, after so many tantalizing calls, letters, and telegrams, to come to the conclusion that we were getting, as the expression goes, "jerked around." And no doubt there were a few in the Bush campaign engaged in that time-honored sport. But my view was that there was a genuine difference of opinion among Bush's top advisers, and that the vice president, after first feinting in one direction and then another, had problems making up his mind. Nancy Bush Ellis, his gracious sister, who lives near Boston, confided to a friend that the vice president was watching "Candidates '88," enjoyed the program, liked me, and, she thought, would ultimately agree to do the January 3 date. She urged him to do it several times. Another Bush friend, Harvard's Grand Marshall, Richard Hunt, urged him to do it. A number of Harvard professors with close contacts to the vice president's chief of staff, Craig Fuller, joined the chorus. Even Treasury Secretary James Baker got into the act. Within the vice president's own staff, Pete Teeley, his press spokesman, told me that he favored Bush's appearance. So did pollster Bob Teeter and others.

But the vice president's media adviser, Roger Ailes—an accomplished professional, clever, funny, unemotional, and tough-minded—vigorously and repeatedly opposed his appearance on "Candidates '88." Once he telephoned and said he was returning my call. But, I replied, though I am happy to talk with you, I didn't call you. Well, he said, trapped, what difference does it make? Let's talk anyway. He then criticized the "media" for its "shallowness" and concluded by saying, "An hour of substantive talk with Marvin Kalb and members of the Harvard community will not advance his candidacy." (I took notes on the conversation, because I found it so interesting.) And Chief of Staff Fuller added other reasons in conversations with mutual friends: The vice president was "tired," and "we have to be careful about not extending him too much," and "he has a 'preppie problem' and a visit to Harvard would only heighten it," and "why run any risks if we don't have to?"

Finally, after many such negative indications, I proposed a change in the format of "Candidates '88." In calls to Teeley, I said that I would accommodate the vice president's fatiguing schedule by taking the show to him: I would go anywhere, at any time, on any day of the week except Sunday, and tape an hour-long interview—no Harvard, no students, no faculty, no travel for the vice president. We'd either slide that interview into the January 3 slot or we'd extend the series a week and run the interview on January 24, 1988. Teeley saw some promise in the proposal; we even discussed two windows of opportunity, for Monday, December 21, or Tuesday, December 22.

But it was not to be. Not Pete Teeley but one of his assistants, Barbara Pardue, called late Tuesday afternoon after numerous prodding calls from me, to state, definitively, that the vice president had decided to skip "Candidates '88," the only one of the candidates to reach that decision. Why? The official reason was that he was "overbooked." The unofficial reasons we already knew—that he didn't want to visit Harvard and that, following Ailes' advice, he felt it was safer for his campaign to sidestep an hour of substantive conversation with me on PBS.

Did Ailes think I would be "too tough" on the vice president? Columnist Ellen Goodman was later to describe my interviewing style as "civilized persistence," but "too tough"? I doubted it. If Bush could handle Rather, as he was later to prove, then he could surely handle Kalb. No, Bush and his aides had obviously decided to run a "safe" campaign. He emerged from the vice presidential cocoon of Air Force Two, the limousines and helicopters, and the phalanx of Secret Service agents only once—after the drubbing Bob Dole gave him in Iowa and before the pro-Reagan Republicans of New Hampshire gave him a new lease on life. For a week, he joined the fray. He drove tractors and kissed babies and acknowledged that though he didn't talk eloquently on TV, he cared, and that was enough. Instead of losing to Dole, as many journalists and a Gallup poll predicted, Bush won by 9 points—a solid victory that so traumatized Dole that on NBC that night, the Senate minority leader accused the vice president of "lying about my record," hardly a gracious way to lose. After New Hampshire, Bush returned to the safe nest of incumbency, riding President Reagan's coattails to a commanding lead in the quest for the GOP nomination. Bush sought to "corner the nomination," in Albert Hunt's phrase, "rather than capture it." The incident revealed a propensity in Bush and his operation for overcalculation, overcaution, and overconfidence—qualities that could create problems for him as his party's nominee or his country's president.

All of the candidates, Republican and Democratic, knew that 1988 was a special campaign. For the first time since 1960, no incumbent was running for reelection. The comparisons were easy, deceptively so. An old and popular Republican President was finishing his second term in office. His vice president sought to succeed him, though some questioned the legitimacy of the inheritance. A new and clever Soviet leader was offering tantalizing proposals. The country was being rocked by a major scandal: in 1960, the U.S. spy plane affair, which destroyed the summit in Paris; in 1987, the Iran-Contra mess, which cracked the Teflon in the Reagan presidency. The economy was shaky: recession in 1960, stock market uneasiness in 1988.

Yet as the candidates were more aware than anybody, the differences were even more striking than the similarities. The old Democratic coalition had been shattered. A black man was conducting a surprisingly successful campaign. The South seemed more Republican than Democratic. The parties had grown weaker and at the same time more coherent: The ideological realignment of American politics had proceeded apace, and increasingly the Democratic party was the "liberal" party, the Republicans the "conservative" one. The number of adult Americans over the age of 25 carrying a college degree in their hip pockets had doubled. They formed a new and volatile voting group—not "yuppies," exactly, but something distinct from either the blue-collar and white-collar voters of old. Between 1972 and 1986, according to the Bureau of Labor Statistics, there had been a net increase of 27.4 million new jobs, most of them white collar and nearly two-thirds of them going to women. Yet individual real incomes had actually declined over that period—a new phenomenon in American life—and it was only the extra paychecks those women workers were bringing home that had kept family incomes flat. Fully half of married women were working. They too represented a new and major voting force, a bloc that could no longer be ignored. Nor could the Hispanic voter.

In 1960, the country seemed optimistic. John F. Kennedy could speak of a rising tide that would lift all boats. Twenty-eight years later, according to the pollster Daniel Yankelovich, "the mood is much more Darwinistic. There are still winners, but you can be a loser if you don't scramble." In 1988, Americans worried about the future, their own and the country's. They worried about education, about economic competitiveness, about their families, about the specter of national decline. Much would depend on the outcome of the presidential election. Yet a vast number of citizens—probably the majority—remained apathetic and uninvolved.

Part of the reason was fatigue with the extraordinary length of the campaign. It tells you something that although the campaign had already begun when we conceived the idea for "Candidates '88," we were able to originate, organize, and carry out a 12-week series—and have it finished and done with before a single ballot had been cast.

Another problem, we were told over and over again, was the quality of the candidates. Rarely in American political history had so many candidates produced so few sparks and so many yawns. The Democrats were described at one point as the "seven dwarfs" and at another point as the "six-pack," and the Republicans, on a scale from one to ten, inched their way toward a three in dynamism, excitement, and substantive illumination of issues on a good day. Such, at any rate, were the judgments of the political pundits; and there was some truth to them. Yet these were and are glib and misleading generalizations. In preparing for each candidate week after week—reading their speeches, watching them in debates, talking with their aides, sharing impressions with reporters on the trail—and then in encountering the candidates themselves, I developed a grudging admiration for almost all of them. The people who ran for president of the United States in 1988 are serious men and sturdy patriots. They are well-educated and well-informed, and whether their prescriptions for the nation's ills are radical or cautious, they are sincerely dedicated to the welfare of their country.

Yet something is obviously broke, and needs fixing. The fault does not lie primarily with the candidates, who are neither better nor worse than the average run of presidential aspirants throughout most of our history. No, the problem is the Rube Goldberg contraption called the American presidential election system. It goes on for too long, it costs too much money, it bores the voters, and it tires the candidates—so much so that when one finally is elected, he will stagger into the Oval Office in a state of such total exhaustion that he will scarcely be able to cope properly with the responsibilities of the job. And there is no other job like it in the world.

The process distorts the ways the candidates feel compelled to present themselves. Understandably, they wish to give as little offense as conscience allows, while at the same time looking and sounding "presidential"—no easy task. They are crammed with set responses to nearly every conceivable question, little mental tape loops twenty seconds in length or forty seconds or even as long as a minute. To go on much longer, to give a subject the nuance and detail it deserves, is to risk getting what vaudevillians used to call the hook. Paul Simon took four and a half minutes to answer my opening question about how he was planning to balance the budget in three years. Click, click, click went television sets all over the country, as benumbed viewers sought relief in football. Maybe that was one reason why Simon, after Iowa and New Hampshire, suddenly found himself out of money—and opportunity. Invariably, regardless of the question or the occasion, the candidates smile as they scan the room for the red eye of the camera, the most coddled and cherished piece of technology in the history of presidential politics. They smile because they believe that the voter likes a smiling candidate, just as the viewer likes a smiling anchorman. And as they explain their policies, all oversimplified, their hands perform a ballet of counting and gesturing and stroking—because always the camera is watching, and the camera is allergic to the static scene. Action, rhetoric, motion—a whirlwind of activity signifying at one and the same time everything and nothing. The candidate who can hold attention, in addition to money and organization, is likely to win—even if what he says and does to hold attention is unworthy of the office he seeks.

The campaign has become, Senator Edward Kennedy has argued, "a grinding cattle show in which all the incentives are to play for short-term advantage." Speaking in the same forum from which "Candidates '88" originated, the senior senator from Massachusetts faulted the press as well as the process. Shallowness, silliness, and a fixation with trivia mark the press's approach, he says, rather than a preoccupation with "principles, problems and possible solutions." But Kennedy must know that for every reporter who plunges into trivia, there is a politician, or a candidate, who cooperates. The process itself is in urgent need of repair. It's reached a point where only one out of every two eligible voters goes to the polls to pick a president, and the trend is down. In 1986, in the off-year election for the House and Senate, only 37 percent of eligible voters cast their ballots. The turnout promises to be slightly better than that in 1988, but it may still be the lowest in any presidential year in our history. We may yet see a time when they hold an election and nobody comes.

The presidential nominating system is a mess because we have allowed it to become one, forfeiting our collective responsibility to take control of our own fate as a nation. There are those who say that we should leave well enough alone, that after all we do muddle through somehow with things as they are, that we shouldn't tinker with something that works, however imperfectly. I find that a dangerously complacent view. The warning signs of public apathy and alienation are too obvious to be ignored.

I don't think anyone would seriously argue that if the Founders of our republic could somehow be magically resurrected and asked to design a system for choosing candidates for president, they would come up with the one we've got. It's hard to imagine James

Madison saying, "I've got an idea—let's force all the candidates to spend a year campaigning in a place called Iowa," or Benjamin Franklin saying, "Here's another brilliant thought—let's make sure the candidates have to spend six or seven hours a day on the phone begging and wheedling for campaign contributions." Our Constitution devotes many lines to the details of where the Electoral College shall meet and how its votes shall be counted. Yet where something infinitely more important is concerned—choosing the two persons who will ultimately compete for the highest office in the land—we are content to leave it up to a crazy hodge-podge of local election laws, chamber-of-commerce boosterism, and party rules designed for short-term factional advantage.

Recent efforts at reform have collapsed. Perhaps they deserved to, because the motives behind them were parochial. For example, Super Tuesday, March 8, 1988, was to have been the way the South reasserted its original clout and selected a Democrat of moderate conservative views who could win in November. In the event, some of the best laid plans of Robb and Nunn went astray, and essentially, the Democratic liberals triumphed again, as quite a few conservatives stayed home or crossed over and voted Republican. But the purpose of reform should not be to guarantee that this or that region, or this or that ideological tendency, has influence beyond its numbers. The purpose should be to guarantee that the American people have an opportunity to make informed, responsible choices—and that the outcome reflects, as best as is humanly possible, their will.

As Robert Kennedy used to say, we can do better. Is it too much to hope that, at some point in the foreseeable future (the spring of 1989, for example), the wise men and women of American politics might gather at the summit and, without turning the event into a media fandango, try to design a system worthier of a great democracy? The goals such an effort might pursue need not be all that controversial: a shorter, more sharply focused campaign; a campaign financing system less exacting in terms of time and humiliation; a combination of "retail" and "wholesale" primaries, so as to keep the process open, but with the opportunity to participate in the early stages distributed among different, perhaps more representative, states in different years. Beyond the issues of 1988 or any other year is the much larger issue of how we go about governing ourselves. That issue deserves to be addressed—and it deserves to be addressed before, not after, some unforeseen catastrophe forces it on our attention.

Candidates '88

A CONVERSATION WITH
JESSE JACKSON

About the Candidate
by Hendrik Hertzberg

This was the year Jesse Jackson became—to borrow a word from the shout-and-response chant in which he has led countless crowds—somebody. Not that he wasn't somebody before: On the contrary, he has been world-famous since 1968, when, to the continuing outrage of some of his colleagues in the civil rights movement, he figuratively seized the banner of the fallen Martin Luther King, Jr. But in 1988 a subtle change seemed to come over Jackson and his reputation. It was as if he had fully achieved the ambition of his youth, and had conceived a set of new, still somewhat cloudy, ambitions. He had succeeded in becoming the essentially unquestioned leader of his fellow citizens of color—the president, so to speak, of black America. Now his sights were set on something more. The notion of Jesse Jackson on a national Democratic ticket no longer seemed outlandish, if not this year then four or eight or twelve years hence. (He was, after all, still only 46 years old.) And in 1988 Jackson earned—indeed, seized by main force—the kind of respect that had always eluded him.

As a presidential candidate Jackson was unique, and not only because of his race. The traditional route to the presidency is electoral: You run for lower office and win, or you serve with distinction in high appointive office, and only then do you run for president. But there is another political tradition in America, the tradition of protest—what Europeans call "extraparliamentary" politics. In our time that tradition has produced such influential figures as Ralph Nader, Betty Friedan, and arguably the most important "politician" of the postwar era, Dr. King. It also produced Jesse Jackson.

Born in humble circumstances in South Carolina, Jackson rose to prominence while still a student at all-black North Carolina Agricultural and Technical University, where he led civil rights demonstrations. His rise in the movement was swift: In 1966, just two years out of college, he was picked by Dr. King to head the labor and economic affairs department of the Southern Christian Leadership Conference. After King's death he moved to Chicago and founded a group called Operation PUSH, which in one form or another has remained his organizational base ever since.

The Reverend Jackson—he is an ordained minister, though he has never had a parish of his own—has been criticized for many things: demagoguery, lack of follow-up, financial irregularities in his organizations, a focus on getting jobs and favors for a few blacks rather than justice for all, and a polarizing confrontationalism. His groundbreaking 1984 presidential race was badly damaged by his reference to Jews as "Hymies" and his association with the anti-Semitic Black Muslim leader Louis Farrakhan.

Things were different in 1988. By the time of his appearance on "Candidates '88," Jackson had already demonstrated that his campaign was better organized than it had been four years before, and that he himself was a calmer, more skilled, less error-prone candidate. Though still on the left fringe of the mainstream, he had moderated his fiery Third World rhetoric and recast his positions to appeal to a broader range of voters. Without forsaking his role as a spokesman for the poor and powerless, he was making a conscientious effort to reach beyond his former base. And as the primaries were to show, he was beginning to make a reality of what he still occasionally called his "rainbow coalition."

The Interview

KALB: Reverend Jackson, you've got a couple of friends here. I'm not sure who stacked the audience, your people or ours.

JACKSON: I think it's because they knew that the New York Stock Exchange is sponsoring this program.

KALB: Indeed.

JACKSON: And they want to make certain you got the grant before the program went on the air.

KALB: That's right. Well, you are a candidate now, but for the purposes of our early round of questioning, let's assume that you are the nominee of your party, and let's even go one step further. It is November 5, 1988, a little over a year from now, and you have been elected president of the United States. What are the first three things you would like to do? The first three things.

JACKSON: The budget deficit and trade imbalance have us in a very vulnerable position because we're dependent upon foreign forces now for capital and energy, and this dependence subjects our military to manipulation. That's why we're trapped in the Persian Gulf now in ways that are not necessarily healthy for us as a nation because of a certain implied threat. We should convene members of the House and Senate and in a bipartisan way drive this budget deficit down, get some grip on our trade imbalance. Reach beyond that to the key financial leaders on Wall and LaSalle Streets and key governors, and have a bipartisan Camp David economic summit meeting. Beyond that, dispatch the secretary of the treasury to key financial markets to assure them that the budget deficit will come down and that we will be moving out of the Persian Gulf or, if we remain there, be part of a more multilateral patrol. I think that driving the deficit down and bringing the trade imbalance in line is important because right now the fact that foreign countries can slow down the purchase of our debt or can slow down the distribution of oil puts us in a very vulnerable position.

KALB: Okay. Now you've mentioned the secretary of the treasury. Give us a sense of your cabinet. Who do you think would be your secretary of state?

JACKSON: Well, it's a bit premature to name names.

KALB: Yes, but you must have some people in mind.

JACKSON: I do have some people in mind, but I would not feel free to project their names in this context. After all, at this stage we're in a Democratic primary, and there is a long list of a variety of people who no doubt would serve in any Democratic administration.

KALB: But what I'm trying to get at is some sense of the way you would govern in a Jackson administration. What kind of people would you have around? Would you seek a balance between liberals on the one side, conservatives on the other?

JACKSON: Well, there must be some sense of balance so as to represent the broad cross-section of the American people. On the other hand, the president must assume the responsibility to project a vision for the country, to give a sense of direction, to interpret the dream.

Two weeks ago when the stock market crashed, I felt frankly that President Reagan panicked in that situation.

KALB: He panicked?

JACKSON: He panicked. The stock market was crashing. He went to one camera and said, "The house is not on fire, and those who say it is are irrational." To another camera he said, "Congress set the house on fire, and all of these programs for poor people represent the fuel." The fact is that if the house is on fire, it's not the time to start determining who is the arsonist. Rather, it's the time to calm the fears of the inhabitants. It's the time to get them to a safe place. It's the time to get an extinguisher.

So what should have happened in my judgment? Convince the country that we do have a problem, but it's not a crisis that is beyond control. Convene key Senate and House leaders and give a sense of a collective leadership with a definite direction. And that did not happen. To me that's real governance. It's vision, it's courage of convictions. It's not panicking under pressure.

KALB: Okay. Now George Bush said a couple of nights ago that he would like to go down in history, if he is elected president of the United States, as the education president.

If you're elected, what would you like to go down in history as?

JACKSON: Well, George Bush, interestingly enough, is the only candidate who in this crisis cannot quote himself, for it was his analysis of voodoo economics that was such a profound one, and President Reagan did not convert him. He hired him, and his silence is a factor in the leadership gap that we have now.

If I am elected, it is significant to me that we stop drugs from coming into this country. Stop jobs from going out, which means economic stability at home and a foreign policy that is coherent and will lend itself to peace and justice in the world. I would project a foreign policy doctrine that would have three basic components. One, support and strengthen international law.

When we, for example, mine the harbors in Nicaragua and ignore the World Court, we destroy that body. So when the Ayatollah does it in the Persian Gulf, we cannot call upon the world because we have violated a very basic principle. Secondly, support self-determination and human rights. And thirdly, provide an economic alternative. If we use that approach of supporting and strengthening international law, supporting self-determination and human rights, and providing economic alternatives to drive down debt crisis in the Third World, that policy applied to Latin America will open the gateway for four million neighbors, allies, customers. Applied in the Middle East, and also in Africa, will make us a much more secure and a much stronger nation.

KALB: Let me ask you this question which relates to the possible way in which you would govern. You yourself have never been elected to public office. There are critics of yours who say that in the Jackson wake is mismanagement. This is a criticism. How, if you're elected president, can you ensure that the government would have a more effective manner of control, of leadership?

JACKSON: First of all, four presidents of the 41 had never held public office. General Eisenhower and General Grant had not held public office. The reach out for Iacocca earlier this year was because of the sense that he had the capacity to shape a consensus and represent a point of view. Well, I bring to bear the capacity to shape a consensus, to build a point of view, and to articulate policy—to communicate, to bring people a sense of assurance. The founding fathers realized very well that all leadership would not come from the elected ranks, that there were ways to become effective leaders other than that. And so it is not establishing any historical precedent in that sense.

I'm convinced that what the leader must do is to project the vision and to have the courage at the point of crisis. And point of crisis is Eisenhower making a judgment about Little Rock in 1957. A point of crisis is President Kennedy making a judgment about Cuba in the early days of his administration. The point of crisis is called a convening at Camp David—an activist president who makes things happen.

I went to Syria to get Lieutenant Robert Goodman and bring him home because it was the point of challenge. It was using minimal resources to get maximum return. I went to Cuba to bring Americans back home, to unify Cuban-American families, and to challenge Castro, as it were.

KALB: Yeah, but you're not really saying, Reverend Jackson, that those are illustrations of governance, of the way you would govern? That is, leaping into a particular situation and extracting an American hostage, which is excellent. I'm talking about the nature of governing an extraordinarily complex environment.

JACKSON: There's several levels, and the first is that presidents must set the tone through initiative. Eisenhower going to Korea was not an example of governance. It was an example of leadership that set the tone for leadership. To be sure, you simply convene a credible transition team of very able and capable people who have had experience in government, some who've not had experience in government, and you lay out your basic direction and expect that cabinet of credible and able people to carry out their duties faithfully.

KALB: But you can't share with us the kind of people you would bring in. Can you give us five names of people you would like to lean on?

JACKSON: I choose not to. What I would do as executive is respect the Congress and not attempt to circumvent it. The idea of selling arms to the Ayatollah illegally and sending him a cake which he does not eat, a Bible which he does not read, is an example of what one should not do. Communicating with the Congress is key because you have this vast body of experience and involvement in the House and Senate. And on critical matters affecting our national interest, to have a bipartisan approach is the way of maximizing a consensus.

Even now in the Persian Gulf situation. The reason why I would hope that the War Powers Act would be respected is because it's a way of saying if the executive and legislative both can agree on a definition of national interest and national security, chances are the American people will follow such an initiation by the president. So it's collective leadership by the House and executive, and the people will then follow.

As it is now, we are dividing ourselves because the vision starts at the executive, separated from the legislative, holding it in contempt, and that is a way to divide our nation and make us weaker.

KALB: Reverend Jackson, let's talk about the use of nuclear weapons, which is something that hangs over any president and his responsibilities in office. When you were four years old, Harry Truman made a very, very historic decision to drop two atom bombs on Hiroshima and Nagasaki. What do you think of that decision?

JACKSON: Well, I think it was an unnecessary dropping of the bombs.

KALB: Unnecessary?

JACKSON: It's left to much debate now, but it was clear that Japan was moving toward submission. The argument, of course, is that the dropping of the bomb sped up the process. I do not identify with that particular decision. Of course, we now have a different set of options because a nuclear strike now will invite a counterstrike, and so first use will induce first response at which time you've chosen mutual annihilation over coexistence. And fundamentally this is the time to make the move toward mutually verifiable reductions in nuclear weapons because the overkill capacity on both sides is really beyond control, and all of us are really living in a time bomb situation, with the ticker getting much louder and much closer. That's why the President Reagan and Gorbachev meeting, as it were, in Washington, December 7, is a—well, put it this way—

KALB: It's a good thing?

JACKSON: It's a good thing. It's a modest step for mankind, a giant step for President Reagan. It's the biggest step, the biggest step he's taken in this direction. Modest because it's a 2 percent cut in the nuclear stockpile. Good because it reduces the whole class of those weapons, and the fact that it would be mutually verifiable takes a step toward deeper cuts. Mutually verifiable.

I'm concerned that what is happening now with the weapons pointing one to the other, that we should not contradict this process by adding on new classes of weapons in the name of modernization. Given our budget deficit on the one hand and our nuclear surplus on the other, why should we contradict that with a Midgetman system costing 45 billion more dollars, Star Wars costing a half trillion to a trillion more dollars, or additional aircraft task forces when we already have 12 to 13?

So I think the meeting is a step in the right direction, but we should not complicate it or should I say contradict it?

KALB: Okay. But I want to go back to Truman for a second. His problem at that time—and it was a major presidential and, in fact, historic decision—was this: His military people came to him and said, "If we do not use these bombs, we may lose a million Americans invading the islands of Japan. We may have several hundred thousand Americans dead. If we use the bomb, we probably avoid that catastrophe in American lives." That was his problem—the balancing of the loss of several hundred thousand Americans as opposed to the use of the bombs themselves. That is the nature of what I'm trying to get at.

JACKSON: Of course, in some sense the president becomes a

prisoner of the information that one receives. Protecting our troops, our national interest is always first. After all, our military function is to do what? Deter war, defend our country, defeat the enemy if we must fight, protect our vital interests. And so, within the context of those guidelines, one would have to do whatever is necessary to protect our vital interest first. I suppose on reflection we can argue the case that information was not as broad as it should have been.

KALB: But that's the information he had. He had to make the decision.

JACKSON: And so he made the best choice he could make with the information that he had.

KALB: But if you were there, would you have gone the other way and not used the bombs?

JACKSON: Well, if I had the obligation to protect the lives of a million Americans, in light of what happened in terms of the attack on Pearl Harbor, I could very well have made that same decision with that information.

I have different information in 1987 relative to this country and the Soviet Union as well as nuclear proliferation in other countries. While Mr. Reagan and Mr. Gorbachev are moving toward an agreement in the Washington scene on December 7, my concern is not just what we would do with a control relationship with the Soviets, but about proliferation of nuclear weapons in countries less stable, which have become an even greater threat because they're forces beyond a president's control. All you can do there is to try to stop the proliferation before the fact. As for the Soviets, we would do well to be aggressive in our attempts to reduce the nuclear stockpile on the one hand. On the other hand, we should begin to look toward an alternative to the cold war—that is, expansion of trade and cultural ties so as to reduce the tensions.

KALB: Okay. But a lot of presidents have tried to do that in recent years and stumbled upon reality in any of a number of ways. On the nuclear issue, do you feel that as president—

JACKSON: I must say that moving toward arms control agreements and arms reductions agreements is reality. It's the most critical reality of our day.

KALB: I'm not arguing that point at all.

JACKSON: Well, I want to make my point.

KALB: Okay.

JACKSON: And we must be tough when it comes to defending our national interest but sensitive when we look at what our real

options are. I think that the shift away from the evil empire
rhetoric, the shift away from exciting the American public and
inciting the Soviets and moving toward the celebration of a signing
represents real mature and strong leadership. More weapons and
more money have made us less secure, not more secure, and that's
the fact of our day.

KALB: Now on the use of nuclear weapons, again, would you
as president be able to hit the button, ignite the weapons that
would destroy the Soviet Union if it was required?

JACKSON: What I'm aware of is that pushing that button
would trigger a counterbutton, which would mean mutual annihilation. It's not a live choice.

KALB: You could not?

JACKSON: Well, I should not have to. We have the choice.

KALB: But if you're faced with it, would you do it?

JACKSON: I am convinced that is not the challenge we have,
because it is the last act of desperation, and one does not become
a hero or a counterhero in the mutual annihilation option. We have
the option now to push guided leadership and not misguided
missiles. That's my concern. I want to represent guided leadership
before the fact and not misguided missiles. Clearly, we have 13,000
nuclear warheads pointed at the Soviets today; 25,000 plus in our
stockpile. They have weapons pointed at us. We have the capacity,
even this day, without pushing the button, I might add. Many of
them are on computers, so that by a human error, by a computer
malfunction, perhaps by an unauthorized agent programming the
machinery, we can have that war right now. That's why there's
such an urgency toward moving away from the trigger and to an
ultimate decision.

KALB: I don't want to drive this point too far, and we'll stop
after one more effort. I just want to know if, in that moment you,
ex-minister, now president, could hit the button to carry out an
obligation that you would have taken as president to defend this
country against all enemies, foreign and domestic. If you had to do
it, could you do it?

JACKSON: I will defend our interests. I will make the intelligent decision, given my options at that moment. We should not
move toward the brink, move any closer toward that brink than we
are right now. I think the decision I really would make is the one
to go to Geneva and Iceland and now to Washington. That's a
bigger decision than saying, "Sure, I would push the button." But
then when we push the button, the Russians would not be crochet-

ing. They will also push a button, and so pushing a button for mutual annihilation does not represent sound leadership.

KALB: Okay. Hang on. Let's switch. Let's switch to the Supreme Court. The man the President has now moved forward as a nominee for the top court is Judge Douglas Ginsburg. Senator Kennedy has called him a clone of Bork. Some of the more facetious characters have called him "son of Bork." What is your own feeling about Judge Ginsburg? Should he be on the Supreme Court?

JACKSON: I do not want to prejudge him. I do not have very much information about him yet. In the case of Judge Bork it was not his age or even conservatism that threatened us. It was his direction. The issue was not conservative or liberal. It was backward or forward. He represented backwardness and he threatened many people. When a woman had the choice between sterilization and a job, he made women feel less secure. A truck driver said, "I don't want to drive the truck. It's unsafe for me with the road conditions." He was fired. Judge Bork sided with the company.

His lack of sensitivity to the need for civil rights threatens a whole body of people and is relative to textile workers and antitrust legislation. So it was his divisiveness that threatened so many people. I suppose that Judge Ginsburg, if he has that same kind of record, will meet that same kind of Senate challenge. But I suspect that if he does not have that kind of a very negative rating, the Senate will be less likely to relate to him the way they did to Judge Bork.

KALB: You have no problem with the president appointing to the Supreme Court a man he feels very comfortable with, who shares his political and economic and philosophical views, do you?

JACKSON: The president should have that option, but the president ought to be sensitive to not just his views but to the views of the entire country. After all, the Supreme Court, to protect its integrity and its credibility, must make people feel secure that they can get justice there—not ideology there, not Democrats there, not Republicans there. That they can get a sense of fairness there.

So beyond academic preparation and the measure of experience, the Supreme Court Justice must give the impression that he or she is capable of being just and fair. Judge Bork did not represent that. He represented an extension of the narrow ideology of President Reagan and Mr. Meese. And it was unfortunate for the country to have to go through the agony of that.

KALB: Let's move on to U.S.-Soviet relations and a question that's on the mind of many of the people who are in this school. Gorbachev is a rather electric figure, a new figure on the international scene. Is it in the interest of this country to help him succeed politically and for the Soviet Union to succeed economically?

JACKSON: Well, the extent to which they are secure, the extent to which we have relations with them, reduces tensions in the world, it is in our interest. It's not in our interest to have a president use the bully pulpit to excite the American public with more fears and incite the Soviets. It's not in our interest to create more tensions because that contributes to the arms race. Every time insecurity rises in the Soviet Union, insecurity rises in this country. When the meeting takes place December 7 in Washington, all of us will feel a little more secure. On guard, but a little more secure. It's better we talk, talk, talk, than threaten, threaten, threaten and fight, fight, fight. That's why meeting once a year with the Soviet leader should become standard operating procedure and not just an occasional dramatic event. We should make mutual interest and mutual security a part of the mandate of the White House.

KALB: You said earlier on in the program, when I asked you what you would do if you were elected president, the first thing you said was that you would convene a major meeting, a kind of Camp David meeting, to deal with the economy because that's in serious trouble. You have also said that you would like to see, and you would initiate, structural changes in the U.S. economy. Give me an example or two of what you mean by a structural change in the economy.

JACKSON: At this point, for example, multinational corporations are beyond the accountability of the U.S. government. There's no sense of regulation, nor are there incentives for them to reinvest in America and retrain our workers. And so GM announces in November the closing of 11 plants, affecting 30,000 jobs and all the small businesses that went with that, and opened up 30,000 jobs in South Korea the same week. There is a tax deduction for opening a plant there; our jobs, our capital, our tax base are exported. South Korea did not take our jobs. GM took our jobs to South Korea. Because they're better laborers? No, because they are cheaper laborers who do not have the right to vote and can't organize free trade unions.

KALB: So what is the—

JACKSON: The same incentives should be applied to merging corporations. Leverage buys and purging workers should be shifted to reinvest in America, retrain our workers, reindustrialize our nation, do research for the development and reconversion to a civilian peacetime economy. And that would be structural change, a shift in incentives. That's a major thrust.

KALB: Okay. Let's talk about politics now. The critics of the Democratic party refer to you and your five colleagues racing for the Democratic nomination as the six dwarfs. Why do you think that image has spread throughout the country?

JACKSON: Because the media has the capacity to perpetuate its myths. That does not make it so. These are very credible men who are public servants wrestling with the great issues of our day, and perhaps some media forces are waiting for the Camelot of their dreams either to build up or to destroy.

KALB: Who do you think that Camelot is?

JACKSON: Well, I do not know who that Camelot is or could be. They go—

KALB: Was he your host on Friday, Governor Cuomo?

JACKSON: Well, he certainly is a credible figure. Some of them have gone from looking for Governor Cuomo to Lee Iacocca to wishing for the return of Roosevelt. They've gone all over the lot, dancing around reality. The reality is that one of the six now running will be the nominee of our party, and that becomes a fact that they must face.

KALB: Okay. Now when you arrive at the convention next summer, you will have a sizable block of delegates. Let us assume that at that time it is set up that Jesse Jackson probably is not going to get the nomination but he's got a lot of power. The question is, What does Jesse want? How is he going to use that power?

JACKSON: First of all, we need not assume that Jesse Jackson will not have the nomination when he gets there.

KALB: I began by assuming that you had it. And I'm now at that point of—

JACKSON: If I had the nomination, then I would use that power to determine who will be my vice presidential choice, and I will determine who my transition team will be as we prepare for an all-out battle with the Republicans for the election in November.

KALB: But my question is, If you do not get the nomination, what is it that you want out of the party's nominee? Out of the Democratic party?

JACKSON: That would be the time to convene the other Democratic leadership and hammer away at a direction that our party must take according to the three keys to our winning in 1988. One, we must expand the party, turn the mainstream into a flowing river, because a stream is too narrow. Enough people can't get in it. The key to victory is expansion. In 1984 critics said I would be divisive. In fact, I was expansive. Two million new Democrats voted Democratic. The reason why the Democrats now have control of the Senate is mostly because of my work, not the competitors in this race. The reason why Judge Bork is now moving toward trivia as opposed to the Supreme Court is because Joe Biden was Senate chairman as opposed to Strom Thurmond, and that was because two million new Democrats voted, put in four senators in 1984, another class in 1986. So the key is expansion. The second key is to build a broad-based coalition. Whether paper workers in Jay, Maine, or meat packers in Wisconsin, or farmers in Greenville, Iowa, or people in urban America, I have pulled together the most diverse body of Democrats of anybody else running. And thirdly, to change our priorities so as to put jobs, peace, and justice in their proper perspective. I'll expect the others around that table to have uppermost the ability to expand our party with more participation, to build a coalition, and to put together priorities that will make a difference on the tables of the average American family.

And, Marvin, people fear the further loss of family farms and with good reason. They fear the exportation of jobs and the importation of drugs. They fear the cutback in educational opportunities for our children and lack of affordable housing. Those are the bread and butter issues that are the sum and substance of the Democratic party, and with that consensus we can together win the election.

KALB: Okay. Reverend Jackson, I have had my turn to ask you questions, but I think that the audience deserves a turn to ask you questions as well. I'd like to start with the dean of the John F. Kennedy School of Government, Graham Allison.

ALLISON: Reverend Jackson, I'd like to ask a complex question that lies at the heart of the center of which Marvin is the director. The question concerns the illuminating as well as the distorting effects of television on politics and government. Last week former German Chancellor Schmidt argued that television is undermining democratic politics and government, turning politicians into, as he said, "great actors and TV anchor men." I'd be interested in your reactions to his view.

JACKSON: Well, TV—

KALB: Be nice to television.

JACKSON: Television does not create the situation. It illuminates the situation. I suppose it's according to what side of the spectrum you're on. It was said, for example, during the heat of the civil rights movement in this country, that were it not for TV dramatizing dogs biting children in the South, it would not have been successful. Well, TVs were not biting children. They were covering dogs biting children, put upon them by people who were unkind and who were mean, and so TV properly used can simply be a medium for mass education.

Often what is a concern of mine is that the agenda of the TV producer may be different from the scene as it really is. For example, every day I face the cultural lag of the TV producer and commentator who says, "But he can't win." That's a very clear statement made thousands of times every day. It has a percentage of lag on the candidacy. That's not said of any other candidate, no matter how low they may be in the poll or how unlikely they are to win. First, let's look at it. As a matter of fact, if this were a feudal country and I was not the president or my daddy was not the king, I could not win. But in a democracy it is not even logical, it's not even accurate, and yet it's said every day as if it becomes the fact of life because it's been projected so much over TV. I got off a plane in Memphis two weeks ago and a reporter came to me, having heard some of the network projection of that, saying, "Reverend Jackson, how does it feel to be stuck at 27 percent?" I said, "As long as my opposition is stuck at 9, it's all right." But that whole query came from a TV projection. It was not the lens. It was the agenda of the producers that distorted reality.

QUESTION: Well, there are also polls that indicate reality as well as make judgments. They give them a snapshot of popular sentiment at that particular time. It's not just a television producer who decides that Jesse Jackson or Pete du Pont or whoever does not have a really good chance of getting the nomination.

JACKSON: As a very American comparison, you should show the very top and the very bottom, just to make your point.

QUESTION: Is access to health care a right, and if it is a right, what should our government do to ensure that Americans really do receive access to health care, rather than being dumped on public hospitals or the elderly being forced into bankruptcy? Should we have some form of national health insurance or a national health service like the British have?

JACKSON: We must have a form of national health service. It is perhaps one of the most disgraceful aspects of the success of the American experiment that we're spending so much money on

medical care and yet more people are denied access to it—like the
38 million without any insurance or millions more who have
inadequate insurance. One of the most shameful scenes I witness
are people who are literally dying in hospital admitting rooms
because they don't have a green or yellow card to go upstairs to a
bed that's empty, waiting for someone with the insurance to get
sick.

Only our country and South Africa have no health safety net for
their people. We can afford to do better. Thus we must restructure
our health system in a way that takes into account people who are
sick no matter what their economic predicament may be. I'm
convinced finally that in this democracy every American should
have the same health options that Mrs. Reagan and Mr. Reagan
are afforded by our government. If it can happen for the very top
in a democracy, it must happen for the very bottom as well.

QUESTION: Reverend Jackson, there has not been much of a
national foreign policy toward the Caribbean region with the
exception of the invasion of Grenada a few years ago. What would
be your foreign policy toward the Caribbean region, particularly
in regards to future elections in Haiti and Jamaica?

KALB: As briefly as possible.

JACKSON: Certainly the position that we must support law.
We must support international law. Secondly, support rights of
self-determination. Since those nations are in our hemisphere,
offer them the aid and trade and assistance they need in order to
become stronger, because any weakness in the Caribbean link is,
in fact, a threat to our national security, and we should handle it
with economic aid and trade before the fact as opposed to military
invasion after the fact.

QUESTION: What do you perceive as the greatest problem of
black America today? Are they the same problems other minorities
face, and what do you propose to do about them?

JACKSON: The public accommodations bill has been passed,
the right to vote bill has been passed and is being implemented,
and open housing laws are now a fact of life. To that extent black
America's basic civil rights problems have been solved. It's a matter
of protection and implementation.

The real critical factor now is not the racial violence of 25 years
ago. It's the economic violence of today. When the plant gate
closes on the worker without notice or the farm is foreclosed, the
lights go out. And when the lights go out, whether you're black or
Hispanic or Asian or female, you can't use color or sex for a crutch
because all of us amazingly have the same characteristics in the

dark. This generation, therefore, must focus on ending economic violence. If we end economic violence—and we can salvage the family farmer, our youth can have scholarships and not just loans, and put America back to work—it will lift the bolt stuck at the bottom. That is why our focus now is on the kind of coalition across lines of race and sex and religion to end the economic violence.

QUESTION: I'd like to ask you several things. First of all, if you would comment on the recent amendment to the AIDS education bill which was put forth by Senator Helms and which passed overwhelmingly this week to limit use of AIDS education money to groups that do not directly or indirectly promote homosexual activity. And I also would like to know if you would support an amendment to the Civil Rights Act of 1964 to prevent discrimination against lesbians and gay men?

JACKSON: Well, first of all, I'm the only candidate who spoke at the gay and lesbian rally October 11 because I thought it was the human and the proper thing to do. I looked and saw six to eight hundred thousand people, and not another candidate was there because they held a blade of grass to the wind and felt it was not politically expedient—it was a little risky to be there. I saw 2,000 people, AIDS victims, dying before my eyes, and no one else there to say, "But you are people, you count." Whatever one's sexual preference is, one deserves equal protection under the law. One deserves due process. We can afford to do no less. Those who hide behind some pseudomoral angle on this issue should remember that the last night Jesus Christ spent on earth, he stayed in the house of the quarantined leper Simon. There's a moral and a legal obligation to concern ourselves with those who are rejected.

As to AIDS education, I must say we cannot simply moralize it, or racialize it, or even nationalize it because the epidemic threatens everybody. It is in our national interest to help rid the world of this disease and, if we do so, we protect everybody, and that would be my commitment: to get adequate research. And as for the AIDS test, it should be voluntary and the results confidential.

KALB: Our next question comes from Nicholas Daniloff, who very shortly will be a resident fellow at the Joan Shorenstein Barone Center here.

DANILOFF: Reverend Jackson, Soviet-American relations, as we're all aware, is a terribly important relationship for the United States but even more so for the whole world. It's a complicated relationship. It's one in which the Soviet Union has a great deal of power which can sometimes be misused to our disadvantage. I think the fact that we had so much trouble getting President

Reagan to meet with Mr. Gorbachev in the United States indicates
the complexity of this relationship. My question is, How would
you handle this relationship? I gather you would push an aggressive arms control policy. You would meet regularly with Mr.
Gorbachev. But what other proposals would you have for protecting American interests while at the same time taking some of the
tension out of relations with Moscow?

JACKSON: I think, for example, the lack of meetings between
Mr. Reagan and the Soviet leadership does not reflect complexity
of the relationship but simplicity of his analysis about what must
happen. In this hemisphere, for example, should we be spending
$10 billion over seven years in many ways trying to overthrow a
government and supporting 15,000 Contras? Or should we, in fact,
see that there are 400 million Latin American neighbors, allies,
consumers, and focus on a comprehensive Pan-American energy
security alliance among Canada, our country, and Latin America
to become less dependent, for example, upon energy from the
Persian Gulf as a case in point? For we, in fact, should use our
leverage of aid and trade to, as it were, get Nicaragua closer to our
orbit and/or remove from them the option, if they're not our allies,
of expanding beyond their borders. Those are what our clear
interests are in that situation. If we use our diplomatic leverage,
follow the vision enunciated by Arias, for example, we can reduce,
if not eliminate, Soviet influence in this hemisphere.

Relative to Cubans we have chosen assassination and boycotts.
Both have failed. If we can break down barriers with China and
the Soviet Union, we can do so with Cuba. We can expand our
influence through diplomacy, aid and trade if necessary of the
military in our own hemisphere.

Secondly, we need to be clear that when we ally with South
Africa, we in fact aid Soviet influence in southern Africa. If we
took the initiative to, in fact, get South Africa out of Angola and
out of Namibia, we could get the Cubans out of Angola, spread our
influence in Angola and in Namibia, build a barrier corridor out of
Mozambique and a railroad, and free up Zimbabwe and Zambia.
We would isolate South Africa, on the one hand, and reduce Soviet
influence on the other. The point is that in these Third World
countries we should be more aggressive with a broader vision.

In the Middle East right now, every day the Iranians can do
nothing but watch our ships escort the most expensive oil in the
history of the world, while Kuwait gives us the option of either
flagging our ships or they will buy nine Soviet ships and perhaps
send oil there. So long as we are that vulnerable, we give the

Soviets leads that they could not otherwise initiate themselves. So an aggressive Third World policy that supports international law, self-determination, and economic alternatives to Third World oppression will, in fact, protect our vital interests.

QUESTION: Reverend Jackson, you're clearly the front-runner. You're clearly the most articulate of the candidates in the campaign. What we continue to hear is that you lack experience. To what extent will your campaign continue to give us specific policies, both domestic and international, to allay some of those concerns, and comment on whether or not you think your challengers should also do the same?

JACKSON: Well, we contend right now that our most pressing issue is to get a bipartisan commitment to drive our budget deficit down. It always was voodoo or irrational to think that those who are most able to pay taxes could be relieved of that responsibility while we double the military budget in peacetime. We simply do not engage in good arithmetic, not to mention calculus. Those who are most able to pay taxes ought to, in fact, pay their share of taxes. You cannot get the additional taxes from people on unemployment compensation. It never did make sense for the top five defense contractors to pay zero taxes and people on unemployment compensation or on welfare to pay taxes. We can't get the taxes from them, or from those who have lost hope. Those most able must pay their share of taxes. If we increase revenue on the one hand, reduce unnecessary expenditures on the other, we can bring that budget deficit in order.

My concern, finally, is this: Today we are overdependent on foreign energy—and on foreign capital. We don't have to be. Any time your vitals are exposed in that way, you can be manipulated militarily, and that becomes real insecurity. What's happening to us in the Persian Gulf right now cannot be protected by a nuclear stockpile. Underneath the umbrella are forces saying, "We can slow down purchase of your debt. We can slow down the production of oil. Therefore, respond to us whether it's in your best interest or not." We must remove that threat.

QUESTION: Reverend Jackson, are you for the Canadian free trade treaty that is presently being proposed?

JACKSON: I basically support the free trade treaty, and if trade is free, reciprocal, and fair and the balance comes down, it's a good situation. However, I could never see and never understand why we would work out a trade relation with Canada and not see the value of doing one with Mexico, which has 80 million people sharing 2,000 miles of contiguous border. We must think hemi-

spherically between Canadians to the north of us and 40 million
Latinos to the south of us. If we think hemispherically, of the
Monroe Doctrine, not just in military terms, but of Jackson doctrine in economic terms and peace terms, we'll be a stronger
nation with a sounder hemisphere.

QUESTION: Reverend Jackson, would you elaborate on the
specific policies you would take to propel the end of apartheid in
South Africa?

JACKSON: First of all, a president must be philosophically
against that system. It seems that this administration, in fact, is
not. It sees South Africa as our geopolitical ally, which is an error
as well as a moral disgrace and does not protect our interests in
that region of the world.

What must we do? Apartheid is not just in South Africa. It is an
empire in southern Africa. We must convene a summit meeting of
front-line leaders as we did of Western European leaders. We must
develop a commitment to full and complete sanctions against
apartheid regimes—perhaps order American corporations to va-
cate these countries as we did in the case of Libya—as a sign of
our seriousness. Thirdly, develop the economic alternative that is
opening up out of Mozambique. Fourthly, negotiate all foreign
troops out of Angola and Namibia. That will substantially isolate
South Africa and put them into a position where they will have to
negotiate in what could be less bloodletting in a progressive
change. Lastly, the front line deserves the least defensive security
from South Africa's constant invading and bombing of their infrastructure.

QUESTION: Reverend Jackson, will you give us a little of your
idea on unions and pension funds and reinvesting in America?

JACKSON: First of all, this President has been a union-busting
president, and that has not been good for the delicate balance
between management and labor. The National Labor Relations
Board has become a kind of scab protection act. So American
workers are either undercut by underpaid workers in this country
or their jobs are taken to repressed labor markets abroad, which
adds to family instability. So the President creates 11 million new
jobs, six million paying $7,000 a year or less, resulting in growth
without opportunity.

Secondly, union workers should have representation on their
pension board and help determine where their pension monies
will be spent. It does not make sense for a steelworker's pension
monies to go when the plant is leveraged or sold out. Or for that
pension worker's money to be used to purchase a competitive meal

in an uncompetitive labor market and close down the mother plant, which means that worker bought the rope he or she is now hanging from. That never was fiduciary responsibility.

I would hope in the future we would take a percentage of public pension funds, maybe 20 percent, with government security and fair rate of return guaranteed, and target that money for infrastructure development. That's how you put America back to work, and as America goes back to work, we generate revenues, we pay taxes, the deficit goes down, and our self-respect and esteem goes up.

QUESTION: Reverend Jackson, the scourge of America is drug proliferation. It has taken away our work ethic. It has divided families. It has broken people. What would you do as president of the United States to deal with this proliferation of drugs, drug trafficking into the country, and the demise of the country?

JACKSON: I have tried to force that as an issue in the campaign. At this point there is no press interest. Therefore, there is no competitor interest. I met with the Coast Guard in Key West, Florida, three weeks ago, where 80 percent of the drug trafficking comes through. Last year 178 tons of cocaine came into our country, as did 20,000 plus pounds of heroin and 66,000 tons of marijuana. Air and sea interdiction has been cut in half.

We must do four things. One, negotiate alternative crops with the countries that are growing it. To do less than that is to make drug trafficking a part of our foreign policy, which is an indictment. Secondly, strengthen the Coast Guard. If we can defend allies' borders in Korea, Japan, and Europe, we must defend our own borders from the number one threat to the youth of our country. Thirdly, provide adequate money for drug education for those who need their minds enlightened before the fact. Fourth, provide adequate treatment centers. But I submit this to you, Mr. Bolling, if I were president, I would cut the supply of drugs because I want to. But also the people must cut their demand for the drugs. It's a two-way street.

KALB: Our last questioner is the dean of the Harvard Divinity School, Ronald Thiemann.

THIEMANN: Reverend Jackson, you have been quite candid throughout your career talking about the way in which your political beliefs have been shaped by your religious convictions. Many Americans, however, often feel as though religiously motivated public figures are not fully to be trusted or that there's a degree of skepticism about those religious motivations, in part because of an attempt to separate church and state or a perception that religious interests are essentially private and should not have a role in the public debate. As you look at the future of your campaign, how do you seek to address that concern about the relation between religion and politics?

JACKSON: Certainly, as a matter of law and fact, we should not be prejudiced against lawyers or actors or people of a given race or a given sex. That's not good. As a matter of fact, my religion makes me political. My politics don't make me religious. I am driven by a commitment to wipe out malnutrition, to be sensitive to the least of us, to see the security interests in peace, and jobs and justice. To know very well there will be no peace without justice, whether in southern Africa or the Middle East or Latin America. There will be no peace without justice.

The Golden Rule is the key to sound foreign policy. Those who believe that those who have the gold make the rule possess a formula for war. And so as a religious person I am concerned about those who are locked out of the inn and born in the stable. I try to convince them that just because you're born in the slum does not mean the slum is born in you. That's the hope that religion brings, and it does not interfere with checks and balances or separation of church and state.

Candidates '88

A CONVERSATION WITH
PETE DU PONT

About the Candidate

The problems of the former governor of Delaware began with his name. Was it Pete du Pont, the regular-guy monicker emblazoned on his campaign brochures? Was it Pierre S. du Pont IV, redolent with hints of old money and ancient lineage? Or was it—worst of all—"The Duper," the prep-school-style nickname affectionately fastened on him by his staff?

It was du Pont's misfortune to be wealthy and well-born in a political year in which pugnacious populism was all the rage. But he toughed it out, proving himself a tireless campaigner, staking out high-relief, controversial positions, and contributing more than his share of daring and intellectual luster to the Republican debate.

Du Pont ran as a candidate of ideas. He advocated a robust free-market ideology that included not only pain-free proposals, such as lower taxes, but also politically risky ones, such as eliminating farm subsidies and making social security voluntary. He backed a voucher system to support private education, a workfare system that would have required able-bodied welfare recipients to take government jobs at 90 percent of the minimum wage, and a program of mandatory drug testing for high school students.

Although he did not choose to do so, or did so only intermittently, du Pont could just as easily have run as a candidate of proven competence. In his two terms as governor of Delaware he compiled a remarkable record. When he took office in 1977 the state was $20 million in the red and had the highest personal tax rate in the country. When he left in 1985 the treasury had a surplus of $46 million, income taxes had been cut twice, the economy was booming, and du Pont had won the respect even of his Democratic rivals in the state. Delaware's turnaround was as impressive as Massachusetts's, and The Duper, like The Duke, had a success story to tell. He had run a government, and he had run it pretty well.

Du Pont, 53, is a great-great-great grandson of the founder of the chemical dynasty. After Exeter, Princeton, the Navy, and Harvard Law School, he dutifully returned to Delaware to work for the family business and begin the long climb up the corporate ladder. In 1968, that year of rebellion, he too rebelled, quitting to run successfully for the state legislature. Two years later he won the first of three terms in the U.S. House of Representatives. His record there was that of a moderately liberal Republican. As a conservative, his zeal is the zeal of a convert.

When he appeared on "Candidates '88," du Pont was in the midst of a struggle with Jack Kemp and Pat Robertson over the mantle of conservative legitimacy. Partly because he lacked either Kemp's long association with the conservative movement or Robertson's roots in the religious right, and partly because the issues he championed struck many voters as marginal, he was ultimately to lose that struggle. But his campaign was nothing to be ashamed of.

H.H.

The Interview

KALB: Governor, let's start with something that is not terribly important, namely your name. I've been forewarned that I'm to call you Pete, and I want to know what's wrong with the long name, Pierre Samuel du Pont IV?

DU PONT: Well, there's nothing wrong with it. And unlike some people running for president, I'm not going to change it.

KALB: Okay, I noticed a couple of weeks ago that the vice president called you Pierre during the Republican debate in Houston, and he seemed, I thought, to get under your skin a bit. I'm wondering why?

DU PONT: I've known George long enough that I'd have thought he'd call me Pete. He was trying to make a point that he had some vision and some ideas and some proposals in his campaign for the presidency, and I was making the opposite point, that he hadn't really told us where he would lead America, that he said, for example, he was an education president. That sounds good. I've put forward a very specific proposal to allow parents to choose which schools their children go to. That will bring competition into our schools and make us the best in the world instead of the tenth best. That's the kind of specific that somebody running for president of the United States ought to put forward, and I don't think George had done that.

KALB: But to get back to the name for a second. Is there something wrong, in your judgment, about running for president of the United States, which has at least a theoretical aim of setting forth an egalitarian society, coming from an authentic aristocratic family?

DU PONT: You know, I don't think it matters, Marvin, much in America who you are. It's what you are. I had a chance to be governor of Delaware for eight years, and for every single family in that state we cut their taxes 30 percent, provided 20 percent more jobs in our state. That's relating to people pretty well. And I don't think, as I say, your name makes a bit of difference. What matters is what would you do as president of the United States? Where would you lead America and in what direction would you take the country?

KALB: Okay, now, let's find out a little bit about you and what some people have regarded as a political conversion. Pete du Pont in the 1970s, if my information is right, voted for higher gasoline taxes. You voted for federal funding for abortions. You voted against U.S. aid to the anticommunist forces in Angola.

A columnist, a former colleague of mine from the *Wilmington News Journal*—Ralph Moyette, who you know—has written, "I'm still looking for something he, du Pont, passionately believes in. He wants to find issues that make people say 'damn right,' and he doesn't care what they are."

DU PONT: Ralph is still very upset that we cut taxes because he's a good old-fashioned liberal who believes in high taxes like many members of the Congress of the United States do. You know and I know, and most of the people watching today know, that if you reduce people's taxes, it increases their opportunity. We increased opportunity enormously by those tax cuts, and Ralph hasn't really adjusted to that.

But let me come back to the questions you raised. We were all different in the 1970s. Ronald Reagan started out as a Democrat. George Bush said that cutting taxes and supply-side economics was voodoo economics. One day in the Congress, Pete du Pont, Jack Kemp, and Bob Dole all voted for wage and price controls. Now that's a bad vote. We were wrong, we've changed. Why have I changed? Because I had a chance to lead. For eight years I was governor, and my job was to lead a state, and that makes you a very different kind of person than when you're in Congress voting on a variety of things in which you're working to someone else's agenda. So I have changed.

KALB: But how does leading a state and having that kind of executive responsibility—or for that matter if you could project ahead, leading the United States of America—really give you the kind of insight that you now feel is required for that job?

DU PONT: Well, consider the vote on the gasoline tax. That was a vote I wouldn't cast today.

KALB: You wouldn't cast it today because you yourself feel it is a bad vote or is it political expediency?

DU PONT: Because I learned in Delaware that if you cut people's taxes, you get an explosion of economic growth and create 20 percent more jobs. I didn't understand that the day I voted that way in Congress because I hadn't been a governor, I hadn't led, I hadn't had a chance to make something happen in the state. So we've changed. We're different.

KALB: But how can you not understand that, and how can you say that someone in his 40s really changes dramatically when he gets into his 50s?

DU PONT: Because you've had a chance to be in charge of a government. You've had the responsibility of not only being for a program, like you might be when you voted in the Congress, you have the responsibility of making that program work, of making it produce results for the people of your state. And that makes you a more conservative person in how you view things, because you have to pick good people to get on your Supreme Court to run your programs. You have to increase opportunity, and that changes.

KALB: Okay, now, you've used the word *conservative,* and that's an interesting point here at the Kennedy School. In January the Institute of Politics is going to have a conference here on the meaning and the value of certain political words like *right, center, left, conservative, liberal.* How important are those descriptions now for really defining what somebody thinks? Because within one person—I have a feeling probably within yourself—you can be both a conservative and a liberal on different issues.

DU PONT: I don't think the words are very important any-more. I think American politics has changed. I don't believe, for example, that allowing a mother and a father a little piece of paper called a voucher to choose the school their third grade son goes to can be defined as a liberal idea or a conservative idea. It's a good idea.

But I use the word *conservative* in a different sense to refer to the values that the majority of the people in this country share, a belief that the individual is more important than government, a belief that the traditional American family is kind of a glue that holds our society together, the belief that American democracy is morally superior to Soviet communism, and they're not equivalent in any way. That there's a difference. The view that in America government's job is to create opportunity for individuals so they can seize a hold of it and the market economy is what makes America unique and successful, not the government that we have. And those are values that all of us share that are, with a small "C," conservative.

KALB: Let me ask you what would happen if you were presi-dent of the United States, and I want to know how your adminis-tration would function. This is, after all, a school of government, so we're focusing on problems like that. Secretary Shultz said during the Iran-Contra hearings that he thought it would be a good idea if every cabinet official had an office in the White House so that there would be authentic cabinet-run government. Would a du Pont administration have that?

DU PONT: With all due respect to Secretary Shultz, that's the kind of silly suggestion that makes no sense at all for a government.

It doesn't matter where a cabinet official sits, for heaven's sake. The question is, Does that cabinet secretary carry out the right policies to increase opportunity in the country?

KALB: Doesn't it have to do really with the direction set by the president?

DU PONT: The president can pick up his telephone and talk to a cabinet secretary any time he wants to. Where the cabinet secretary's office is doesn't matter, and that's the kind of window dressing philosophy that I think has gotten this government into trouble.

KALB: But how do you then avoid in government what we saw happening in the Reagan administration within the last year and a half? That a lieutenant colonel in the United States Marine Corps could actually take charge of a major element of American foreign policy.

DU PONT: You had that happen because the chief of staff for the President wasn't doing his job properly.

As governor I had 12 cabinet secretaries whose job it was, yes, to run their departments, but secondly, to implement the policy that our administration was advocating. My chief of staff's job was to make sure that the cabinet secretaries did that and did it on time and that they followed the policy and made the changes they were supposed to make in their department. I think in Colonel North's case that his goal was the correct one, bringing—

KALB: His goal was the correct one?

DU PONT: Bringing freedom to Central America, but his mechanics in reaching that goal were way out of bounds, and the chief of staff should have been following up to make sure—

KALB: Where was the President of the United States through all this?

DU PONT: Well, the President of the United States, through his chief of staff, should have been doing that.

KALB: No, what about the President?

DU PONT: Well, he should have been following up to make sure that wasn't happening too. But he says to the chief of staff, "Look, Don, are they carrying out our policy?" And Don's job is to say yes or no or partly or we're going to do it next week or whatever the answer is.

KALB: What does it say about President Reagan, that all of this could take place on his shift? He lived and worked at the White House.

DU PONT: The same thing that it said that Jack Kennedy—

when Jack Kennedy had the Bay of Pigs—that somebody wasn't paying attention.

KALB: Who's the somebody?

DU PONT: In that case I don't know who it was.

KALB: No, I mean now.

DU PONT: Don Regan, the chief of staff.

KALB: In other words, you're absolving the President of responsibility?

DU PONT: No, the President takes responsibility, and his job should have been to have a chief of staff who did the follow-up in government.

KALB: How would you populate a du Pont administration? Would it have only conservatives following the ethical and moral values that you set forth a moment ago, also the political values, or would you have other people in there as well to give you some kind of balance?

DU PONT: I want to have a room full of advisers who reflect different viewpoints, who get to me the inputs from people all across the country of different persuasions so I can make the best possible decision. I would not have a litmus test for service in my administration. But I would have people who are able, people who are dedicated to making the changes in government that we want to make, and want to help me do that.

KALB: Governor, you've taken a very strong stand against drugs. You have advocated, recommended strongly, random mandatory testing of high school students. There is some question among a number of the people I talked to in preparing for this program as to whether that is constitutional, whether it is not a really unnecessary and illegal invasion of privacy.

DU PONT: I want to answer that question. But let me ask you a question first: If it was constitutional, would you be for it?

KALB: No, I ask the question, you answer.

DU PONT: I tried.

KALB: No, no, that's all right. That's perfectly fine. But you're a lawyer. Are you concerned in any way this may be an invasion of privacy?

DU PONT: Of course. And I believe it's going to be found constitutional. Every circuit court of appeals in this country that's ruled on random drug testing so far has found it constitutional. For transportation workers, for jockeys—I mean, that's far down the line.

KALB: Except for jockeys.

DU PONT: I believe it's constitutional because the Fourth Amendment says that we are protected against unreasonable searches and seizures, and the operative word is unreasonable.

Before you could go to school as a youngster, state law required that you be vaccinated. Was that an invasion of your privacy? Of course it was. But that invasion of your privacy was held to be reasonable considering the desire to keep disease out of our schools. When you return to the country from abroad your baggage and your person can be searched. Is that an invasion of privacy? Yes. But the Supreme Court said the value of keeping contraband out of America outweighs the temporary inconvenience of the search of your person or luggage. I would argue that asking a student to take a random drug test once a year is far outweighed by the value of getting drugs out of our schools, which today are being used by one teenager in four, by one truck driver in six, by 40 percent of young doctors in America who work in a hospital. We've got a serious problem in this country, and we better start addressing it with young people.

KALB: Has the problem gotten worse in the last six or seven years?

DU PONT: Infinitely worse. Drugs are cheaper and more plentiful than ever.

KALB: What does that say about the value of White House rhetoric? Because certainly there's been an awful lot of that.

DU PONT: Our proposal is that rhetoric and posters of Mean Joe Greene on the wall aren't enough. What we need is a policy that says to young people in this country that drugs are not okay. They are not something that is chic. They are not something that our society is for. They're illegal substances. We're against using them. They'll destroy your opportunity, and you ought to get them out of your life.

KALB: In your view was the revelation about Judge Ginsburg having used drugs in the '60s and '70s a valid reason on his part, as far as you're concerned, for having pulled out?

DU PONT: Well, I don't know about Judge Ginsburg's part. He'll have to speak for himself. But I think that's a valid reason not to offer him to the United States Senate for a seat on the Supreme Court. Here you had an individual who while a professor of law was breaking the law, and for a Supreme Court nominee, I think the standards are a little higher than they might be for others.

KALB: What does that say about the White House system for raising these people and advancing them?

DU PONT: Now we're back to the question you asked a moment ago.

KALB: I'm trying to get your view.

DU PONT: I was a governor, and I had to nominate cabinet secretaries and Supreme Court nominees and various people for different positions in the government. My chief of staff was always instructed to ask, "Have you paid your taxes every year?" "Do you have a criminal record?" Those are the obvious questions. And the final question always was, "Is there anything in your background, Mr. Kalb, that, when we take you before the Senate, is going to prove an embarrassment to you or to me?" That's an important question. That focuses the nominee's mind a little bit on the confirmation process.

KALB: I can tell you in answer to your question, no, there is nothing.

DU PONT: You answered my question this time. That's progress in the show. Now come back to whether you think drug testing is okay if it's constitutional. Will you answer that? About testing?

KALB: No, not at this point. I'll answer it later.

DU PONT: But we're getting your views on this question.

KALB: No, no, but I want to get yours. I think that's more important. You're running for president. I'm not.

I would like to know why it is when I give you two, three, four, and I think a half dozen opportunities to be even slightly critical of President Reagan, you duck that opportunity and put it off on the chief of staff in your administration or in his administration. What is it about Ronald Reagan now that even a conservative cannot possibly criticize? Is he some kind of political totem pole that has been set up to be worshiped?

DU PONT: Let me be critical of the President.

KALB: No, I'm not asking you to be.

DU PONT: I'm going to be. Let me tell you, speaking as a governor who had the same kind of responsibility, that I think two weeks ago he made a tactical and a substantive mistake by saying to the Congress of the United States, yes, we'll accept a tax increase. When you give legislators the eye of a needle, they'll drive an 18-wheeler through it. And he's going to see the biggest tax increase on his desk that the Congress thinks they can possibly get away with. He ought to veto it. I hope he'll veto it. And I don't think the President in that specific case made the right decision.

KALB: Right now, on the front page of every newspaper today, you have stories saying that Treasury Secretary James Baker is proposing, as part of the deal with the Congress, higher taxes in order to lower the budget deficit.

DU PONT: And that's a serious mistake. Taxes don't lower budget deficits because they slow economic growth. And I've not met in my campaign a single family in America that claims they're undertaxed.

You recall, that was Walter Mondale's position in the campaign and that was rejected 49 states to one.

KALB: Was that what was rejected?

DU PONT: A tax increase? That was the starkest element of his campaign.

KALB: Let me again get to the shape of the du Pont administration on economic matters. Do you feel that the effort to reduce the budget deficit should be the prime preoccupation of your administration?

DU PONT: No. And the reason is, Marvin, that we haven't got a crisis. We have a challenge. In the year in which the budget deficit dropped $65 billion dollars, we suddenly had the market give us a signal of no confidence in the future. It didn't give us that signal while the deficit was rising. If you read the newspapers in America today and watched television, you'd think the only issue in America was $23 billion out of the federal deficit. That's not what the country needs to face up to. It needs to face up to the long-range challenges that we have in the country. We need, first of all, a high-growth economy so people can work, and we have one. We need a low-inflation economy so people's savings are worth something, and we have one of those, too. America isn't falling apart. We have the best performing economy of any nation in the world, and the preoccupation of the Pete du Pont administration is going to be to keep taxes down, keep inflation down, and try to further peel back regulations that stop entrepreneurial people from creating opportunity, and thus make the whole great.

KALB: You are probably aware, Governor, that on Friday, *USA Today* and CNN put out a poll which said that Republicans and Democrats believe that lowering the budget deficit should be the prime preoccupation of any administration, Republican or Democratic. Are you saying that the American people in this respect are wrong and Pete du Pont is right?

DU PONT: Yes. I'm saying that that is status quo thinking. That is just not correct—to have blinders on, to believe that all that matters is $23 billion out of the deficit. And I have a couple of opponents like that in this race, not to mention six Democrats who are pessimists. You listen to those Democratic candidates call for more taxes, more regulations, higher protective tariffs, all of which take away freedom from people and destroy opportunity in the country. And that's a prescription for economic disaster in our country.

KALB: You know that most of Western Europe—if one believes what is in the newspapers, and I tend to—believes that the United States must now change its economic policy. If I can quote the British Chancellor of the Exchequer, who demands slashing the budget deficit and raising taxes, he says, "Both are necessary in economic terms, but also because this has now become the touchstone of whether the United States has the political will to make hard choices."

You say that your administration would have that political will. Europe, our allies, are depending upon the United States now to raise taxes in order to lower the deficit. You're saying that's all a lot of hogwash?

DU PONT: One expects that the Europeans would like America's economy to be like theirs. And heaven help us from getting into that state. Their economies aren't growing. They're not creating new jobs in Europe, I don't believe, a tenth as fast as we are in America. They have, particularly on the Continent—leaving Britain aside for the moment—a static economic situation in Germany, in France, in Italy. We don't need to Europeanize America's economy. Sure, we need to get the deficit down. How do you do it? You do it by reducing spending. How do you do that? By phasing out those agricultural subsidies that cost the taxpayers of this country $26 billion a year and don't help farmers. There's a $26 billion bite that our campaign for the presidency supports, and not one Republican or one Democrat among the other 11 running will touch it. And one wonders whether they're really serious about getting the deficit down.

KALB: Let's take the other side of that coin, on two issues, welfare and social security, major pillars of your economic proposals. Is welfare, by your estimate, going to cost an additional $7 billion?

DU PONT: No, you've got that backwards. It's going to save $7 billion. Once it's implemented, it's going to cost $5 billion in the first year, $3 billion in the second, even in the third, and $7 billion a year—

KALB: But at the very beginning—

DU PONT: It will cost $5 billion.

KALB: Five billion, not 7. I take it back. On social security overhaul your estimate is at the beginning it will cost $20 billion. Every year. Every year it will cost $20 billion. So already we're adding $25 billion, right?

DU PONT: Yes.

KALB: What's the sense in that?

DU PONT: Marvin, I think your view of the presidency and mine are diametrically opposed.

KALB: I don't have a particular view.

DU PONT: Yes, you're a bean counter. All these questions have been about totaling this, and you're worried about the $23 billion deficit.

KALB: Aren't you?

DU PONT: This is not a nation of bean counters. This is a nation trying to get economic growth in the country, replacing welfare with work and giving the poor today, who have no opportunity, a chance to go out and become a part of America and not have to use food stamps, which is a horrible experience for an individual. Have a chance to get a job, wake up in the morning and feel a part of America. Have some self-respect and a shot of opportunity. That's far more important in this country than worrying about whether you're going to get $23 or $22 billion out of the budget. I just think you have it backwards.

KALB: No, I'm not sure I have it backwards because all I'm doing is asking the question. You're providing the answers. My question is a simple one. I assume you want to lower the deficit?

DU PONT: Certainly.

KALB: Okay, you're only saying, according to your plan, it will take a while before you do that. Somewhere down the road if this works out well—

DU PONT: I told you that reducing the deficit is third in the economic priorities of a Pete du Pont administration. The first is low inflation. Because a 10 or 15 percent inflation economy destroys opportunities for the poor, the investor, and all the working families of the country. That's a disastrous policy. That's Jimmy Carter's policy, and that was the bleakest period in economics America has seen. The second priority is keeping taxes down so there are enough jobs so everybody in America can work. I wouldn't trade a $23 billion deficit for 10 percent unemployment, and I don't think you would either.

KALB: Probably not. Let's switch to foreign policy.

DU PONT: We're making some progress.

KALB: A little bit. Although this is not a session in conversion, it is a Sunday.

On the issue of strategic defense, you have said on the President's program on strategic defense, "This is the first opportunity since Hiroshima that gives the United States an opportunity to build a defense against the most dangerous circumstance of our age." My question is a very simple one. How do you do that?

DU PONT: Well, I know two things: First, that there are 15,000 Soviet missiles this afternoon facing America. I know that there is some chance that someone like Colonel Khadafy also has a missile, and if one of those missiles is fired today by mistake, aimed at Boston, that there's nothing the government of the United States of America can do about it. We can give these good people in the audience 15 minutes warning, and then we watch it land. I don't think that's protecting our freedoms or our families. And the second thing I know is that there is a technology that can destroy that missile, that is, has been proven to work twice, and we ought to research it, and build it, and we ought to deploy it because we'd be safer tomorrow than today if we're protected against one missile fired in mistake or 100 fired in anger.

KALB: I want to be clear that I understand what your vision is on strategic defense. Is it the same vision that the President advocated in 1983 when he said this would be a wonderful plan for the U.S. and make nuclear weapons obsolete? Are you looking toward an absolutely foolproof system of strategic defense?

DU PONT: That will be very hard to achieve.

KALB: Then how— Maybe one of those warheads could still get through to Boston.

DU PONT: Yes. But wouldn't you rather have defense against one or ten or a hundred than no defense at all? I would.

KALB: Okay, but what percentage of leakage would you accept and still call strategic defense successful?

DU PONT: I'd be glad to have the protection against one. And it's going to be a few years before that can be accomplished.

KALB: What do you think this will cost?

DU PONT: I'll come back to the cost in a minute. Once this is accomplished, after 10 years you might have a defense against several hundreds or thousands, and someday you might have a defense against them all. But today we're absolutely undefended and that's not right.

What would it cost? About $5 billion a year over perhaps the next 20 years to accomplish that. The Pentagon has listed 30 military bases in America that are unnecessary to the defense of this country that would save $3 to $4 billion if you closed them down, and the Congress won't let them do that. That is a better thing to do than not build the strategic defense initiative.

KALB: A question about what happened this past week in China and the Soviet Union. Do you believe that we are witnessing in both communist giants a significant, major, meaningful change in the way they do business?

DU PONT: Perhaps. I don't think we'll know that for a long time. The change in China's leadership is so recent I think it's difficult to tell what it means in the long term. In the Soviet Union the change has been going on a little longer, but it's a little easier to understand, because Soviet Russia today is in danger of becoming a third-class world power. They have fallen technologically way behind America. They are falling behind Japan, behind nations in Western Europe perhaps. And I think Gorbachev is worried about that, and that's why he tried to change the economic policy of the country. It is not easy to change a bureaucracy in America, let alone in the Soviet Union. And I think he's going to have a difficult time.

KALB: Governor, before we go to the audience for its questions, I want to run through something. Give me the first adjective that comes into your mind while I tick off the following names.

Kemp.

DU PONT: A good friend.

KALB: Haig.

DU PONT: A good general.

KALB: Robertson. Good minister?

DU PONT: Well, perhaps, but that's not what comes to mind. What comes to mind is that Pat Robertson has a very powerful message in his presidential campaign that neither Kemp nor Haig has, and that's a message of bringing morality into government. Whether you agree with it or not, he is delivering a message that is very powerful in terms of the people of this country because it's something they fundamentally agree with, whether they agree with his particular religious beliefs or not.

Jack Kemp used to be an innovator. He had some good ideas in the Congress. He started in Washington the tax cutting that we'd already begun in Delaware. He has ideas for letting public housing tenants own their housing. That's a good idea. So in his background he has some bold ideas. I don't see any in his campaign, and that's one of the differences between the two.

KALB: Two more names. Dole.

DU PONT: Bob Dole is a very effective legislative leader.

KALB: Bush.

DU PONT: Vice president of the United States who so far in this campaign has not given us his vision of where he would take America, how he would get us there, and it's really important that a candidate say those things, because one of the things we've learned about the presidency and about leadership in government is that you can only accomplish in office what you campaign for as you're trying to get to office. And George hasn't given us that.

KALB: Governor, one of the distinctive things about this program is that the host doesn't ask all the questions. The audience gets an opportunity to ask questions, and that time has now come. Let us begin first with the academic dean of the John F. Kennedy School of Government, Albert Carnesale.

CARNESALE: Governor, next month we're going to have a summit meeting, and it appears the centerpiece is going to be a treaty eliminating medium-range nuclear weapons globally. That's going to relegitimize arms control, in the view of many, since a conservative such as President Reagan will be reaching that agreement. It may even pave the way for a further agreement limiting by more than half, reducing by more than half, the number of long-range weapons that can reach the United States. Is this a road that's being paved that you'd like to see us travel or not, and why?

DU PONT: I would like to see us try to negotiate arms control agreements with the Soviet Union that are verifiable. That would be a part of the Pete du Pont administration. But arms control is no substitute for defense. It's part of a defense program, not a substitute for keeping America militarily strong so our freedoms are defended. I can't speak to the long-range negotiations, because they haven't really progressed very far yet. The short-range missiles in Europe, though, and the negotiations that are producing an agreement there, are of great concern to me, because first we haven't seen the agreement yet, we haven't read it, it hasn't been written. I believe in reading agreements before we commit to them, not in signing now and negotiating later. I want to see that treaty before I support it. Secondly, removing short-range missiles from Europe, I do not believe should be allowed to happen unless there's a redress of the conventional imbalance that exists in conventional forces.

Soviet forces on the eastern side of the line—the Warsaw Pact and Soviet Union's forces—are twice as strong as Western forces if you measure in tanks, three times in artillery, five times in tactical aircraft. I think there has to be a codicil added to that treaty in the United States Senate that says it doesn't go into effect until there's a conventional force imbalance reduction. Otherwise, I think we're putting Western Europe at risk, and we've been there twice in two lifetimes to try to help, and I hope we don't have to go there again.

QUESTION: Could you tell me, if elected president, how will you respond to 25 million gay and lesbian citizens who are demanding their civil rights?

DU PONT: I would respond by saying they have civil rights under the Constitution of the United States and our government will make sure those constitutional rights are protected.

QUESTION: Mr. Governor, you've talked about the family being the glue that holds our society together. You also talk about abolishing welfare. That would force poor women to leave their children with a sitter and go off and wash dishes. Do you feel that it's more important for a poor woman to be washing dishes than being home with her small child?

DU PONT: I think it's most important of all that every woman in America have opportunity. And I don't believe you have any opportunity by sitting home getting a check from the government. Nor do I believe that an able-bodied person in America has a right to be supported by the government. If you're handicapped or disabled, or ill, or over 65 and on social security, yes, governmental support is important and right. But if you are an able-bodied person, this is not a country in which the government supports you. This is a country which gives you the opportunity to go out and work. And the work is a value in this country. The work ethic started not very far from here in the Massachusetts Bay Colony. That's an important value, and today we're denying poor people that opportunity, and that's wrong.

QUESTION: Again, my question is, Isn't caring for a child work, and isn't that important for the child and for society?

DU PONT: Yes. But think of all the working mothers in America who aren't on welfare, who get up at 6:00 in the morning, get their children into day care, to school, and go out and create opportunity for themselves and their communities. That's important. And I think that giving people the opportunity to work by saying to them, "If you're an able-bodied person and you want to earn money in America, you have to work for it," is not only presenting opportunity for people, but it's the right value in America.

QUESTION: You propose giving drug tests to teens as a precondition for receiving a driver's license. Given that the establishing of standards for driver qualifications is a state prerogative right now, how would you compel the states to adopt these tests without infringing on the Tenth Amendment, or is this another case of an infringement that's okay given the cost of drugs in society?

DU PONT: I'm glad to hear there's someone who's heard of the Tenth Amendment in Cambridge. Perhaps this school is doing better than I thought, Marvin.

KALB: I have a feeling it is.

DU PONT: Well said. We have in America today a right turn on red law that says that Massachusetts and Delaware and every other state in the union loses federal highway money if it does not enact a right turn on red law. Don't you think driving kids out of the classrooms is a little more important than making people have a right turn on red law? I do. And I would say to the states, you have an obligation to get your federal educational funds, to have equal access for handicapped people, to have a nondiscriminatory policy in regard to race and sex in your school system. I would add to that, you also have to have some kind of a program to drive drugs out of our schools, and I'd suggest to you the driver's license program, and it's up to you to choose one and implement it. But if you want our help and educational funds, you have to have a program like this one.

QUESTION: Governor du Pont, in today's deregulated financial markets, we've seen billions of dollars move across the exchange market from one country to another within seconds. In this environment, can American presidents still pursue independent economic policies or should you coordinate policies more with powers such as Japan and Germany?

DU PONT: I don't believe there exists in today's economy the Balkanization of the world that used to exist in the '50s and the '60s. We are competing today in an international economy. American automobile workers are producing automobiles that compete with Japanese ones. American farmers are growing grain that competes with Canadian grain and Argentine grain. We are an integrated economy. That's why protectionism is such an awful idea. It limits people's choice and denies opportunity in America. It won't work in an international economy. The answer to your question is, We're all in this global economy together. America has to stick to its market principles. It ought to help other countries develop market economies, but, of course, we have to coordinate and understand the international aspects of our economy, or we won't survive in a world market.

QUESTION: Mr. du Pont, I would like to have your view on international law. The World Court in The Hague ruled that the mining of the harbors in Nicaragua was against international law. President Reagan discarded this decision. Are you going to respect international law?

DU PONT: I'm going to respect international law, but the first responsibility of the president of the United States is to look after security interests of the United States of America. I don't know what the international law situation was when President John F. Kennedy put a naval blockade around Cuba, but he did the right thing because it kept Soviet missiles out of Cuba. If I were president of the United States and saw similar missiles coming into Nicaragua, I wouldn't hesitate to use the Navy to blockade it, because the first responsibility is to protect American security.

QUESTION: What use do you see in having international law if you only follow it as you choose to?

DU PONT: Well, as I said, the first responsibility of a president is to look after America's interest and take care of our country. We have a United Nations. It can be useful. We should work with United Nations health organizations and others, for example. But the United Nations is no substitute for a military force, for example, to defend America.

QUESTION: I'd like to return to your welfare reform proposals.

DU PONT: Yes.

QUESTION: You pointed out that many women get up at six A.M. and take their children to day care before going to work. This assumes they have available and affordable day care. How does your policy proposal deal with those women taking minimum-wage jobs? What kind of day care proposal goes along with this?

DU PONT: Let me explain the proposal a little bit so you understand it better. The proposal is to say that six or nine months from now, welfare checks stop and paychecks start. You go out and find a job. If you can't find one, you come on down to the local government office and we'll find you a job. We'll put you to work working in a day care center, sitting with an elderly patient in a veterans hospital, being a hall monitor in a school classroom so teachers have the time to teach, cleaning up a park, whatever. There's lots of work to do in America. We'll supply you with a wage and an earned income tax credit and a Medicaid card that gives you health benefits and economic opportunity greater than you have today on welfare, on the average by about 15 percent. We'll also provide day care for you at an affordable price, and you can avail yourself of that or you can keep the money you're earning and put your child at your sister's house or make some other arrangement. What we're trying to do is give people opportunity. Today people on welfare have none. It's a prison. They're trapped there. The government is holding them there with a system called welfare that's denying them opportunity and impoverishing them generation after generation. What we have ought to be scrapped, and we ought to start over because what we have isn't working.

KALB: Our next question comes from Claire Fleming, the chairperson of the student advisory committee of the Institute of Politics.

FLEMING: Today you talked about your commitment to education and the call for an increase in the quality of education, and you've also touched on your policy for allowing parents to choose where they would send their children to school. What I'd like to ask is, if you were president, would you increase funding for college loans so that college students would be able to have that choice of where they could go to school? And a second question, do you believe in merit pay for teachers?

DU PONT: I believe that a good teacher ought to be paid more money than a not-so-good teacher. And one of the reasons is that that encourages people to become better teachers. Everyone else working in some other job is evaluated on his or her merit in our society. Teachers can be, too. You know, I had a teacher say to me once, "The trouble with your plan, sir, is that I don't test very well." And I said, "Ma'am, I made that argument when I was in the fourth grade, and no teacher ever seemed to think that argument was worth very much." And I don't think it's worth very much now.

I believe that no American should be denied the opportunity of a college education because of a lack of money. So if I were president, I would set up a national schooling and training bank that allows a young American coming out of high school, or a somewhat older American who may want to go back to school, or a laid-off automobile worker aged 45 who needs a new skill to get a new job—any of those individuals, regardless of age and income— to go down to a bank and borrow the money they need to go to school, and the government would guarantee the loan. That would ensure access for everyone in America who wants to go to college or go back to college. That would be good for the country and bring opportunity to a lot of people. You have to pay it back yourself because it's your opportunity and responsibility, but nobody ought to be denied schooling because he doesn't have money.

QUESTION: You said you'd like to reduce the risk of a nuclear weapon landing on Boston. How would you respond to Mr. Gorbachev's proposal to eliminate all nuclear weapons by the year 2000?

DU PONT: That's a wonderful goal. The challenge is in the fine print. Can we verify it? Will it work? Can we be sure if we reduce our defenses that the Soviet Union reduces its offenses? If we can, I'd move in the direction of negotiating such an agreement.

QUESTION: Governor du Pont, I have trouble with your idea of a voucher system for education. Don't you feel this will give up the long-term goal of mixing diverse elements of our society through public education?

DU PONT: I think your long-term goal and my long-term goal are different. My long-term goal is to get the best education I can for every youngster in America, not to make sure that the government properly assigns people to schools. We're talking about saying to the poor woman in Cambridge, "Look, we want your son or your daughter to have the best education in Cambridge. Send him or her to any elementary school you like." As a matter of fact, Cambridge has an open choice plan among its high schools. As a parent in Cambridge, you're allowed to send your child to any one of the public high schools, with some technical qualifications. That's a good thing that empowers people to make decisions best for their family. We're running an education system to educate kids, not to please bus drivers or bureaucrats.

QUESTION: So your idea is that parents could just as easily send their child to a Catholic school as a public school.

DU PONT: If they thought that was in the best interest of their child, that's the kind of power to give to parents in America.

QUESTION: Governor du Pont, my question is that we've had tremendous success at job growth over the last few years. But I see an increasing number of the homeless. Why is there this discrepancy, and what's the answer?

DU PONT: The answer is good programs for people who need physical care or mental care, to get that care to them. And the answer is to continue to expand the number of job opportunities in our country and to think in terms of that economic growth as our first priority as opposed, Mr. Kalb, to worrying about $22 billion or $23 billion.

KALB: Hey, to you 22, 23 billion dollars is nothing. To me it sounds like a lot of money.

QUESTION: In your view, what is the goal of U.S. policy in Nicaragua? Do we want to negotiate with the Sandinistas or overthrow them?

DU PONT: Neither of those is the goal. There are three goals in Nicaragua. First, to bring freedom to the Nicaraguan people, as we want to bring freedom to everyone around the world. That's part of the legacy. Second, to make sure that the fragile democracies that surround Nicaragua aren't subverted by it—that the communist infection that is in Nicaragua is not spread to Honduras or Costa Rica or Panama, or ultimately to Mexico. The third goal is the most important of all, and that is to make sure that offensive Soviet personnel and equipment in Nicaragua do not pose a threat to the security of the United States. Missiles would, MIGs would, Soviet submarines would. We want the communists out of Central America. We want them back in Soviet Russia. So our program has to be to try to achieve all three of those goals.

QUESTION: Governor, you're not saying the communists who are in Nicaragua who are Nicaraguans should go back to the Soviet Union.

DU PONT: No, I said, I think, Soviet forces and Soviet troops.

QUESTION: Governor, you seem to be saying people ought to have the opportunity to work, and that's a cornerstone of your campaign. The 20 million gay men and lesbians referred to earlier across the country are being systematically denied employment rights by both the federal government and by countless employers around the country. Do you believe a person denied employment based only on sexual preference ought to have recourse under an amended Civil Rights Act of 1964?

DU PONT: I don't think we need to change the Civil Rights Act in that regard. I don't believe we need to change the Constitution in that regard. We have an equal protection amendment. We have the Fourteenth Amendment. I think those amendments apply and protect all Americans. And I would not change our Constitution or the civil rights.

QUESTION: If it's not working, if people are not, in fact, being protected by those, and if in fact they're being fired or not hired, what would you propose the government do to protect their rights from employment?

DU PONT: To answer that question, I'd have to know something very specific, that is, I'd have to know about the individual case. But I don't think we need any more special constitutional provisions for gays or for others in America. We have a good Constitution, and we ought to enforce it.

QUESTION: As president, sir, what foreign policy would you advocate in the Middle East, in specific, with reflagging of Kuwaiti tankers and the complications of the Iran-Iraq war?

DU PONT: Well, I'm going to take you back. Can I be a historian for a moment, Marvin?

KALB: Where better?

DU PONT: You are old enough to remember Harry Truman.

KALB: I'm old enough to remember anything.

DU PONT: When Harry Truman was president in 1948, the Soviets closed the border to East Germany. They signed an agreement with us that Berlin was to be an open city with the French and the English and the United States and the Soviet Union. They closed that border. Harry Truman is sitting in the White House, and you can almost visualize the scene. An adviser rushes in and says, "Berlin has been sealed off, and surely, Mr. President, you're not thinking of risking American boys' lives by trying to get them food there or you're not thinking of using the American taxpayer's dollars to fly flights in there. What difference does Berlin matter? It's not economically important. It's not strategically important. Let it go, Mr. President." Harry Truman was smart enough to know that sometimes you have to stand on principle. He said, "The principle of a free Berlin is important. And so I am going to risk American boys' lives and spend taxpayers' dollars. I'm going to fly 70 planes of food a day in there until that blockade is lifted." He did the right thing.

We're doing the right thing in the Persian Gulf for an equally important principle. And that's the principle of freedom of the seas. But in the Persian Gulf there are two other things. There's an economic interest—oil. There's a strategic interest in that we don't want the Soviet Union or the madman in Tehran controlling South Asia. So I'd keep American ships there. I'm glad there are ships of five other nations helping us there, and I'd send the entire bill to the Japanese.

KALB: We have less than three minutes to go, and I'd like to call on Professor David Ellwood of the Kennedy School of Government.

ELLWOOD: I'd like to return to the question of social security, which Mr. Kalb raised earlier. Elsewhere you expressed concern about the future of social security, that in the next century we may not have enough money to pay all the retirees. And your plan, in effect, gives tax breaks to people who save now for their own retirement in exchange for less retirement in the future. All the estimates I've seen, even the conservative ones, suggest social security is going to be secure at least until 2040, 2050. And quite possibly maybe forever. On the other hand, the current costs of giving the tax breaks now range from your estimate of $20 billion to as much as $100 billion.

My question is, Why is it so important and responsible to cost ourselves $20 or $100 billion now, when the deficit is clearly a massive problem, and, you yourself acknowledge, for a potential revenue problem that may never arise, and even if it does, it won't arise until 2050?

DU PONT: Let me give you a somewhat different set of facts. Certainly social security is solvent. It's going to pay the benefits for Marvin and for young people. It's going to pay the benefits for Marvin and for all of those who are retired today. But in the year 2017, according to the Social Security Administration, the cash flow turns the other way because that baby boom generation is so much bigger than the generation ahead of it and the generation behind it. And you know there's nothing in a shoe box in Washington today that says Marvin Kalb. All that's in there are some IOUs. And the answer is, in 2017 roughly we'll either have to double social security taxes on young people or reduce benefits. So there will be a significant tax increase in that year unless we start now. And my argument is that allowing people some tax credits to start saving for their own retirement is far better than either cutting grandma's check in half or doubling taxes on our kids.

QUESTION: Isn't it the case that we're going to be building up that trust fund and will have a large trust fund by 2020, when we start to draw it down, and that it won't get exhausted until 2050?

DU PONT: No, because there's nothing there. The day the trust fund is called upon, the government has to raise taxes or sell a bond to get the money to pay it, because today's social security contributions are going out to grandma, and the surplus is being spent by the Congress. And that's why we better act right now to ensure the retirement of an entire generation of baby boomers. I think that's important, and I think the next president has to lead us in that direction.

A CONVERSATION WITH
ALEXANDER HAIG

Photo by Martha Stewart

About the Candidate

Unlike George Washington, Andrew Jackson, William Henry Harrison, Ulysses S. Grant, and Dwight D. Eisenhower—the generals-turned-president he hoped to emulate—Alexander M. Haig won his greatest triumphs not on the field of battle against foreign enemies but in the corridors of power against bureaucratic rivals. He rose to giddy heights, virtually running the country as President Nixon's chief of staff while Nixon was crippled by the Watergate scandal, and proclaiming, "I am in control here," from the podium of the White House press room while President Reagan lay wounded in a hospital after the assassination attempt in 1981.

Al Haig was Reagan's first secretary of state, and it was in that job that he formed the animus toward George Bush that seemed to provide much of the underlying motivation for his own presidential race. As Haig himself was perfectly well aware, his chances of winning were slim: He had no constituency, no experience as a political candidate, and no money. But he turned out to be a surprisingly good campaigner, especially in the televised debates. He also revealed a hitherto antic side of himself, laughing and joking his way along the campaign trail. Apparently, it took a hopeless bid for the presidency to turn the dour general into a happy warrior.

Haig saw combat in the Battle of Ap Gu in Vietnam in 1966, for which he earned a Distinguished Service Cross, but his real forte was staff work. His first assignment after West Point was as administrative assistant to General Douglas MacArthur's chief of staff in Japan in 1949. He also served on the NATO staff and did graduate work in international affairs at Columbia and Georgetown universities. In 1969 destiny came calling in the form of Henry Kissinger, who tapped him to be his military assistant in the Nixon White House. He rose quickly; during what came to be known as the final days, he ruled the ruins as chief of staff.

Nixon fell, but Haig kept on rising: President Ford made him Supreme Commander of NATO. President Carter kept him on the job until 1979, when he left the army for a stint as president of the United Technologies Corporation. Then came Reagan, and Haig was back in power as secretary of state. His tenure at Foggy Bottom was marked by incessant struggles for power with the White House staff, at which, given his experience on the other side, he proved surprisingly inept. Forced out in 1982, he wrote his memoirs, bided his time, and decided to run for president.

Haig's strength as a candidate, unsurprising, was foreign policy. As he showed in his appearance on "Candidates '88," his scorn for

Bush, whom he had observed at close quarters in the White House Cabinet Room, could be withering. Ultimately, a few days before the New Hampshire primary, he withdrew and endorsed Bob Dole.

H.H.

The Interview

KALB: How are you enjoying this running round from one city, one microphone, to another running for president of the United States?

HAIG: I've never had so much fun in my life. If you don't enjoy it, you shouldn't do it.

KALB: Somebody told me you've got to be a little crazy to do it.

HAIG: Well, I meet that criterion.

KALB: A quote to begin with: "In politics when you're running for óffice, you've got to deal with people whom you wouldn't tolerate for 30 seconds. You have to learn to tolerate fools." You recognize the quote?

HAIG: It seems familiar.

KALB: Now, how are you doing tolerating fools these days?

HAIG: Well, no better than I ever did. Sometimes I find myself not tolerated, which might put me in that same category. No, this is a very, very interesting experience. I've done a lot of things. As you see, I've had trouble holding a job over the years, and this is just a new dimension to something I've been closely associated with in the last 20 years. But to see how it works is rather fascinating.

KALB: To go back to the word *fools* once again, who are the fools really? And I don't mean to hold you to that. But are we talking about the American people? Are we talking about politicians, both Democratic and Republican? Or are we talking about the press? Who are the fools? All of the above?

HAIG: You're asking me to commit public masochism here today. I'm not going to do that.

KALB: Just suicide.

HAIG: Let me just suggest that people who are in the business for money, as distinct from those in the business from conviction, I find something less than highly qualified and reliable in many respects.

KALB: Well, in your own campaign you have used Uncle Sams on stilts, you've used clowns. A couple of months ago in Washington, to the press corps you even handed out Chinese fortune cookies, and in one of them it said, "Cookie is delectable, Haig is electable." Did you think up that one?

HAIG: No, I didn't. But it was a family product, and my wife's here today, and I think she's probably chuckling along with my daughter-in-law about it.

KALB: Is this a way to run for president of the United States? It's a serious question. What has happened to the process that makes a serious man like you with your background do that? And all of the candidates are doing it in order to attract attention. Is there something wrong with the system?

HAIG: Well, I wouldn't want to condemn the system out of hand. I do think it has become rather frivolous in that it's all image-making—it's compression personality, profile. There's not enough focus on substance.

KALB: All right. Now image-making. You used the term. You're the boss. Why don't you stop them? Why do you listen to a huckster?

HAIG: It's like Walter Mondale suggesting we should have taxes a few years ago. He was probably right, but it killed him politically, and I don't think any politician—aspiring politician, especially a novice like myself—can walk away and ignore the advice of the pros even though you in some instances may chafe at it.

KALB: No, but what I mean, what makes their advice so sensible at this point? What is so terrific about having a clown walk into a serious meeting? And you're perfectly capable because I have covered you and I know this. You are very capable of doing a very substantive speech and having a substantive conversation. Why bother with the other stuff?

HAIG: Well, it simply doesn't work. I just left what I call a Republican coronation in Orlando yesterday, and I have never seen anything like it in all my life. The two candidates who had it locked and cased for six months before the event must have spent a half a million dollars in balloons and cardboard caricatures. It was really an incredible sight to behold. It's fun, people like it. That's what attracts them to politics. You have to get attention. Unfortunately, the country doesn't go out looking and thirsting for the most highly qualified candidate, nor are they blessed with the most highly qualified public officials who are appointed to the political system, and that also is a tragedy.

KALB: On the serious side, you have been associated in the past with a number of personalities and a number of issues, and I want to link the two. You've been associated with Henry Kissinger in pursuit of détente with the Soviet Union, with Henry Kissinger in the matter in which we got out of Vietnam, with Richard Nixon on Watergate, with Gerald Ford on the pardoning of Nixon. I assume you did all of those things because you thought they were right to do at the time. But there are questions that emerge, and they have to do with whether you were doing them as a good military man following orders from your commander in chief, whether you truly believed at the time that they were the right thing to do. Is this a prescription for presidential leadership?

HAIG: Well, first, Marvin, that litany of experiences you describe would suggest each and every one was wrong and some kind of a failure. I don't agree with that. You know as well as I, having been intimately involved, that politics is the art of the possible. Somebody asked me the other day what the most tragic experience of my life was. And I would say it was having to go along with the Vietnamese peace treaty the way it was constructed. It was a tragedy, but it was the only decent hope to get America extracted from that conflict, even though I suspected at the time that we would be double-crossed, as we were.

KALB: It was a humiliation.

HAIG: The humiliation, but the humiliation that was facing us, did we not settle that war, was even worse with the Congress voting us out directly.

KALB: What about the commander in chief? You were working for Richard Nixon. He was the one giving the final orders on what was happening in Vietnam, wasn't he?

HAIG: Of course.

KALB: Wasn't there another course that could have been taken?

HAIG: Frankly, one is not always totally comfortable with policies that one is associated with, but it is the art of the possible that gives an institution like the one we're in today its life blood, analyzing and reanalyzing. I think it was a mistake to leave Vietnam in the way we did, but unfortunately we were faced with either an impeachment or a limitation on any military operations in Vietnam, and that was in July, following the signing of the peace treaty. So it was politics.

It's like Ronald Reagan today flirting with a peace proposal that spun from the Arias plan, which clearly is a formula for no success from the American point of view, and that's what we're faced with. Otherwise, he'll find himself unable to support the Contras at all, and he's walking a very tight tightrope.

Now I don't have to burnish my credentials here with you, Marvin, with respect to my willingness to stand up on a matter of critical importance. I left Ronald Reagan on that. There were a host of them, including the Middle East, in which you subsequently found yourself involved, where American policy accomplished the impossible. We snatched defeat from the jaws of victory by mismanagement of American diplomacy. I don't know of any leader I've ever worked for, from Robert McNamara on one side to Richard Nixon on the other, who wouldn't tell you that when Al Haig had a point of view, you heard it. Now it is true that as you develop in a career and progress at lower levels, you're confronted with frequent conflicts with your conscience. But you are more willing to tell yourself, "Well, if I just hang in there, perhaps at some point I can make a difference."

KALB: Give me an example of one of those moments.

HAIG: I think very much so on the Vietnam peace treaty. I was profoundly disturbed with it. As you gain experience and as you acquire greater responsibilities, you see the consequences of these misjudgments—and very often history doesn't tell you what would have happened had you done it the right way. That's the great foible of the human experience. But as you go up, then you know. If our vital interests are involved or lives are involved, if you can't have your way, you'd best disassociate yourself from that policy. That's what I have done. I think you did something of the same thing.

KALB: That's true. That's true. Alas.

When you were secretary of state and before you left, I know from aides of yours, you'd go into a rage sometimes at some of your colleagues. I'm told that you would refer to Defense Secretary Weinberger as "incompetent." You would refer to President Reagan as "that poor old man." Do you feel that the President is a poor old man?

HAIG: First, let me tell you to beware of third- and fourth-tier creeps who would talk to you about such things.

KALB: Creeps?

HAIG: They probably didn't know anything about what I did in the first place. It's always very flattering for the press in the State Department to be given these little homilies, these little gems, because it shows that the guy giving it to them is somehow more influential than his job justifies or his pay scale would confirm.

KALB: Would you be surprised if some of these people were actually in the room with you?

HAIG: I would be very surprised if they ever heard me call Ronald Reagan "that poor old man." And I don't agree with that.

KALB: Why did you leave?

HAIG: It is no question I had a certain amount of frustration with Mr. Weinberger, who, in the early part of his tenure as secretary of defense, wanted to be secretary of state more than he did secretary of defense. Maybe that's why we have that zoo over there in the Pentagon that we have today, where billions of dollars of American taxpayers' money is being squandered. That place needs a complete overhaul.

KALB: How would you do it if you were president?

HAIG: Put in somebody who knows something about it like a Bill Simon or somebody of that character who has a track record for management and efficiency.

KALB: What does Bill Simon know about the military?

HAIG: He knows quite a bit. I've been very close to him and discussed it over the years. He knows quite a bit.

KALB: Who would you put in as secretary of state?

HAIG: Are you available?

KALB: You've got a deal. No, I like it here. I'm in charge here. You regret saying that back in 1980?

HAIG: Not one bit. You know I'd have died if you hadn't raised it.

KALB: So would I.

HAIG: Let me tell you, there are many today who look back with nostalgia on that event. But it is also rather important to understand what really happened, and I think I can cover it very quickly.

KALB: Please.

HAIG: The vice president was out of the city. The president was seriously wounded, far more seriously than we could or should have told the American people at the time.

KALB: Did you know it at that time?

HAIG: Yes, I knew it. Jim Baker told me in his first discussion with me. He asked me to go over to the White House and orchestrate the things that had to be orchestrated as he and Deaver and Meese and Mrs. Reagan sat by the President's side, where they should have been. The acts that were done were all a result of a cabinet group that I convened at the White House including recalling Vice President Bush, who hadn't even been notified and was happily preparing to land in Houston, Texas. In the process, there were premature and very dangerous alert measures taken unilaterally within the Pentagon with respect to our nuclear forces.

KALB: By Mr. Weinberger?

HAIG: By the secretary of defense, yes. We had quite a brouhaha about that, and at that point Mr. Speakes, the new acting press secretary, wandered into the press room and was asked, "Have we taken any alert measures?" Clearly the stringers from the field had already alerted some. The answer was "Gosh, I don't know." When he was asked, "Who's running the government?" Answer, "Gosh, I don't know." This was the spokesman for the President, and the whole world was watching every moment on live, real-time satellite television. It was absolutely essential to go upstairs into the press room and correct the impression that we had some kind of a runaway government. And, incidentally, there was a little mischief in the press—at least in one network where they clipped what I really said at both ends and only showed, "I'm in control here," and said this crazy maniac thinks he's going to be next in line to be president.

KALB: You've identified the network as CBS, if I'm not mistaken?

HAIG: Well, I think I named the fellow who did it. His polls have dropped suddenly, recently.

KALB: Actually he's back on top.

HAIG: You're not working for him now?

I hold nothing against him. That's the game. But you know, I had presided over—at least been very closely involved in—the removal of a president and a vice president, and any experienced network commentator should have known that I knew the pecking order for succession. It was never a question of that. It was a question of whether we had a functioning, effective executive branch with the vice president away and a president seriously wounded.

KALB: Mr. Secretary, you've explained it all very well now, and I'm sure we do understand it better, but why has that statement plagued you as it has over the years?

HAIG: Oh, well, it's not hard to plague me anyway. I'm not a fellow known for my humility or my shyness. Only those who know me closely, like you, know a heart beats inside of this exterior.

KALB: Once every week.

Let's talk a moment about the press because there are a couple of innuendos that you have been making here. Do you feel that the press has been doing a good job in this particular campaign?

HAIG: Yes, I do. I have certainly no complaints about the press. They've treated me very, very fairly and perhaps more fairly than I deserve to be treated. I'm not a politician. I started this campaign about seven months ago. The two front-runners have been at it for years, 12 years in the case of George Bush and eight years in the case of Bob Dole. They've both been around the circuit two or three times. Jack Kemp as well, eight years. So I'm as green as the newly mown hay, but I must say the press has not seized on that. Oh, there are ideologues, of course, around the circuit on either side of the spectrum who are always looking for a turkey to carve up.

KALB: What about the issue of sex or drugs? Do you feel there's been too much of an emphasis on that?

HAIG: Well, the only thing I can say to you is that if you ask me a question about it, I'll say it's none of your damn business. And I think that's what the candidates should have been saying. That's not to suggest that, in a contemporary sense, an aspirant for the office of president who is publicly abusing the standard codes of morality in America shouldn't be called to account—and I think that was right in the case of the Bimini kid.

KALB: Let's talk about foreign policy—the Middle East. And I want to take you back to June 1982. We were in Bonn. It was during a presidential trip to Western Europe. The Israelis had just moved massively into Lebanon. Question: Did you give the Israelis the nod—the wink to go ahead?

HAIG: I've seen that, speaking of turkeys resurrected, several times with some help from the White House staff and some help from labor circles in Israel. The facts are precisely the opposite, and the record is so clear that it's excruciatingly so. That involves messages sent by me to Mr. Begin before the entry of the Israeli forces, the two-year-long discussions we'd had with their foreign minister, their defense minister, and Prime Minister Begin repeatedly. There was no question about it, including the latest visit in May of Minister Sharon, when we had both a public discussion of it and a private one-on-one discussion of it in my office. He verified that, incidentally, to the great Washington seat of wisdom, the *Washington Post*, in an interview when he was there.

KALB: In other words, you made it very clear to the Israelis that they were not to go into Lebanon?

HAIG: No, no, no. What you make clear to them is that you won't lie and say that they don't have a right to protect their vital interests, Marvin. And the day you get into that business you're in deep trouble. What you do tell them is if they are going to go into Lebanon, it's going to be in the face of a provocation which is understood and accepted globally, and their response will be

proportional to that. And that was a two-year—almost two years—
10-month position that I gave to Mr. Begin when he first raised it
with me. Incidentally, he raised Lebanon with me, the potential
of going in there, during the funeral of Anwar Sadat in Cairo, and
at that time I gave him that answer and it never changed.

KALB: I remember in Bonn, we journalists were alerted to get
ready—the secretary of state wants to go to the Middle East. Did
you want to go? Who stopped you from going? And what would
you want to do there?

HAIG: Well, of course I wanted to go because I was convinced,
and Begin had called me at 4:00 that morning while we were
outside of Bonn and implied that if I could go there, he could use
that visit to bring under control what were clearly some problems
in Israel, too, on that subject and to bring a halt to the fighting. I
don't know who overruled it. It could have been anyone of the
Meese-Deaver-Baker combination. It usually rotated among the
three or sometimes in collusion, sometimes separately. All I know
is that when I raised it with the President, within a few moments
Mr. Meese gave a press conference saying that there would be no
trip to the Middle East. It had never been discussed with me. That
was just one of the many issues which caused me to resign from
the administration. It certainly was not the most important.

KALB: If you were to become president of the United States,
under what circumstances would you feel that you could commit
American forces to combat? What criteria would you apply?

HAIG: Well, if you're asking me to give you a Weinberger
checkoff list, don't do that, because I won't. And I don't think any
president can answer that question. Clearly, the vital interests of
the American people must be involved—not only in a subjective
way but in a fairly clearly recognized way and a consensus established before such a decision is made, including participation by
the legislature.

KALB: A couple of weeks ago I asked Jesse Jackson if he would
be able to use nuclear weapons if he were president of the United
States. I'm not quite sure, I must tell you, that I understood his
answer, but let me put the question to you directly. Would you, as
president of the United States, be able to use nuclear weapons in
defense of American interest?

HAIG: You must have stayed up late last night developing
these questions.

I don't think it's a question that can be answered in a frivolous
environment of this kind and off the cuff.

KALB: This is not frivolous. This is a very serious university.

HAIG: It's getting that way. You haven't heard the rest of me.

One thing that is clear is that if the United States ever conveyed the impression to the Soviet Union or to our allies, who depend on our guarantees, that this is not a possibility, we might as well wrap up and come home and get ready for what could be a major challenge from the Soviet Union. So no responsible public official would make such a statement, although I know of several who have, including the President. Now—

KALB: I just want to be clear.

HAIG: That you would never use a nuclear weapon? Those statements are not made. I'm fascinated by the nuclear dialogue in America because it lurches from the moral question of the kind you just asked to war-fighting scenarios. And you know, in our debate at Houston, George Bush said, "Your grandchildren and mine will want to know how many nuclear weapons we have done away with." That's the wrong question. What my grandchildren and your grandchildren will want to know is how many wars we prevented. That's the important question. And these nuclear questions and this posture that the American leader takes are so critically intertwined with our ability to prevent conflict that they just cannot be dealt with in isolation, with the kind of question that you asked. I'll tell you another thing to reassure you about my martial air, and that is, I do believe there are things worth fighting for.

KALB: I have to remark that you really are not—do you want to leave the impression that you may use nuclear weapons and the Russians should have that in their minds because that's the essence of nuclear deterrence.

HAIG: That's exactly right.

KALB: But you don't choose to answer the question though?

HAIG: Well, what I'm saying is that you ask such a question devoid of the circumstances and the conditions which would shape a decision of whatever kind to use them or not to use them.

KALB: No. All I'm asking is, Would you be able to use them? I'm not asking you to spell out a scenario.

HAIG: You're asking me to give you a little private confessional on whether or not my character is such that I could or could not. My answer would be, probably I could in extremis.

KALB: Let me ask you this: Congressional committees will come out within the next couple of days with a report on the Iran-Contra scandal. If you were writing that report, what would be the one or two major points you feel should be made in that report regarding the administration's policy?

HAIG: Well, first reread my book *Caveat*, written in 1982, where I predicted precisely this kind of thing. It was inevitable. Secondly, I think the real misjudgment was the failure of the President in the early hours of this crisis to step up and tell the American people, "I did this. I'm responsible. You hold me responsible. I'm going to fire those who mucked up my wishes, carried out my policies. There is going to be no congressional investigation. There's going to be no orgy of self-flagellation here in America. I've cleaned house," and I would have cleaned house and said, "You hold me responsible," much like Jack Kennedy did after the Bay of Pigs—and get on with solving the problems of this country. We lost almost half of a year as our economic crisis was brewing and crystallizing, as our diplomacy was stalled out in Central America.

Let me tell you, we are not in government to have these periods of self-entertainment, where we bring our public officials to the docket every five or six years. Let's get public officials who know what responsibility is and what leadership is, and that is that the buck stops on that president's desk. And if Ronald Reagan had said in November last, "I did it badly. If you don't like it, impeach me," you know no one would have impeached him. And I've been through this with another president, who I think would have done it very differently if he had it to do over again.

KALB: How would you compare Reagan and Nixon?

HAIG: I never give report cards on presidents I've served.

KALB: Okay, but you have been giving one on Reagan though.

HAIG: If you ask me about an issue about any president, I'll be happy to give it to you, but not to presume to psychoanalyze them.

KALB: One final question or area of questioning, really. Look ahead several months. Who do you think is going to be the Democratic nominee?

HAIG: Well, I have a harrowing tale I tell to my Republican colleagues. At the end of Super Tuesday the Reverend Jesse Jackson will emerge as the plurality candidate in the Democratic party, with 25 to perhaps 30 percent. I think the remainder of the Democrats are going to muck around, and I said that I cried when I looked at the paucity of the quality in the Democratic field.

But I'll tell you one Democrat who is not crying. That's Mario Cuomo. He's laughing because he's sitting in the catbird's seat, and either just before or after he sees Jesse Jackson emerge as the plurality candidate, why he's going to make himself available as the unifying savior of the Democratic party. And he's really anguishing, not with whether he'll run, but with the timing he'll use to throw his helmet into the ring, to use that nasty phrase you quoted.

KALB: And you feel that Cuomo may do this after Super Tuesday?

HAIG: Well, no. I think there are a lot of pluses and minuses for him to preempt Super Tuesday, because when people put their vote on the line for a candidate, sometimes by law they can't change it and some are reluctant to do it anyway. Or he may prefer to wait right up until the convention when this gaggle of candidates haven't produced a decisive front-runner and then allow himself to be drafted. Now I hear a lot of skepticism about that, but it's happened before. It happened with Adlai Stevenson, as you'll recall.

KALB: And the Republicans right now. Do you feel that they are realistic about their chances of beating a Democrat next year?

HAIG: I think the Republicans are badly overconfident today. And, as I say, I understand the reason for that. One is the poor qualifications of the Democratic candidates thus far surfaced. And they are poorly qualified. There's no question about it in terms of experience, age, and what a man should bring to this job.

Secondly, you know I think most Republicans believe quite rightly that we Americans do feel better about ourselves in 1987 than we did in 1980. This is no longer going to be adequate, and I've made the point repeatedly that just feeling good about ourselves risks a surrealistic character that faces us with the kinds of things we saw Monday a few weeks ago. And it's time to infuse excellence into American government once again. I think Republicans haven't totally grasped the significance of this.

KALB: Mr. Secretary, we're at that point in the program where I stop asking the questions and we go to the audience to ask the questions. The first question goes to Dennis Thompson, a professor of political philosophy here at Harvard.

THOMPSON: Mr. Secretary, you've been quoted as saying politics and soldiering are very, very close, that they're both fields in which a man lays everything on the line to win or lose. There are other military metaphors—Marvin started with the helmet— the famous Saturday Night Massacre comment to Bill Ruckelshaus, "Your commander in chief has given you an order"—Bill Watts earlier over the Cambodian invasion. I guess we would like your reflections—not so much your own attitudes on courage and standing up to orders that you may or may not disagree with or agree with—Marvin asked about that earlier. But if, as president, you would take some steps or what steps you might take to ensure that your subordinates, if I may use that term, or your colleagues in the administration would, in fact, have some room for dissent, independence of thought and accountability not only to you as commander in chief but to the American people?

HAIG: Professor, first let me comment that I suspect you have a rather selective reading list. Secondly, let me suggest to you that that alleged comment of Mr. Ruckelshaus is a total farce and totally untrue. It might surprise you to know that the whole sequence of Elliot Richardson's and Ruckelshaus's decision to resign was pre-cooked in the President's office that morning in my presence with Ronald Reagan and the attorney general.

KALB: Ronald Reagan?

HAIG: I mean Richard Nixon and the attorney general. I've read Freud too. Now what I'm really saying to you is to be very careful in assessing the character of a man, and don't go to sources which are self-serving and wrong, and that happens to be one and it didn't, incidentally, come from me, the attorney general, or Mr. Ruckelshaus. It came from what I call one of these millions Marvin was quoting about my operations in the morning and in dealing with my staff. And Mr. Watts is a primary case.

THOMPSON: That's why I'm going to you, as a source I'm asking you.

HAIG: He raises questions or he had raised questions which were to me rather shocking in the context of their inaccuracy and their bias. Now I've spent my life running organizations, not just military organizations—big corporations and my own small business—and I've been a bureaucrat par excellence over my 40 years of public service. And let me tell you, the worst mistake that a president or an executive can make is to insist that his staff be a mirror image of his own thinking.

You know, Henry Kissinger, as secretary or as national security adviser, went out and got the most diverse spectrum of political thinking that I have ever seen drawn into a single office. And, boy, did it create a cacophony of horrors. But let me tell you, if you can live with those horrors, if you can listen to those diverse views, chances are you're going to be able to decide the best course of action, which is a reflection of the broad spectrum of thinking in America, but you will also have some soundness because no individual in a complex matter of the presidency is infallible. And the minute he thinks he is, we've got problems.

QUESTION: General Haig, the government of the Philippines under Mrs. Aquino is undergoing difficult times right now. Considering the United States interest in promoting democracy and maintaining the U.S. bases in the Philippines, what would be your foreign policy towards the Philippines, and how does that differ from President Reagan's policy?

HAIG: Well, I don't know that it would differ too much from President Reagan's foreign policy. The United States is now very importantly committed to the success of Madam Aquino. That doesn't discomfort me. I think we are going to have to do all we can, but there are limits. And when we Americans think we are entitled to determine for the people of the Philippines who they will or will not support, then we're re-creating a lot of the fallacies of the '70s, and I saw a lot that sometimes have the unfortunate consequences of making matters worse rather than better.

I think we all know that Madam Aquino is an endangered species today in the Philippines, but we can do no less than wish her well and to help her in every way we can as long as we don't step beyond the line of proclaiming the right to determine the internal affairs of the Philippines for the Filipino people. We don't have that right, and we must avoid it.

QUESTION: General Haig, I would just like to know where you stand on SDI?

HAIG: Where I stand on it? I support SDI for the simple reason I don't believe we have the luxury of turning over a monopoly in outer space to the Soviet Union, which has been actively engaged for the last 20 years in this area, as have we, incidentally. Now having said I support SDI, I was appalled when the President gave that speech in March of '83. He oversold it; he undercut our deterrent. He made it harder rather than easier to get the resources that a president will need to really conduct prudent SDI research and development. And I must say, more importantly, he distorted the arms control dialogue by hyping this SDI system and politicizing an issue which never should be politicized. You never politicize the profound. And national security issues must be bipartisan and totally devoid of political ax grinding or posturing.

QUESTION: What do you mean by that, Mr. Secretary? Could you spell that out a little bit more?

HAIG: On SDI?

QUESTION: Well, on the posturing that you're alleging the President has been engaging in.

HAIG: Having been there and having spent most of my life in this business, as a Republican, I'm not very proud of our record in the nuclear area. We inherited a consensus from the Carter administration to deal with the most important deficiencies in the American strategic inventory with the deployment of 200 MXs. We recoiled from doing so. We still haven't done it. That created a need in political and psychological terms and strategic terms for some kind of a solution to a problem that we were unwilling to politically confront here at home, and that's to deploy more ballistic systems. And then the SDI became some kind of a panacea for this cop out. So we oversold it. We undercut the morality of our deterrent. We unnerved our allies. We gave the Soviet Union an unprecedented vehicle for distorting arms control, which they have done with a vengeance and may do again on the ninth or seventh of December. That's what I'm talking about. No president should talk about sensitive security matters which are still at best no more than a dream on a drawing board and speak of them as though they were achievable and in hand. That's wrong, and it was wrong, and we're going to pay a heavy price for it.

QUESTION: General Haig, I'm a citizen of West Germany, and I got the impression myself, as you did, that many of the West European leaders are indeed unnerved by the INF treaty. In my opinion the treaty will run out—

HAIG: Mr. Bush doesn't believe that.

QUESTION: In my opinion, the treaty will increase the possibility of war in Western Europe instead of lowering such a risk. Now my question is, Assuming the treaty will in fact be signed and ratified by the Senate, what would a Haig administration do to enhance the security of Western Europe and thus the whole world in the face of the overwhelming Soviet superiority in conventional weapons?

HAIG: Well, I think first with respect to the double zero, I'm not quite confident it will be ratified by the next inauguration. I suspect it will not be. I don't think it's possible now, despite the flaws in this double zero option, to cast it aside. The price of that in Western Europe, incidentally, might even be heavier in political terms than to go ahead with it. But what we should do is play the Russian game. Every time Mr. Gorbachev makes a concession, a day or two later he comes and says, "By the way, you have this if you meet these following conditions." He did it with the Pershing 1s in West Germany, of course. And we played his game. What we should say is that we're going to take out half of these Pershings because they're the crucial weapon. But if we don't have an agreement for substantial reductions which correct the imbalances in central strategic ballistics systems, we're just going to have to keep those systems in and in the meantime let both sides go along proportionally with the withdrawal plan.

And secondly, I think there should be an agreement on an approach to the conventional question. But this is a very complex subject, and it must deal not only with numbers of troops, like we seem now to mindlessly be dealing with numbers of nuclear weapons, but the disparities and the anomalies and the differences between the United States here and the Soviet Union right on the borders of Western European powers.

QUESTION: General Haig, there are many high-exposure issues in the campaign—INF and budget deficit reduction. But my question is on domestic poverty, which is a very important issue but doesn't have much exposure. This week is the 25th celebration of the book *The Other America,* which discusses domestic poverty. And as we gather here, there are 21 percent of kids under age 15, which is 11 million kids, living in households of poverty. Does this have a high priority with you, and if so, what specific measures would a Haig administration take to address this problem?

HAIG: It has a very high priority with me, and I'm not at all happy as a Republican. When I served Richard Nixon in the early '70s, roughly 14 percent of our households were below the poverty line, and today some 20 percent are, despite all the bombast about our great supply-side economy. Clearly, this is a matter of utmost concern. You know, we simply have to be able to conduct our statecraft in such a way that we can bring our poverty-level citizens above that poverty line. I like to talk about three rungs of the ladder—the family; education and the kind of opportunity, especially among our minorities, that we the majority have enjoyed; and access to credit, access to start up businesses and availability for jobs. No, I think this is a very important thing.

QUESTION: What, if any, conclusions do you draw about the health of our economy from the instability in the world financial markets?

HAIG: I'm worried, but I'm not panicky. And there's been a little bit of panic injected in the system, some of it politically motivated, of course. But you don't know what to do about these twin deficits unless you know how we got them, and I haven't heard a candidate on the stump describe how we got them. I think I know because I sat at the cabinet table and watched it happen.

We instituted two directly contrary schools of economic theory simultaneously—a growth theory supply-side and the Laffer curve from California—deregulation of tax rebates, enough to get our engines turning and provide the revenues we needed. But Paul Volcker, facing 13 percent double-digit runaway inflation, knew that he had to get that under control. So he launched a constraint school of economic theory—monetarism, tight money, high interest—to squeeze inflation out of the economy, and he did it with a vengeance. And God bless him for doing so. He was right. But it was like putting the economic engine in first gear and reverse at the same time, and the grinding you heard was the mounting national debt.

And we have doubled from $1 trillion to $2.3 trillion as I speak today on our national debt. And most importantly—and here's what most Americans haven't really gleaned yet—we have transformed America from a creditor nation to a debtor nation, and that very act has lost for us a measure of our nationhood and nothing enjoys the urgency, in my view, as getting that situation corrected.

QUESTION: In your long career as a public servant, Mr. Secretary, you've always been a creature of the executive branch and you've never had to deal with the legislature in any kind of a major way. If you were elected, sir, what would your relationship be with the Congress? Would you treat them as a partner or as an adversary?

HAIG: That's a very important question, and the facts are as White House chief of staff, I bet I spent 70 percent of my time in legislative affairs. So I've had extensive experience with it. And let me tell you what is really the problem of our federal government today, if I may in my view, and that's the collapse of a partnership of responsibility between the legislature and the executive branch. I think the worst thing a president can do is to run it as a tactical scorecard. All I heard in the first three years of this administration is that the President rolled the Congress again. The President rolled the Congress again, and now they're sitting in the catbird's seat, and they're crowing the same message.

You're got to sit down with these congressional leaders of both sides of the aisle—committee leaders—every Monday morning and deal with every problem you face and hammer out a consensus. It's tougher today because the Congress has lost its discipline. I don't mean that in a frightening sense. It's one man one vote, and the more outrageous the junior member of a committee is, the more attention he's going to get from the media and the more likely he'll be revoted back into his sinecure.

QUESTION: Secretary Haig, you've brought up the matter of your heart, and I'd like to ask what conclusion voters should draw about your tenure and your reliability in office given triple bypass surgery?

HAIG: Right. First, it was double bypass. And the day that I called Henry Kissinger after his triple, he said, "Al, how many did you have?" And I said, "Two." And he said, "Well, I had three!" Well, let me tell you, I've just come back from the Houston Heart Center. My operation was done by Denton Cooley and my cardiologist, Bob Hall. I've had a similar examination at Cornell Medical Center in New York. I came out with flying colors, and I think both of the specialists involved said that I'm in better shape than most 62-year-old-men who haven't had a double bypass, and I'm willing to take my chances on that. You'd be surprised how many chief executives running our biggest corporations in America have had it. The chief of Signa in Philadelphia, Bob Kirkpatrick, who's been playing tennis with me regularly since, had his done the same day I did. So don't read too much into it.

KALB: He plays a pretty wicked game of tennis too.

HAIG: When the good Lord is going to take you, he's going to take you.

KALB: Our last questioner, Sissela Bok, associate professor of philosophy at Brandeis University.

BOK: Secretary Haig, I want to say that I think a lot of people here and in the public have a strong sense of sympathy for the prolonged and intense scrutiny that you and the other candidates are undergoing with respect to character and other issues. At the same time, however, I think it's also true that they don't feel they know very much about the candidates yet, in particular, not at all about how they think candidates will, in fact, respond once they're in office. In part this has to do with what you mentioned—image-making—which I think is very destructive for the public and for the candidates.

But my question is whether you would agree also that in part, and perhaps in very large part, the problem resides in a tremendous sense of betrayal that the public now experiences, namely, a sense that people have been manipulated, the American public has been lied to, disinformation has become an overt policy of this government, to the point where many people don't want to vote any more, and others simply are very troubled and pursue this kind of probing that is probably inappropriate when it goes too far?

HAIG: I'm not sure I would want to endorse everything that you've said. Let me answer your question by saying that having served seven presidents, I haven't found any particular one of them to be particularly notorious in violating the trust of the people in the context of your question. One thing I have left the experience with is a profound sense, not of the power of the presidency, but of the limitations on the power of the presidency. And his real power, and I guess James Madison knew this as he sat down with his brethren in Philadelphia 200 years ago, is the sharing of power with the courts and the legislature, and the president's real vehicle is the bully pulpit. Because it's his ability to communicate with the people regularly, consistently, reliably, and honestly that really determines what is the president's power and that determinant ultimately is the trust of the people as you so wisely point out. And for too many years poll taking, day to day popularity, pandering to the consensus whim of the people has become the centerpiece of statecraft in the Oval Office.

Well, I would suggest that a lot of our students here might reread Edmund Burke. I think he had some wise observations to make in that regard, and I happen to be an avid admirer of his point of view. What really earns a president credibility, trust, and effectiveness is his track record. Has he solved the problems of the people?

Candidates '88

A CONVERSATION WITH
RICHARD GEPHARDT

Photo by Martha Stewart

69

About the Candidate

Every now and then some member of the House of Representatives mistakes power on Capitol Hill for popularity on Main Street, decides to run for president, and falls quickly by the wayside. For a while it looked as if the campaign of Richard A. Gephardt of Missouri would meet that fate, joining the Wilbur Mills effort of 1972 in the annals of forgotten futility.

It didn't turn out that way. Although Super Tuesday ultimately ended his dream of becoming the first congressman to go directly to the White House since James A. Garfield in 1880, Dick Gephardt surprised the pundits and pollsters by putting up a far tougher fight than they had judged him capable of. He offered something that is still consistently undervalued, even in the wake of Reagan's political success: a clear, powerful message. That message was economic nationalism, with strong anti-establishment overtones and a heavy dose of protectionism.

Gephardt, 47, was an unlikely figure to lead an anti-establishment revolt (which only underscored the political appeal of what he had to say). He has never been a rebel. Beginning as an Eagle Scout in the blue-collar St. Louis neighborhood he would later represent in Congress, he always sought to please. At every stage of his rise from ward committeeman to city alderman to congressman to member of the inner circle of House leaders, his pattern has been to ingratiate himself with his senior colleagues and then, when something came open, move up to the next level with their support.

Gephardt has unquestionably been an effective and influential congressman. His most noteworthy achievement was coauthorship, with Senator Bill Bradley, of the Bradley-Gephardt tax plan, which became the basis for the 1985 Tax Reform Act. By the time that passed, however, he had switched his focus to trade issues, and as chief proponent of the Gephardt Amendment he has become perhaps the nation's leading advocate of sanctions against trading partners which limit American imports.

A founder of the centrist Democratic Leadership Council, and perhaps the most conservative Democrat in the race by background and experience, Gephardt has moved to the left on such issues as abortion and aid to the Nicaraguan Contras. This opened him to damaging attacks as a "flip-flopper," though he really had no choice if he was to have any hope of nomination. On "Candidates '88" and elsewhere, he consistently denied that his trade proposals amounted to simple protectionism. Yet there was no doubt he had struck a chord, as his impressive victory in the Iowa caucuses would show. In the end his opponents would afford him the sincerest form of flattery: By springtime, both Michael Dukakis and Albert Gore had appropriated, for their own purposes, the Gephardt theme of economic nationalism.

H.H.

The Interview

KALB: Congressman, let's start by talking politics. The latest Gallup poll, and I quote, concludes with the following sentence: "No topic has received less public attention than the 1988 race for the White House." We hear about a Democratic six-pack. We have heard about dwarfs. We see Mario Cuomo being terribly coy out of New York, and we even hear that Gary Hart may once again reenter the race. What is it about the Democratic candidates? Uninspiring, poor choice, brilliant people who are not yet recognized for their brilliance. What is it?

GEPHARDT: I think two things. First, you have to remember that none of us is really worthy of being president of the United States. I think we want someone perfect to be president, so none of us, no matter who runs, is going to really reach the mark. We want someone supernatural. So whoever gets in the race will become another human being and disappoint us to some extent. Second, I think as time goes on, people are going to see there are good candidates in this race. I think that as they get to know us— we've had a lot of debates, a lot of chances to talk about the issues that affect this country—people will see there are good candidates.

Remember back in 1976, no one really knew who was in the field, and there was always talk of who else would come in the race—even after Jimmy Carter had started to win in Iowa and Jerry Brown from California got in the race, Frank Church got in the race. And Jimmy Carter finally won it. So I think that as time goes on, you'll see it will be a race like that one. Someone will catch fire in the early days and go on and win this race and be the next president.

KALB: In preparing for this conversation, I have read a good deal about you. And I want to tick off some of the adjectives I have read more than others. There are five that come to mind. Cool, competent, opportunistic, pandering, pragmatic—but not passionate. That word didn't come up. And apparently not capable really of arousing passion, or so some of the people who have been following you seem to feel. Does it worry you that people have the impression that you yourself are not passionate about issues and are incapable of arousing passion in the electorate?

GEPHARDT: I think that people who have been following me recently in the campaign—I'd say over the last six to eight months—have seen speeches and talks that do arouse passion, and I certainly do feel very strongly about what we need to do in this country. I'm running because I want our country to meet the challenges that I think we face, and I think they are considerable. And I have worked in the Congress, probably harder than anybody in this race in either party for issues and causes that I believe in, whether it's tax reform or trade or improving the health care system, keeping social security strong, doing something about the energy issues that we face, nuclear test ban treaty, fighting aid to the Contras. I led the fight on the floor eight times, convinced some of my colleagues that we should take that on. Fighting the Senate version of Gramm-Rudman which would have been the realization of Reaganomics. Those are issues I have fought on and feel very deeply about.

I think there's a difference between being ideological and having strong feelings and sometimes getting something done. I'm a person who likes to get things done. If you have an idea, if you have something you feel strongly about, then it's got to be important enough to you that you can get it done. I think I can get things done. That's been my record in the Congress, and I think that's what we need in a president in '88.

KALB: Let's talk about Iowa for a second. You visited all 99 counties. You started campaigning in that state in 1985. In May of this year the *Des Moines Register*—you're smiling already—which is certainly the best newspaper, the most prominent newspaper in the state, ran a poll. Among the Democrats, in May you were number one, and your approval rating was 24 percent. Last week the same newspaper places you number three, approval rating 14 percent. Obvious question: What has happened to Dick Gephardt's campaign and popularity in Iowa?

GEPHARDT: Well, first, you can't believe every poll you read. Some of them—

KALB: Well, you believe the one in May.

GEPHARDT: I believe that one a lot more than the last one. I think we're doing very well in Iowa. We've worked very hard. We're competitive in that state. But I'll say this. I think my campaign is the only campaign that is competitive everywhere. We're competitive in New Hampshire. We're competitive in Iowa. We're competitive in the South. I compete against Simon and Dukakis in Iowa, against Governor Dukakis in New Hampshire, and against Jesse Jackson and Al Gore in the South. To win this campaign you've got to do well enough everywhere. And I think we're going to do well in each place, and I think I'm going to be the next nominee.

KALB: There is still the perception among some political experts that your campaign seems to have plateaued. And I'm not talking just about Iowa, but throughout the country. Does that worry you at all?

GEPHARDT: Every campaign has an ebb and a flow. You can't be up on top throughout this whole thing. There's no question that as other campaigns have come along, people look at those campaigns. Some people get attracted to them. But the fact of the matter is the great majority of people in Iowa, and I suspect in New Hampshire and in the South, are undecided. The big winner so far in Iowa is still undecided.

KALB: Undecided, I thought, came in second in Iowa behind Paul Simon.

GEPHARDT: No, no.

KALB: Twenty-four percent to 20 percent, wasn't it?

GEPHARDT: I don't think so. I think if you really look at it, undecided is still winning, and most people are still making up their minds.

KALB: Your hometown newspaper, the *St. Louis Post Dispatch,* refers to Paul Simon's campaign now as a rocketship. Is he now, in your view, the guy to beat in the Democratic party?

GEPHARDT: He's doing well at this particular point, and he is, I think, becoming known by more voters as we go along. But this is a long marathon contest. This is a three-year proposition—at least a one-year proposition—and it takes time. People judge us, scrutinize us, and decide who they want to be the next president. That takes a lot of time, and as time goes on, people will see Paul, they'll see Governor Dukakis, they'll see the rest of us, and they'll make judgments. The time you want to peak is not November the 15th. You want to peak on February the 8th in Iowa, and then a week later in New Hampshire, and then in the South. I think that's what I'm going to be able to do.

KALB: We're talking about the people who are formally in the Democratic race. There is the governor of New York who sits on the sidelines. And I wonder whether you think it is fair for Cuomo to sit on the sidelines and tantalize everybody with the possibility that at some point down the road he might be enticed into becoming a candidate and being drafted?

GEPHARDT: I think he's just being honest. He has said over and over again that he doesn't want to be a candidate, that he's the governor of New York, and he thinks that's inconsistent with what you have to do to be a candidate. When he's asked, will you make the Shermanesque statement, he says no, and I don't think he should either.

KALB: Why not?

GEPHARDT: Because he doesn't know if we're going to wind up in a muddled situation, which isn't likely, where no one has near enough votes and the party has to look for someone else. I don't think that's going to happen. He doesn't think that's going to happen, and it probably won't happen. But for him to have to say, "No, I would not be president under any circumstances," I think would be unrealistic. So I think he's just trying to be honest, and I think we ought to take it for what he says.

KALB: But if he's trying to be realistic, isn't he at the same time leaving open the possibility that all of you get just a bit more nervous, that the people who write about the campaigns, press people particularly, get more and more tantalized by the possibility that this man may eventually become a candidate? And I wonder whether it is fair. I go back to that word. If he is in any way serious about this, don't you think he ought to jump in?

GEPHARDT: First of all, I'm not nervous about it. I decided a long, long time ago that I wasn't going to worry about who was in or out of this race. I have to run my race. I have to say what's in my heart and mind about why I want to be president, and let the rest of the campaigns do their own thing. Second, I really think that as in '76, there's always going to be press speculation about someone. No one will ever be content with whatever the field is. There's always going to be somebody else who could come in. In '76 there were other candidates always lurking around the outskirts of the field. But this is a process of winning delegates, and if you're going to be the nominee, you have to go out there and run, put yourself in front of the American people and ask for their vote. Somebody's going to win enough delegates to be the nominee, and I doubt that it's anyone who's not in the race today.

KALB: We care a lot in this school about process, trying to understand process. You're right in the middle of the process of trying to become president of the United States. What do you think about the way it happens? What do you think about the validity, the wisdom, and logic of the process that you are experiencing and we're just watching?

GEPHARDT: It has some logic, and I think it has some merit. First of all, it starts in small places—Iowa, New Hampshire. You can argue whether it should be in other places and if we should move it around. But the facts are that's what we wound up with. And it does allow someone who's unknown like myself and probably most of the other candidates to get in the race. It allows you to go there and campaign over a long period, see voters and have a chance to get yourself into the race. I think that's good.

Second, by having it start in those kinds of small states, it allows voters, as we're doing here today, to have a chance to appeal to the industrial North, but conservative enough to appeal to the South.

KALB: Which one of those candidates now running—and I really want you to surprise me with your answer—do you feel has that kind of balance?

GEPHARDT: Well, obviously I think I do.

KALB: That was right over the plate.

GEPHARDT: That's right. I could see that one coming.

KALB: Okay, you've answered it, but let's go beyond it. When you look at this, you, for example, have had any number of votes against abortion, against busing, against gun control. Can a Democrat with that kind of voting record really appeal to the liberal wing in the Democratic party?

GEPHARDT: I think you have to go to Iowa and New Hampshire and say precisely the same thing there that you would say in the South, or say anywhere else. The speech in Alabama has to be the speech you give in Iowa and New Hampshire and all the other states. I believed from the beginning that if I could run the same campaign in the early states that I wanted to run everywhere else, I'd have a chance to get nominated and I'd have a chance to be elected president. The Democrats cannot win the presidency without winning our share of the South and our share of the West. I think I can do that. I think I'm the one candidate in this race who can run everywhere and win everywhere.

KALB: Why is it that every candidate, if I would ask that question, comes in with the same answer?

GEPHARDT: Well, obviously we all believe we have to and we can.

KALB: Until 1985—let's deal with the abortion issue for a second—you were for a constitutional amendment against abortion. Then you began running for the presidency, and your position on this issue began to shift. Now you are against a constitutional amendment, but you're still against federal funding for abortion except in cases of rape, incest, and where a mother's life is in danger. That seems to many people like political expediency, and if it isn't, could you explain it?

GEPHARDT: My beliefs have never changed. I think that what you have to look at is how you get to your beliefs. How do you get what you want to see happen to happen? For some time I believed that a change in the law was appropriate. After 14 years of fighting about this issue legally, I come to the conclusion that we've got to address the underlying problems. How do we really encourage people to avoid unwanted pregnancies? How do we get people to choose options other than abortion? And I think even the legal fight we've been undergoing has prevented us from getting people together to do better on those issues, to do better on sex education, on family planning, on giving people viable options to abortion. So I came to the conclusion before the '86 election, before I had to stand in front of my constituents in St. Louis, that that's what we should do. I announced my change. I said exactly why I was doing it, and that's my position. I think we really can do better, and I think that's the way we have to go at this problem.

KALB: You were saying a moment ago that you're still—perhaps you're changing the tactics, but you're still approaching essentially the same goal. What did you mean by that?

GEPHARDT: The goal of trying to give people options to abortion. Cut down on the use of abortion. I think everybody in our society thinks abortion is not a good outcome, not the preferred outcome. So if that's what you believe, then you can do it legally, you can try to affect the outcome nationally, or you can do something to affect the underlying problems. I also became concerned that the people who were advocating a legal change were some who were against increased funding for family planning, were against the very things that I felt could really change the outcome in reality. And I really became concerned that we were not doing what we could do. So I think to continue the legal battle, constitutionally or judicially, is not going to get us to the real outcome that we need to effect.

KALB: But philosophically or maybe even religiously, do you feel that abortion is the killing of life?

GEPHARDT: I think everyone, even the Supreme Court in *Roe* v. *Wade,* said that at a certain point an abortion is improper. So we can have disagreements, and obviously we always will, about where the line should be drawn. But the fact is, I think all of us believe that abortion is not the preferred outcome. So the question is what do you do about it? How do you practically effect a better outcome? And it seems to me now that the best thing to do is to try to do better with family planning, sex education, maternal health, welfare programs to really begin affecting the problem.

The other point is along about 1982 or '83 even the people advocating legal change changed to a states rights amendment, which would have put us back, I guess, to where we were before

Roe v. *Wade*. So they would have left us in a position where some states allow it, some states don't, and you're back to the underlying problem. That's what we have to go at.

KALB: Why, in your view, is abortion such a difficult political issue, particularly for someone running for president?

GEPHARDT: Because we don't agree on it. There's a profound disagreement in the country, but I really think the majority of people want to move on with what are realistic solutions to the problem. That's what I've been trying to talk about.

KALB: Assuming for a minute that you win the nomination and the election, how would you structure the White House staff so that there would be no possibility of an Oliver North emerging to run his own foreign policy?

GEPHARDT: I'm not sure that the structure or the process is that important in the outcome. I think you have to be a president who knows what you want to do and sets those goals with your subordinates and the people working with you and then makes them accountable to you, so that they're carrying out those goals in a way that you think is appropriate. I think you also have to say to the National Security Council people and to the people at the CIA that you don't want a foreign policy implemented in those agencies, that you want it done in State, and to some extent in Defense, that you want there to be proper coordination, which the National Security Council is supposed to do, and you want proper intelligence information developed by and dispensed by the Central Intelligence Agency.

KALB: How would you ensure that that would happen in that way?

GEPHARDT: Well, first you bring in people who are willing to work with you and are not independent agents, as I think are some of the people we've seen in this administration.

KALB: I think you'd agree that Oliver North and John Poindexter felt they were very much working for the President, serving his interest certainly.

GEPHARDT: But they seemed to have a blank check. We had a president who was not engaged, who was not making them accountable, who was not talking to them frequently enough or finding out often enough what they were doing. So it really comes back to the President. This President has had a sign on his desk that Truman had that said, "The buck stops here," but it turns out that about nine cents of the buck stopped on the President's desk.

KALB: On that particular point, do you believe John Poindexter when he says that he wanted to provide the President with deniability, and therefore on his own stopped critical information about the diversion of funds to the Contras from going to the President?

GEPHARDT: I don't know the answers. Obviously, the report that we have now doesn't really know the answers to that either. We can all have conjecture and we can surmise what was going on, but there are no hard facts that the President participated in any of that, but obviously he is negligent. He's guilty of negligence in what was happening in his own administration. There's no denying that. And that, I think, is an indictment of his leadership. And that's what you elect a president for—to lead. To lead the country, to lead his own people, to lead the Congress. This President hasn't done that.

KALB: On foreign affairs in general, you have been quoted as saying, "We should think about other countries as we do of local politics. The people running those other countries are just like us, politicians." Now do you really think that Mikhail Gorbachev is just like Dick Gephardt?

GEPHARDT: In many, many ways he is. He has to hold power. He got to power by being a successful politician in his own context, in his own system. But clearly, he is someone who is acceptable enough to the party leaders all over that republic. And he is right now, I think, backtracking from some of the things he started out with because he's trying to keep his political power. Se we need to recognize that. We need to approach him or any other leader with an understanding that all of us have to have a certain amount of acceptance from the people we're trying to lead. And I think we have to look at other countries as they are and not so much as we would like them to be or as we think we are. I think we often look at other countries—in trade, for instance—through our own eyeglass. We see them as we are, and we think they're going to respond to the same things we do. And the fact is they don't. They're different. They have a different culture, a different history. I think we have to look at all that as we look at them as political leaders as well.

KALB: Now you mentioned trade. Again, you are quoted as saying, "80 percent of the $160 billion trade deficit is our own fault." If that is the case, and many economists agree with you that it is, why then are you in the forefront of pushing what is described as punitive trade legislation through Congress,—it may not get through Congress, by the way, but at least you're pushing that through Congress—when four-fifths of the problem is right here at home?

GEPHARDT: Well, the fact that the majority of the problem may not be unopened markets is not enough reason to forget that issue, or not to make it an issue. I never said anywhere that that is the only thing we need to do. We face tremendous challenges economically to be excellent, to be productive, to be strong in a world marketplace. But I think one of the places to start is to be able to say to American business and American workers, "We've constructed a level playing field for you. You have a fair chance if you can make good products to go into the world marketplace and sell those products." We can't say that with a straight face today. And there are a lot of people who believe that more than 20 percent of our problem is unopened markets. So it is an important problem. It is a place to start. And one of the things government can do is construct an environment in which businesses and workers in this country can be successful. So why do we constantly put it off to the side and say it's not a problem? One last thing, the bill is not punitive. It's against protectionism. It is a foe of protectionism. And it's trying to construct what we should be, a world common market where trade between all countries is as fair and as free as it is between the states of the United States.

KALB: I used the word *punitive*. I didn't say protectionist— although that word is applied very, very often to describe your particular amendment.

GEPHARDT: By people who haven't read it and don't understand it.

KALB: The President and the Congress have now come to a two-year, $75 billion compromise on the budget deficit. Does that seem to you to be a good proposition, a good thing to have happened? Or does it seem to you that possibly the big, tough economic decisions are still being postponed until after the '88 election?

GEPHARDT: Well, the answer to your last question is the big decisions are still being put off. This is not an optimal solution. But it's better than the other two alternatives right now. One would be doing little or nothing, and that could have happened. The other would be having the Gramm-Rudman automatic cutting procedure go into effect, which would have been 50 percent defense, 50 percent domestic, but all cuts, no revenues. So given where we are, given the fact the President is not leading on the budget issues, he's not on almost every other issue, this is about as good as we're going to do. Understand that the Congress, not the President, is leading in this situation. And it's very hard for a committee of 535 people to lead. That's what's happening. Now all the specifics are probably not going to be very acceptable or very positive. But given the situation, given the lack of presidential leadership, this is a pretty good outcome.

KALB: Let me ask you a couple of questions about space. President Kennedy, at the beginning of the '60s, said that it would be a magnificent goal for the United States to put a man on the moon by the end of the decade, and the United States was able to do that, and it was really a tremendous event. Made everybody feel good. And it was also technologically an extraordinary achievement. Could you yourself proclaim some glorious new goal in space for the United States?

GEPHARDT: I don't think there's a glorious new goal. We've got some goals out there. I was in Alabama the other day at the Huntsville Rocket Center. And I went through a mock-up of the space station that we've been talking about and working on for a long time. It's supposed to go up in the early '90s, and if it goes up, it would be a good next step in our space program. In about a year we're going to put up the new space telescope which will allow us to see into space 300 or 400 times better than we can today. That's going to be exciting. So those are good next steps. Nothing unexpected there. But I think they should be continued. We can't, in this budget, really spend a huge amount of money on some grandiose space project at this point. But that doesn't mean we can't make good progress.

KALB: You have said that you can't even spend any more money on space.

GEPHARDT: If we keep the funding we have now, we can continue the programs that we see.

KALB: But it seems as if the Russians are just zooming ahead of the United States in space now. Since the *Challenger* disaster, the United States has done nothing in space. Is the U.S. simply to accept second place at this time?

GEPHARDT: Let's talk about other goals that we might want to set that might be more important than putting a person on Mars or taking a trip to wherever that could be grandiose and akin to what Jack Kennedy did in 1960. I want to state a goal for the country in my inaugural address in January of 1989. I want to say that by the year 2000 we will have the best educated people in the world. Now that's a goal that's going to be harder to reach than putting a person on the moon. It's going to involve all the American people. It will cost lots of money. But when I look out over the next 20 years and see the challenge we face, economically and every other way, I think the only way we can meet those challenges is if we have the best educated people in the world. We can do it. We must do it. And that's the kind of challenge that I'd like to set for America.

KALB: I think that everybody would probably agree that's a very noble goal. But you just said about space and I imagine about just about everything else that we don't have the money to do it. We keep facing the necessity of cutting back, not expanding the amount of money. This kind of a program on education that you care about so deeply is going to cost what? Ten billion dollars is one estimate I've seen.

GEPHARDT: We spend $10 billion a year now federally on education. We're going to spend $11 billion this year on corn subsidies. So I think our priorities aren't quite right. We can do better with the Harkin and Gephardt bill, and with farming, to give farmers a fair price for their product from the marketplace. Cut back on that, and put money over in education. Leadership is about setting priorities. We can't do everything. I've been very clear about that. I've said we've got to decide what's important. But as I look out over the next 20 years, having better mental capacity, having better prepared people is going to be the most important thing in our future.

KALB: Congressman, let's widen our circle, so to speak. I will not ask any other questions for the remainder of our hour but invite members of the audience to ask questions. And let us begin with Edith Stokey, a lecturer in public policy here at the John F. Kennedy School of Government.

STOKEY: Welcome to the school, Congressman Gephardt.

I'd like to push you a little further on the Gephardt Amendment. You've been pursuing this cause for two years now, maybe more than two years, and it's finally passed the House. It's in conference committee. But let's face it. The prospects don't look enormously good that it will come out of the conference committee in any form that you would recognize. But during these two years the world has changed a lot, and, in particular, if you think about what's happened with the dollar, the fall that began in early '85, we're beginning to see the picture changing. We're beginning to see a turnaround in the sorry state of the current account balance. Given these changes, and given the likelihood that your amendment is not going to make it through, and given the free fall of the last month, which will make matters even better as far as the current account is concerned, do you plan to offer the amendment again in the next Congress?

GEPHARDT: First of all, the conference is between a bill that I passed in the House which requires the president to negotiate with other countries generally about opening markets and then gives the president the option of using penalties if there's no progress. The Senate passed a very similar proposal. And let me explain what I think this whole concept is about and why I think it's important. Under present law if you have an unopen market or an unfair trade practice, the way you complain about it is to go to the International Trade Commission and make a case, and if there is finally a hearing and a decision, you then can get your grievance redressed. It takes a long time. It's inefficient. It's very slow. And by the time you get action, you're usually out of business anyway. It's not very effective. So my approach says, let's take this on a country by country basis. Let's look for a pattern of unfair trade practices. Let's ask the president to negotiate with that country on the whole spectrum of things that are wrong, and let's give pressure or power to the president if he or she wants to use it to begin penalizing a country that won't begin in a general way, in a wider way, to open their market to us. It also encourages them to open their market to everybody else.

Now what's the goal, and how is the world changed? The goal is to get a world common market. We've got to get other countries to open up to a much greater degree. I don't think we're ever going to achieve that on a piecemeal, commodity by commodity basis. I think we've got to move to the kind of negotiation we recently had with Canada, where we got a free trade treaty between our two countries.

If my amendment or the Senate amendment, or, more likely, something in between is passed, I think you'll see more treaties like the U.S.-Canadian trade treaty. And that to me is the wave of the future. That's what we've got to be accomplishing—it will be good for us, and it will be good for the whole world.

One last statistic. If you look at Third World countries and their export of manufactured products, today they export 62 percent of their manufactured products to the United States, 7 percent to Japan. There's got to be an opening up. There's got to be movement in world markets so that trade between all countries is as free and as fair and as easy as it is among the states of the United States. That's my goal, and the Gephardt Amendment will get us toward that goal.

QUESTION: Congressman Gephardt, there's been a lot of talk of Jesse Jackson being a power broker at next year's convention. If you're the front-runner at the convention but you don't have the majority of delegates and you need Mr. Jackson's support to win the nomination, what kind of concessions would you make to Mr. Jackson in exchange for his support, and would you agree to make Mr. Jackson your running mate?

GEPHARDT: I'm going to get enough votes to win before the convention starts. No one today is prepared to say who would be their running mate. I would decide on two grounds. First, who would be a good president, and who could help us win the presidency in 1988. Those are the two criteria.

QUESTION: What will the government's role be in encouraging and promoting new manufacturing and industrial technologies?

GEPHARDT: Well, first we've got to create an environment in which there can be economic growth, so all of the usual suspects have to be looked at. The budget, tax policy, monetary policy, energy, agriculture, trade. We have to create an environment in which businesses new and old can grow and prosper. Second, we have to help produce the kind of workers and the kind of managers who will make us excellent, make us productive, make us high in performance. Third, we've got to have the kind of capital available in our society so that young, growing businesses can start. And finally, we have to have a role in research, new ideas, new technologies, and in my view, a lot of the research that's going on today on the defense side has to be moved to the civilian side to make that happen.

QUESTION: Representative Gephardt, within your plan to bolster education, do you see merit pay as key to that? And if you do, who's going to determine the standards with which the teachers will be judged?

GEPHARDT: The president and the Congress should not be the national school board. Questions like merit pay, how much to pay teachers, and how long the school day and school year are should be decisions that have to be decided at the state and local level. But from the federal level I would like to back up my goal of having the best educated people to say to state and local school boards, "If you can improve your educational outcomes, we will give you extra federal money for education. You figure out how to do it, but we want to make you accountable with dollars to get the outcome we need as a country." I think that makes a lot of sense.

QUESTION: Excuse me, Congressman, I'm a visiting fellow from the USSR, and it's interesting. What is your opinion about the possibility of Gorbachev's speech in Congress?

GEPHARDT: Well, I'm a leader in the House. I'm chairman of the House Democratic Caucus. And while I don't condone everything that the secretary has done, while I don't agree with everything the Soviet government does or wants to do, I don't think we should let an opportunity pass to have the leader of the Soviet Union, if he's in the United States, communicate. And I would hope it would be a two-way communication with the members of the Congress.

KALB: To the best of my knowledge, the White House has in effect said that is not going to happen.

GEPHARDT: It can happen in other ways, and I would hope we could find a way to do that. And I want to be aggressive and enthusiastic about trying to figure out how to do that. There are other places where that communication could take place, and I hope it will take place.

KALB: You mean within committees?

GEPHARDT: Within committees or informally, in the House Democratic Caucus. We had a meeting with President Arias that was a joint meeting of the House and Republican caucus. I have a sense that the Republicans aren't too interested in using their caucus to do this. I don't see what we can lose by this. He's here. He doesn't come here often. What are we going to lose? We don't condone everything the Soviet Union has done in its history, and I'm sure he wouldn't condone everything we've done either. I think it would be good if our President could go on television as was talked about in the Soviet Union. We need to talk. I'm a good listener. I like to listen to people. I also like to communicate my thoughts. I think it's a good chance to do that.

KALB: A question now from Pete Sidebottom, a student of the Harvard Business School and a member of the student advisory committee of the Institute of Politics.

SIDEBOTTOM: Congressman Gephardt, the Gephardt-Harkin Bill, I've heard it said that what it does is shift the payments from the government to the consumer by instituting production quotas and therefore heightening prices and allowing the farmers to make the money from the consumer rather than from government. Would you respond to that charge? And how do you think the Gephardt-Harkin Bill is going to help the consumer and get the government out of the subsidy business?

GEPHARDT: Well, right now we're paying for an oversupply of corn and wheat and other commodities through the tax system, through the budget. As I said a minute ago, we're paying $11 billion this year in corn subsidies alone. The whole agricultural program is about $27 billion. We're spending more on unwanted corn than we are on education at the federal level. So there's got to be a better way to do this. And I can tell you, the farmers in the Midwest do not like this program where they're farming for government checks more than they are for a price from the marketplace. So I think it would be better for everyone if the consumer paid a fair price for products.

Now how do you do it? Greater supply management is what the Harkin-Gephardt Bill is about. You let the farmers vote in every commodity. If they vote for greater supply management, we do it by bushels rather than acres so they can better manage their land environmentally, and we get the supplies down. We try to reach agreements with other countries so they can bring their supplies down, so that farmers worldwide can get what everybody would like to have—a fair price for their hard work. I don't think that's too much to ask.

QUESTION: Congressman, I want to ask you a little bit more about trade. I've always been a little bit nervous of what I perceived as your sort of "let them have it with both barrels" approach to rectifying our trade imbalance. And since black Friday last month, I'm scared to death about it. I mean, I look at the situation right now, on Wall Street the markets are in a tailspin. In Washington there's now emerging a bipartisan consensus for fiscal conservatism, and out on the prairies, you and some of your colleagues and marching up and down campaigning and looking through what seems to me a fairly reactionary trade policy. My question is this: Isn't this the 1930s all over again? I mean, must we stagger from Reaganomics to Hoovernomics? Can you allay my concerns that this is the same pattern that we saw in the '30s?

GEPHARDT: Let's put the ghost of Smoot-Hawley away. Halloween is over. We really don't need to bring him out again, or them out again, because we're in a new world. We have different challenges. It's a new day. We're in a modern time, and we have to begin addressing the problems we face today with solutions that will really work. Now nobody is talking about protectionism. Nobody is talking about anything that even resembles or comes close to what we did back in the '30s. In fact, what I'm talking about is 180 degrees away from what we did back in the '30s. I'm trying to open markets, not close them. I'm trying to get us a world common market, not shut down the American market, which is what Smoot-Hawley did. So we've got to get our thinking out of the past, we've got to get off the labels and stop trying to scare one another with ghosts from the past, and talk about what will work in 1988 and beyond. And we really do need to open these markets. For the reasons I just said, we've got Third World countries that can't sell their manufactured products in Japan, in Taiwan, in South Korea, or in Europe. They need to be able to sell them so their standard of living can go up. Let's all understand, world trade is synergistic. If we can really open it up and have competition, we're going to get everybody's standard of living to go up. That's the goal. That's what my trade amendment tries to do.

QUESTION: Congressman, you've talked tonight about leadership. In regard to your ambitious objective for education, you've said that leadership involves setting priorities, and in particular budget priorities. Those of us here at the Kennedy School believe leadership is more than just setting budget priorities, and in particular it has a lot to do about changing the way people think about an issue. What do we have to do to change the American people's thinking about the education issue in order to achieve your objective?

GEPHARDT: I think we have to get people to see the nature of the challenge we face in the next 10 to 20 years. We're the only country in the world trying to be the best economically and the best militarily at the same time, and we're now in a world marketplace where we're competing against countries that often have a standard of living much lower than ours. So the goal for us is to remain strong from a security and economic standpoint and to compete in a world marketplace and hold our standard of living. If you look at that for just a moment, you really can begin to see how the mental capacity of our people is the key to being able to pull off that challenge, and when I look at what our education system is producing, I get full of anxiety about where we're headed in the future. Twenty-five percent of our youngsters are not going to get their high school degree. We're turning out half the number of mathematicians and scientists as the Japanese and many other countries. We have a huge challenge in front of us. And if people can begin to see that and understand why mental capacity is so important to what we have to do, then I think we can get people excited about investing our wealth in better educated people.

QUESTION: My question is about the elective process and fund raising and about imagery and about reality and about democracy.

GEPHARDT: That's a tall order.

QUESTION: How much money will your campaign raise? What percentage of that will go to manufacture television commercials? What image do you seek to project in those commercials? How real is that image? And is the democratic process served by all this?

GEPHARDT: First of all, we believe we will raise between five and six million dollars by the end of this year. And with the matching funds we'll be at seven or eight or nine million before the first event begins on February the 8th. That is not the biggest budget on the Democratic side by far, but it's an adequate budget and one that I think will get us to the nomination, if we can do well early and then add to that later on. Not much of it will go toward television, at least in the early stage, because so much of the campaigning in the early states is face-to-face campaigning and meetings like we're having tonight. So a lot of your resources go to organization, to travel, to putting on the kinds of meetings and events that you need to do retail politics and retail campaigning. When we do ads we will try to get across the things I believe in, what I care about. I've been more specific in this campaign than I think anyone. We've put out white papers on every issue, white papers on issues I've been working on for 11 years in the Congress. I think that's what the American people want in 1988. They don't want glitzy TV ads, "It's morning in America" and a lot of other stuff that they don't believe anymore. They know better than that. They want real answers to real problems, and that's what I'm going to try to give them in person and on television.

QUESTION: Congressman Gephardt, for most of your political life you've been one of some 400-odd members of the House. What should make us believe that you're going to be effective at taking hold of a rather large number of agencies in the federal government? What executive experience should make us believe that you can do that? It's more than just issues, but being an executive leader.

GEPHARDT: First, I've been a leader in the House. I haven't just talked about tax reform and trade and a lot of other issues. I've put my ideas on paper, and I've been able to take the paper and make it reality. We passed tax reform. We passed the trade bill. We cut off aid to the Contras. We passed the nuclear test ban treaty bill that I worked on for about four years. Second, I'm chairman of the House Democratic Caucus, and I've got 80 members of the House who are supporting my candidacy. If we were in Great Britain, I'd be almost halfway to being prime minister. And I think that's important. We need a president in 1988 who not only can run the executive branch and see that we bring people to the executive branch who can run the agencies, we need a president who can inspire and galvanize the American people and the Congress. I know I can do that. I've done it. And I think that kind of leadership is what we need.

QUESTION: On a PBS special recently Bill Moyers indicated that the Iran-Contra affair, as horrible as it is, is the tip of an iceberg that goes back over 25 years of a secret government that exports terrorism and imports drugs, among other things, in the name of the American people. At the Harvard Law School recently, Attorney Daniel Sheehan spoke of this. My question is, Are you aware of the lawsuit that will be filed in the spring in Miami that will bring these charges to court, and what implications will it have for the image of the United States in the world and our efficacy as a nation?

GEPHARDT: I'm aware of it. I've read about it. I don't know that we need a lot more information to know that, at least in the last seven years, this administration has not been in control of its own government—that we had a secret government carrying out policy that supposedly the President didn't even know about. I suspect though that in the Jimmy Carter period a lot of this didn't go on. I won't say that none of it went on, but I would say a lot less of it went on because we had a leader who was in charge, one who had a CIA leader who was in charge of that body and really did try to bring it under greater control. I believe we can do that. I think good leadership would solve a lot of the problems that we face today. But we haven't had it, and we sure do need it in 1988.

KALB: The final questioner is Richard Haass, a lecturer in public policy here at the John F. Kennedy School of Government.

HAASS: Congressman, as you know, one of the principal tenets of the current administration's foreign policy is the so-called Reagan doctrine, support for freedom fighters around the world. You've made known your views about Central America, about Nicaragua, but what about the other three principal manifestations of the doctrine? Do you support continued aid to the guerrillas in Afghanistan, to the resistance in Cambodia, to the resistance in Angola, and if so, how do you justify this support as opposed to your opposition to aid for the Contras?

GEPHARDT: Well, I think you take each case on its own merits. You don't announce some dogmatic policy that we will never do it or we will always do it, and you approach each case on its own facts. We probably don't have time to go through each of them. But I think clearly in the case of Afghanistan what we've done has been right and proper. These were people who were fighting their invaders with rocks before we finally decided to do something to aid their cause. They had been invaded by an opposing force. There was clearly no legal or moral justification for what had happened. So in that case with no other way to really resolve that conflict, I think you can make a good argument that we should move forward. In the case of Nicaragua, we have not clearly stated a goal. We did not have an invasion coming from another country across a border. We did not use diplomatic options before we went to the military option. And I think what we've done has been clearly wrong.

QUESTION: Congressman Gephardt, would you consider support to the Afghans if, for example, there was very little evidence that if they won they would establish a democracy? Or by contrast, would you change your position on the Contras if the current peace approach breaks down and you were more confident that they might establish a democracy?

GEPHARDT: You can establish all kinds of hypotheticals, and we could sit here and go through hundreds of them. I think the point is you take each case as it comes; you try to find out as much about it as you possibly can. Maybe we could get the Central Intelligence Agency back into the information business and out of the foreign policy business so that we could make sound judgments. It seems to me in all of these you want to try to exemplify and live the values that are expressed in our Constitution, in our Declaration of Independence, and also be competent, be sensible, be in touch with reality. And if we'll do that—put diplomacy first and military action last—I think we can have a much better foreign policy than we've had in the past seven years.

QUESTION: A quick final question. Why were you so fast off the mark in saying no way to the Contras?

GEPHARDT: Because I felt that we had never stated a goal for what we were trying to do. I still don't know what we're trying to do. What is our vital interest in Nicaragua? Is it to have *La Prensa* open, or is it to get rid of the foreign military influence that threatens us or our neighbors, or is it to keep them from interfering with their neighbors? I think the last two are vital interests. But I think you first try to do it diplomatically, and finally militarily. We've not clearly stated the goal, and we have the cart before the horse. We use the military first, rather than last.

Candidates '88

A CONVERSATION WITH MICHAEL DUKAKIS

Photo by Martha Stewart

About the Candidate

Nobody had to give Michael Dukakis directions to the John F. Kennedy School of Government for his appearance on "Candidates '88." Dukakis is the K-School's favorite son, and he knows his way around the place. In 1978, after his shocking defeat for renomination as governor of Massachusetts, Dukakis could have settled into a lucrative law practice. Instead, he chose to join the Kennedy School's faculty as a lecturer in Public Policy and director of the State, Local, and Intergovernmental Center. His wife, Kitty, still works there as Director of the School's Public Space Partnerships Program.

The Kennedy School was not just a place for Mike Dukakis to hang his hat for three years while he plotted a political comeback. He was an active, conscientious, and by all accounts excellent teacher. Apparently, he learned a few things, too: In 1982 he took back the governorship, compiled a widely acclaimed record, and was reelected overwhelmingly to a third term in 1986.

For Dukakis, that 1978 defeat at the hands of Ed King, a conservative Democrat who has since become a Republican, was almost the only setback in a lifetime of uninterrupted success. Some say it was the best thing that ever happened to him. It humbled him, softened his righteous edge, and taught him the virtues of compromise and consensus.

Dukakis, 54, still lives a few blocks from where he was born in Brookline. As a student at Swarthmore College he set his sights on the Massachusetts State House, and two years after he got his law degree from Harvard he won election to the legislature as a reform Democrat. During the turbulent 1960s, his great achievement was the enactment of the nation's first no-fault auto insurance system. As governor, he has presided over a spectacular economic recovery, and the controversy over whether he is really responsible for the "Massachusetts Miracle" does not seem to have hurt him.

"The Duke"—the nickname connotes more respect than affection—is a man of formidable intelligence and discipline. Although he got into the 1988 presidential race relatively late, he amassed the biggest treasury in the history of Democratic nominating politics. He was hard hit by the forced resignation of his top aide, the widely respected John Sasso, after Sasso helped torpedo the presidential campaign of Senator Joseph Biden of Maryland by circulating a videotape showing apparent plagiarism in Biden's speeches. But Dukakis recovered quickly, and a string of primary victories beginning in New Hampshire made him, by spring, the front-runner for the nomination.

If Dukakis is comfortable on television, it's no wonder. For the two years before his first race for governor, he served as moderator of "The Advocates," a nationally broadcast public TV series. That series, by the way, originated from—of all places—the John F. Kennedy School of Government.

H.H.

The Interview

KALB: Governor, can you successfully and effectively both campaign and run a state?

DUKAKIS: Marvin, if you're in your third term, if you have a very good team of people working for you and with you, if your legislature is 5:1 Democratic and as supportive as any legislature in the country, and if you spend a lot of your flight time during the half of the week that you are campaigning working on your governor's responsibilities, then you can do it.

KALB: I guess I asked the question because if you look back at recent American history, the last three of the last four American presidents have not been in office while they were running full time for the presidency. They won. So I guess there's an obvious lesson that could be drawn there: Can you run the risk of doing both? You may fail.

DUKAKIS: Well, if you fail, you fail. You still have your job as governor, and it's a good job. But I think there's something troubling about the notion that you have to be out of office in order to run for the presidency.

KALB: Why troubling?

DUKAKIS: Because it almost puts a premium on not being there, on not making decisions, on not having to make the tough choices, on not confronting the kinds of challenges that you have to confront as president. Nobody suggested that John Kennedy leave the Senate, for example, in 1959 and 1960. In fact, we'd have been shocked if anybody had. So it seems to me if you have a situation which I'm fortunate enough to have in a state that has had a great deal of success and is doing well, then this is a very good base from which to run, and so far I seem to be combining the two responsibilities pretty well.

KALB: Governor, the centerpiece of your campaign seems to be that you would like to transplant what you have called "the strategy Massachusetts miracle" from this state to the other 49.

DUKAKIS: I don't want to transplant it. I want to leave it here. But—

KALB: You want to leave it here, but—

DUKAKIS: I want to leave it here, but I want to grow more of those flowers elsewhere.

KALB: Okay, fair enough. What makes you think you can do that?

DUKAKIS: Well, obviously every state, every region of the

country, has a different mix of things, which in some cases makes for an energy-dominated economy, a mining-dominated economy, a farm-dominated economy, an industrial-dominated economy. But I think what has happened here, Marvin, is at least an example of the kind of thing we can do all over the country. I inherited a state that was an economic and financial basket case—a massive deficit, the state with the second highest unemployment rate in the country—and I think what we've demonstrated is that you can take public resources, combine those public resources with private initiative, and literally transform an economy. That's the kind of aggressive economic leadership we have to have in this country, beginning with somebody who knows how to balance budgets and make tough choices on spending but also can put together a strategy for growth of this country, one that will be successful, will create jobs and economic opportunity for all of our citizens.

Populist message

KALB: But when you found that basket case and you began to take steps to correct it, you were voted out of office the next time around.

DUKAKIS: That's always a risk you run. I think with the benefit of hindsight and a certain amount of experience, I might have done things a little differently. And when I came back in 1983 and inherited another deficit and a state where one-third of its communities had double-digit unemployment, I think I did things better and more effectively in part because of the experience I had in my first term.

KALB: Okay. Now you have claimed credit for the Massachusetts miracle. You've done it again this evening.

DUKAKIS: In part.

KALB: Okay, but a number of your former—

DUKAKIS: Let me say this—

KALB: But a number of your former— I'm sorry.

DUKAKIS: Obviously, it isn't just one person or one thing that has made the difference here, and it won't be one person or one thing that will make the difference, not only in dealing with this massive federal budget deficit, but in putting together a strong and vibrant economic future for this country. But every team has to have a quarterback. Somebody's got to call the signals and throw the ball. You're not a successful quarterback unless they're blocking for you, unless somebody's downfield to catch your passes. But that's what a president does. That's what a governor does. But it's been teamwork in this state that has made the difference. It's been bringing business and labor and the educational community together with state government, with community leadership, that has made the difference. And I think that's the same kind of leadership and the same kind of teamwork we must have nationally.

KALB: Well, a number of your former colleagues here at the Kennedy School have questioned the job that you have done as quarterback. One of them, Robert Reich, a lecturer in public policy says, "It would be a miracle if Massachusetts didn't do as well as it has. Mike Dukakis has helped at the margin." And in a special report that was done here on the state's economy—you know it, you're smiling already—Ronald Ferguson and Helen Ladd say, "State policy probably played at most a marginal role in producing the state's economic miracle." So on reflection, do you think that maybe some of the credit that you're reaching for and articulating may be unjustified?

DUKAKIS: Well, let me say again that a lot of things went into this. I didn't create Harvard and MIT and 118 other colleges and universities. I'm not responsible for a very special quality of life that this state has, but all of those things were here in 1975, and they were calling us "taxachusetts" and "the new Appalachia." Something had to make a difference. And if you go out across this state and ask people, I think they'll tell you that a very aggressive state government role, a very aggressive state economic development program, made a difference, especially in those regions and communities in this state that were hurting, were declining, were depressed, and today are enjoying new prosperity, new growth, and very good jobs for their people. That, I think, is the unique contribution that state government has made, and it's the kind of presidential leadership that I'd like to bring to the presidency. I think we need it.

KALB: In 1975 the state was getting about $3 billion in government military contracts. It's now getting, I am told, $9 billion. Now will you acknowledge that that $6 billion in additional revenue might have had a good bit to do with the economic prosperity in the state?

DUKAKIS: Not very much actually, Marvin. In the total scheme of things, we've created about 650,00 new jobs in the past 10 years in the state. Less than 5 percent are defense related. And as a matter of fact, the number of defense-related jobs has dropped a little bit this past year. Now we do a good deal of military R & D, and I hope that one of these days we can move some of that military research and development money into civilian research and development purposes. But the strength of this state's comeback economically has been in our diversity, not as a result of the military buildup. And I hope it remains that way. I want us to make our contribution to the national defense, but I never want to see this state again become so dependent on the Pentagon budget that when people start making cuts, we get into trouble.

KALB: One of the jokes about Michael Dukakis is that he has never met a weapons system that he liked, that he's never met a defense budget that he wouldn't like to cut. Would you give credit to the Reagan administration over the last seven years for having built up America's defense?

DUKAKIS: Well, let me respond to the first comment before I go on to the second. I want this country to have a strong national defense. I'm not sure after the expenditure of billions and billions of dollars that we have it. And I'm very concerned about what's happened to our conventional defense capability. We have a massive nuclear deterrent, and we need a nuclear deterrent. Twelve thousand strategic nuclear warheads, enough to blow up the Soviet Union about 40 times over. They have 11,000. And in the meantime I have serious questions about what's happening to our conventional defense capability—to the weapons, equipment, ammunition, support, training, air-lift and sea-lift capacity that we're giving our conventional forces.

What we all know—in the face of the kind of severe fiscal difficulty that this country is in—is that defense budgets are not going to grow over the course of the next year or two or three. I think we all understand that. So the job of the next president is going to be to make some hard choices within what is a fairly fixed defense budget. And given the strength of our nuclear deterrent, when you make those choices, I think we've got to put some of those resources into strengthening conventional defense capabilities. So that's where I want to put my emphasis as president, and that's what I think the country's national defense requires.

KALB: But at this particular point, Governor, if you were president, would you also seek to cut back on the defense budget, or keep it more or less where it is now?

DUKAKIS: Well, I think at this point if we can simply keep that defense budget stable, we'll be doing well. Obviously, if we're successful in negotiating with the Soviet Union deep cuts in strategic weapons and the test ban treaty, and conceivably reductions in conventional forces, then maybe you could cut that budget. But just to keep the defense budget stable, Marvin, is going to require some significant cuts in weapons systems. I'd cut Star Wars back to where it was before the President announced his initiative in 1983. I think it's a fantasy. I don't think it is worth the expenditure of money that is involved.

KALB: Can I interrupt you when you say things like that? It jumps into my mind, and I'm sorry.

DUKAKIS: That's all right.

KALB: How do you know it's a fantasy?

DUKAKIS: Because based on the information I have and on analyses done by people whose judgment I respect, I think it is highly unlikely that this system will ever work. And in any event, testing it and deploying it is illegal under the ABM treaty, and I don't believe this country ought to be engaging in unlawful activity, particularly under a treaty which we pushed on the Russians and which was our initiative. But I wouldn't do Star Wars. I wouldn't do two $18 billion supercarriers. I wouldn't spend $50 billion on the Minuteman missile. I wouldn't spend hundreds of millions of dollars on a three-hour space plane from Washington to Tokyo. I think these are things which are neither necessary nor desirable, particularly when there are serious questions about our conventional defense capability, and we simply aren't putting the resources we need into that. And that's something which I think ought to be a priority.

KALB: I want to go back to my question that I started this series with. Do you give any credit to the Reagan administration for building up America's defenses in the '80s?

DUKAKIS: I think our forces are probably somewhat stronger. I'm impressed, for example, that the qualifications, the pay, the training of our fighting forces are better, and I think we're getting a more qualified, a better recruit than we did seven or eight years ago. I'd like to build on that and expand on it, but I am also very concerned about a Pentagon which today, as you know, is in chaos, an outgoing secretary of defense who refused to accept the fact that that budget was not going to increase, an incoming secretary of defense who has acknowledged that he has a massive job to do to get that place back into shape, to manage it, and to get some value for our defense dollar.

KALB: Why do you think the Russians have returned, one, to the negotiating table, two, to accepting the President's 1981 proposal on the zero option on the medium-range missiles in Europe if it were not for the significant military buildup of the United States during that time?

DUKAKIS: That may have played some role, but I think the reason Mr. Gorbachev is at the negotiating table is because the

Soviet Union as a society is in very deep trouble. It's a closed society. It's a society that's failing. It's a society whose economy has stagnated for the past 10 years—very serious social problems, health problems. Non-Russian ethnic groups comprise a majority in the Soviet Union for the first time since the Bolshevik revolution. I think what you have in Gorbachev is new leadership which is less ideological, more pragmatic, and which understands if they continue to devote 16 percent of the GNP to the military, they're going to become a second- or third-rate economic power. That's what I think really has brought them to the table. I don't deny that our military buildup has probably added to that, but I think it's very serious domestic problems in the Soviet Union which have brought forth this new leadership and new leadership which seems to be significantly different from what we've had in the past.

KALB: Governor, in one of your position papers on arms control it is said, "We have a shared interest"—we and the Russians, I assume—"in doing all we can to discourage either side from being tempted to launch a first nuclear strike." Now the Russians have already said publicly that they will not be the first to launch a nuclear strike. Would a Dukakis administration make a similar pledge?

DUKAKIS: No.

KALB: Why?

DUKAKIS: I would pledge no early first use. But I don't see how you can have a credible nuclear deterrent and make that commitment, especially when Russian conventional forces in Eastern Europe and in the Soviet Union far outbalance Western conventional forces under the NATO alliance.

KALB: Governor, obviously one of the biggest problems you'd have as president would be the manner in which you dealt with the Soviet Union. It is the only country in the world that can inflict mortal damage on this one.

DUKAKIS: Right.

KALB: Do you feel that you have a sufficiently good grounding, a sufficiently good understanding, about the reality of the Soviet Union, its leadership, its people, economy?

DUKAKIS: Yes, I think I do. Obviously, if one were president, one would have access to even more information, more knowledge, more intelligence, but—

KALB: Sure.

DUKAKIS: I've been a student of foreign policy all my life even though my experience has been at the state and local level. I must say I think what's happening these days in the Soviet Union is intriguing, to put it mildly. Obviously, the winds of change are sweeping through the Soviet Union. Where it's going to end, whether Gorbachev himself can survive, what the significance of the Yeltsin affair is, all of these things are fascinating, and I'm not sure any of us, at this point, can tell. But I don't think anyone looking at the Soviet Union over the past two or three years can help but come to the conclusion that something is different, and I would dearly love to be the president who pursues the opportunity for what conceivably could be a very significant breakthrough in arms control, arms reduction, and in our relationship with the Soviet Union.

KALB: Have you yourself even met a Soviet leader? Have you ever met Gorbachev?

DUKAKIS: No.

KALB: Or Brezhnev? Khrushchev?

DUKAKIS: None of the—

KALB: Of the top leaders?

DUKAKIS: Of the top leaders.

KALB: Have you yourself ever spent any significant amount of time in the Soviet Union?

DUKAKIS: In the Soviet Union? No. But I'm not sure that that's necessary—

KALB: No, I just wanted—

DUKAKIS: —to be a strong international leader. No.

KALB: Who are your advisers on Soviet affairs?

DUKAKIS: A few of them are in the room here, but I'm not sure they'd want to be identified out there. One of the great advantages, Marvin, of being the governor of Massachusetts is there is a state department in exile, an arms control and disarmament agency in exile within about 10 miles of the State House in Boston. So I'm in a position to draw on an awful lot of people, not just in this institution, which I happen to be very close to, but in institutions throughout the metropolitan area. I also have a very good group of advisers in Washington and others around the country. I'm somebody who, as most people who know me will tell you, generally makes up his own mind. But these are very, very good people, and I've gained a great deal from having had access to them and having been able to consult with them.

KALB: Have you read any of the almost best-seller-type books on modern-day Russia such as the Hedrick Smith book on the

Russians, the Robert Kaiser book, or perhaps even Marshall Goldman's book on the Gorbachev challenge?

DUKAKIS: I read some of Marshall's things, although generally in the popular press and some of his monographs and articles
and so on. But I've found some of the latest commentary to be not
only interesting but rather intriguing. I thought Gorbachev's
speech, which was never delivered but which was released on the
future of the United Nations and the International Court of Justice,
was one of the most extraordinary documents I've ever seen. If the
man believes what he said in that speech, then there is a basis for
very serious negotiation with the Soviet Union. Time will tell, and
he's going to be challenged on that. But I would love to be in a
position to see whether he is serious about building the United
Nations as a peace-keeping agency, as an antiterrorism institution,
mandatory jurisdiction for the International Court of Justice. Kind
of sounds like the kinds of things that we were suggesting in the
'60s, and if in fact he's serious, these are very significant documents.

KALB: Okay. Then let me ask you this: How would you define
the problem with the Soviet Union? Is it an ideological problem?
Is it the compulsion of great Russian nationalism? Where is the
conflict between the United States and the Soviet Union?

DUKAKIS: I think it's all of the above. It's partly ideological,
it's partly geopolitical. It's partly the clash of two great Super
Powers. I think ideology plays a major role, and one of the
interesting questions is whether or not, at least under Gorbachev
and the new Soviet leadership, ideology is now beginning to take
a back seat to pragmatism and to a serious concern with very deep-
seated economic and social problems in the Soviet Union. Now I
think that's what's happening, but we won't know until we have a
president who's prepared to challenge him on some of these things
and negotiate seriously.

KALB: Okay. Would you be prepared to invite the Soviet
Union in to negotiate the future of the Middle East?

DUKAKIS: They're there. I mean, this notion that we can
exclude the Soviet Union from the Middle East in my judgment is
absurd. The Soviet Union is all over the Middle East.

KALB: So that you would invite them into an international
conference?

DUKAKIS: It's not a question of inviting them in. I think, for
example, that a multilateral peace-keeping force in the Persian
Gulf might be one way to end that conflict.

KALB: I'm not talking about the Persian Gulf. I'm talking about the Arab-Israeli problem there. Would you invite them in as a participant, as the United States is, in a negotiated solution of the Middle East problem?

DUKAKIS: I think Shimon Peres's proposal for an international conference under the aegis of the Security Council makes sense but only for negotiations that are conducted bilaterally between and among the parties, presumably Israel, Jordan, Egypt, and responsible elements in the Palestinian community who—

KALB: Let me ask you about the Palestinian community. You have also been quoted as saying that there can be peace in the Middle East without a homeland for the Palestinians.

DUKAKIS: Right.

KALB: Give us your vision of what a Middle East peace would look like, and where in that peace is there room for three to four million Palestinians?

DUKAKIS: Well, I'm not sure how precise one can be. But let's assume that there was such a conference where Israel, Jordan, Egypt, and responsible elements in the Palestinian community who accepted resolutions 242 and 348 were present and were negotiating bilaterally. I think it's conceivable that consistent with the Camp David Accords, it might be possible to come up with a plan in which there was an autonomous region under the jurisdiction of Jordan which was available, if you will, for Palestinians, as a place where Palestinians could live.

KALB: You think that would be a formula for peace?

DUKAKIS: It's conceivable that it would be. There's no way that I or you or any of us can make that judgment, but my sense is that there might be a basis for that in accordance with the Camp David Accords and with what at that time we hoped, I think, would be progress toward that kind of a settlement. Now only the nations and negotiators in question can make that judgment. And at this point, as you know, Israel itself has been unable to develop a political consensus to even join in such a conference. But in my judgment, such a conference would be a constructive step forward.

KALB: You have been described as a truly rational man, highly intelligent—

DUKAKIS: I'm not sure my children would agree with you on the question of rationality.

KALB: All right. But who sees a problem and feels there has to be a solution.

DUKAKIS: Sometimes. I'm less rational than I used to be. I'll put it that way.

KALB: Oh, I see. Okay. In that case in the Middle East, for example, a number of people feel that there may be a set of problems there for which there are no solutions.

DUKAKIS: That may be. That may be. I don't rule that out. It may be one of those things where it will be years before there can be a settlement. I'm encouraged by the fact that Egypt, Jordan, even some of the other Arab nations that have just come out of this latest conference seem to be adopting a somewhat more moderate stance. That, at least, may give us a ray of hope that it's possible to come up with a solution which is consistent with the Camp David Accords and what we hoped we were achieving then. But there's no way of telling, and this kind of a settlement is not going to be imposed from on high. This is something that has to be worked out by these nations and by the parties to these negotiations.

KALB: Let's switch to Central America, and I appreciate that I'm going to ask you a hypothetical question. But it has been speculated about for several years now. If Nicaragua were to suddenly find itself in possession of sophisticated Soviet hardware like a jet fighter, like a missile that could hit a neighbor, would you as president be prepared to use American military power to stop that kind of buildup?

DUKAKIS: Yes. I would do so, as John Kennedy did in the case of the Cuban missile crisis. On the other hand, I see no evidence that that's happening, and as a matter of fact, all of the information we have indicates that the Soviet Union has no interest in that and has enough problems back home without getting involved in Nicaragua. I think the Arias plan is the best hope for peace and for the economic and social reconstruction of Central America we've had in a long time, and I would like to see the United States getting enthusiastically behind the plan. As you know, that's not happening. We have the anomalous situation of the Speaker of the House acting as the secretary of state of the United States pro-tem because there is such an enormous vacuum in Washington. But I think the Arias plan is where we should be. I think we should be supporting it enthusiastically, and if we did, as Arias himself said when he was here in Boston not too long ago, it would succeed.

KALB: Western Europe. For the last couple of decades now the United States has maintained a force of about 325,000 troops, most of them in West Germany.

DUKAKIS: Right.

KALB: Would you be prepared as president to begin a withdrawal of American forces from Western Europe?

DUKAKIS: No. Particularly if the INF agreement is signed and ratified, I would be opposed to withdrawing or reducing the U.S. commitment in Western Europe. It seems to me that if that agreement is signed and if it's ratified and if intermediate- and short-range missiles are taken out of Western Europe, then there is an even stronger case to be made for maintaining the U.S. commitment to NATO and to Western Europe.

KALB: Let me switch to another subject, namely, back at home and politics for a moment. Let's assume you get the nomination. You've got to select a vice president. Would you give serious consideration to a woman?

DUKAKIS: Sure.

KALB: Do you have any in mind?

DUKAKIS: No. But let me say this, and I really haven't thought about it. I've got all I can do to go out there and win this nomination. But let me say this. The single most important criterion for selecting a running mate, far more important than politics or region or anything else, is whether or not that person, if, God forbid, something happens to the president, can be a first-rate president. Everything else pales by comparison. That's where you start. If you find a person or persons who clearly met that criterion, then where they come from, who they are, whether they provide additional strength for the ticket and to the administration if you're elected—those things are relevant, but—

KALB: Are you open to the selection of a black as vice president?

DUKAKIS: Sure.

KALB: Jesse Jackson as a vice president?

DUKAKIS: I wouldn't rule anybody out.

KALB: Including Jackson?

DUKAKIS: I wouldn't rule anybody out. Or in.

KALB: Was the "in" with reference to Jackson?

DUKAKIS: No, to anybody.

KALB: There's a school of thought—you've heard it before—that a Democrat is going to have an awfully hard time winning next year. Do you share that concern?

DUKAKIS: No. As a matter of fact, shame on us if we lose given the economic mess and the managerial mess and some unbelievably bad foreign policy decisions we've had over the course of the past seven years. On the other hand, it isn't going to be handed to us on a silver platter. And since I believe that the issue of jobs and economic growth will be the single most important issue in this campaign, the Democratic nominee had better be somebody who is not only strongly committed to jobs and economic opportunity for the people of this country, but has a track record and credibility on those issues. I think that's one of the strengths I bring to this campaign. But that's the Democratic party's stock and trade, and that's where we are, that's where we've got to be, and that's the message that we have to communicate to the American people. If we do, then a Democrat is going to be the next president.

KALB: I want to ask you about the impact of television on your campaigning—on everybody's campaigning, for that matter. In this room if I'm not mistaken, in the early '70s, you were doing that early PBS program "The Advocates."

DUKAKIS: Faneuil Hall and here.

KALB: Okay.

DUKAKIS: I guess not here. Maybe this place wasn't here in the early '70s.

KALB: Has the experience that you picked up doing those kinds of programs been an asset to you in running for the presidency?

DUKAKIS: Yes.

KALB: In what way? Tell us.

DUKAKIS: Well, I think—

KALB: Why is it so important that you be on a first-name basis with a camera?

DUKAKIS: You've been in the business a long time.

KALB: But I'm not running. You are.

DUKAKIS: You still have your union card, and I still have mine. I think when you have an opportunity to do what you've done for years and what I did for a few years, you're just a lot more comfortable in front of that camera. You're less intimidated by it. I think you can speak to it and to the American people with a certain amount of ease and persuasiveness that maybe you don't have when you don't have that kind of experience. On the other hand, anyone who's been in politics five, ten, fifteen, or twenty years— and most of us have who are running—by this time probably should be pretty comfortable in front of a camera.

KALB: There was an interview today or yesterday that I read with George Bush in which he said that he doesn't do terribly well on television, he feels, and that therefore he may not wish to appear on programs, or he's going to cut back on that kind of thing, and he has certainly been there for a long time too. So there is something special about the relationship that an individual has with that camera. Is it that powerful a force in American politics?

DUKAKIS: It's a powerful force. It's not everything. It's no substitute for substance. It's no substitute for good grassroots organizing and thousands of people across the country working for you and organizing and going out and asking others to work for you, but it is probably the most powerful medium of communication we've ever had in the history of this planet and if you're running for the presidency, it's something that you probably ought to feel pretty comfortable with.

KALB: You're making the point here that you've got to have substance as well.

DUKAKIS: Yes.

KALB: My favorite question on this relates to Moses, who led the Jews out of Egypt and, according to the Bible, stuttered. Now if there had been television then, could he have succeeded as a great figure?

DUKAKIS: The waters would never have parted.

KALB: The waters would never have parted. It is that powerful?

DUKAKIS: It is today. Now I think it can be exaggerated. We've had a media presidency for seven years, which is beginning to crumble because there isn't much substance there. But if you're somebody who has substance and also can communicate effectively via television, I think that's an extra plus.

KALB: Governor, we're at that point now where I stop asking the questions, the audience begins to ask the questions, and I know three people here who are going to be asking questions. And why don't we start the questioning with Thomas Schelling, a professor of political economy here at the Kennedy School of Government?

SCHELLING: Governor, welcome back to the Kennedy School. I feel completely engulfed by Soviet-American relations. We have a summit coming up. We have an INF agreement that may come up for us. We're interested in glasnost, the opening up of communication, and perestroika, the restructuring of the Soviet economy. Twenty years ago, 30 years ago, equally important in American foreign policy preoccupations was the People's Republic of China, which has been going through its own glasnost at least on the scale of the Soviet Union and a perestroika which I think may be even more dramatic than anything that Gorbachev has yet accomplished. And yet I can't find that the United States has any attitude toward, any policy toward, China. And my question, sir, is does the United States have a policy toward China? If so, what is it? Would you, if you were president, change it or add to it? Specifically, do we want the Chinese to succeed in what they're trying to do? And specifically, would we prefer that the Chinese have good relations with the Soviet Union or bad relations with the Soviet Union, or doesn't it make any difference?

DUKAKIS: That's six questions, Tom.

SCHELLING: At Harvard we allow you to answer any three.

DUKAKIS: I'll answer three if you help my wife to stop smoking. This man is an apostle of antinicotine in our society.

KALB: Governor, answer the question.

DUKAKIS: Yeah, I think we have a policy which has been a fairly bipartisan one, actually, going back to the Nixon opening, if you will, which is to try to develop and maintain good relations with China, to encourage this movement toward reform, to encourage good trade relations. This state alone has got a very strong and expanding relationship with Guangdong Province, which is a province of 70 million people, and I've been there leading trade missions. They've been back, and that's part of a much larger picture. And in general, I think even in this administration, which often is so obsessively ideological, there's been a substantial amount of good, pragmatic, bipartisan policy on China. I don't think any of us are happy with Silkworm missiles being shipped to Iran and being used to add to the conflict and exacerbate the conflict in the Persian Gulf. And I gather that the Chinese have now stopped that or said that they're going to stop it. I'm somebody who believes, generally speaking, that good relations between and among nations generally is a plus. So I don't have a problem with a notion of better relations between the Soviet Union and China, just so long as it doesn't involve some kind of an alignment which is then turned against us or other free nations. But I think, generally speaking, that better relations between us and China and improving relations between China and its neighbors, whoever they may be, is a good thing. And I think we ought to encourage that so long as the motives for such improving relations are sound.

QUESTION: Governor, a number of issues concerning the status of women will come before the Supreme Court, including sex discrimination, abortion, adoption, and issues affecting women in the workplace. Are you willing to pledge now to search for a qualified woman for the U.S. Supreme Court if a vacancy occurs during your presidency?

DUKAKIS: One of the things that you get from one who's been a chief executive for nine years is a record, not just promises—look at my administration, at the way I select judges. I have the same authority as governor of Massachusetts to select judges for life that the president has at the national level, and I don't even need senate confirmation. Once my nominations go to the Executive Council and they're approved, these appointments become life-time appointments. I think what you'll see is a record of the appointment of very good people, and by the way, people who I've met before I appoint them. As a matter of fact, and I don't think this is a radical suggestion, I not only have a judicial nominating council that screens all candidates for judgeships down to and including district court judgeships, but they recommend three finalists to me, and I interview every one of those finalists person-ally. And I would hope and expect that in selecting justices for the highest court in the land I would at least do that, and probably a good deal more.

QUESTION: Sounds like an outrageous idea.

DUKAKIS: Well, there's a lot to be recommended, a lot to be said for it. In any event, I think my record speaks for itself, and obviously I would be seeking qualified women to sit at every level of the federal judiciary.

QUESTION: Governor Dukakis, I agree with you that if you've been governor for 9 of the last 13 years, you do have a record. And according to the federal government, Boston Harbor is the most polluted harbor in the country. Our prisons are the most over-crowded in the country. Many of our mental health facilities have been decertified by the federal court. My question is, with a 4 to 1 Democratic majority here in the local state legislature, are you really a can-do governor that can get things through Congress?

DUKAKIS: Yeah. I didn't pollute Boston Harbor, but I'm the guy who's cleaning it up. And we've made more progress in the past three years toward the cleanup of that harbor than we have in the past hundred. Yes, we have overcrowded prisons. So does just about every state in the country. We also have a state where crime has dropped more in the past four years than in any other state in the country with one exception, and that wasn't an accident. I take my responsibility to enforce the law seriously in this state. I feel very strongly about violent crime. We've been very tough on violent crime while observing and being committed to due process and the Bill of Rights, and that's one of the reasons this state has one of the best anticrime records in the country. And we are now embarked on probably the most ambitious program for improving the staffing and the condition of our state mental hospitals and our state mental health services of any state in the nation. Now all of those things have happened in the past four years, and I think it's one of the reasons why this state is viewed as being one of the most effective, one of the most progressive, and one of the most successful states in the country.

QUESTION: On the question of energy policy, it's clear that our long-term petroleum supplies are limited and the price can only really go up over the long term. At the same time we've seen you come out against projects like Seabrook in New Hampshire. My question is, How will your energy policy as president address our long-term needs for both inexpensive and plentiful energy as we go into the next century?

DUKAKIS: We have all kinds of energy supplies, energy resources, and the possibility for additional energy in this country without committing ourselves irrevocably to nuclear power. Now I'm not ideologically opposed to nuclear power. My problem with Seabrook is, as anybody knows who knows anything about the area, is that it is just impossible to evacuate that area in the event of a serious nuclear accident. I mean, you can't evacuate it on a Saturday afternoon in July without a serious nuclear accident, let alone if something happens down there. That's my problem with Seabrook. And unless and until somebody finds an acceptable and safe way to dispose of high-level radioactive waste in this country, I think it's unconscionable to continue to build more and more nuclear plants. We still don't have an answer on that problem.

Having said that, we have three hundred years' supply of coal and clean coal-burning technologies that are available now. We have 150 years' worth of natural gas, and believe me, I'd love to generate electric energy in Massachusetts with natural gas. And there are a lot of people in Texas who would like to sell it to us. And it doesn't cause acid rain, and it's clean and efficient. We have photovoltaic energy, which, in my judgment, is only a few years away, with some federal investment, from becoming cost competitive with regular forms of energy. We have an emerging cogeneration industry which has unbelievable potential. And just to give you an example without going on at great length as to just how much energy there is out there, when the Boston Edison Company a few months ago issued a public request for proposals for energy to the small power-producing industry, they were looking for 200 megawatts. They got 66 proposals for a total of 2,054 megawatts at prices half or less of what energy will cost if Seabrook is ever opened up up there in Seabrook, New Hampshire. That just gives you some sense of what's going on. There's plenty of energy out there. The question is, Do we have the will and capacity to go out there and get it?

QUESTION: Governor, currently there are five voluntary national service bills pending in Congress to encourage students to serve their community. Many link service to tuition aid. If you were elected president, what would your position be on the issue of youth national service?

DUKAKIS: I'm not for mandatory service. I think that's a bad idea, almost a contradiction in terms. You can't mandate people to serve in the kind of way and for the things that you and I, I think, would like young people to serve. But I am very anxious to try to bring back some of the spirit of the early '60s. John Kennedy had an enormous impact on many of us who were just coming out of college and graduate school at that time. He literally transformed the environment for public service in this country, especially for young people.

I'm particularly interested in reviving the National Teacher Corps. Half of our public school teachers in the United States are going to retire in the next five to ten years. Half of them. And I go to colleges and universities and high schools and ask how many students are seriously interested in a career in public school teaching? And if I get five hands going up out of five hundred, I'm lucky. I want to revive the National Teachers Corps and make it a Peace Corps for teaching. I want to give young people an opportunity at least to try out a teaching assistantship, a teaching internship. That's just one example of the kind of voluntary national service I would like to encourage, and I think we could do a lot more at very modest cost. So I'd like very much to do that. And I hope I can.

KALB: Governor, our next question comes from Art Rublin, a member of the student advisory committee of the Institute of Politics.

RUBLIN: Governor, I'm particularly interested in the area of nuclear proliferation policy, and I was interested in what your view was on how the Reagan administration has done in this area, and what changes you'd make.

DUKAKIS: How they've done? They've done nothing. And I'm very concerned about it. I think this is very, very important. It isn't just that the Soviet Union and the U.S. possess this incredible nuclear arsenal that we do. It's that a number of nations already have this capability, more are going to get it, and there is a very solemn responsibility on the United States and the Soviet Union to take nuclear proliferation seriously, and not only to be serious about our responsibilities under existing treaties, but to exercise the kind of leadership that both of us must, in this case together, if we're serious about stopping the spread of nuclear weapons. And I take that responsibility very seriously. I've seen very little evidence in the past seven years that the current administration does at all, and that for me would be a very important priority.

QUESTION: Governor, a question that President Ford almost had to deal with directly. If a terrorist organization were to prove that they had nuclear capabilities and were to make an outrageous ransom demand to you for the city of Boston and gave you 24 hours, and it was determined that they definitely did have that ability, how would you handle that situation? Specifically, they have no particular geographic base that they operate from, which would make retaliation a very difficult situation indeed.

DUKAKIS: Let me talk more generally about terrorism. I think this country and the international community has got to be very tough on international terrorism. International terrorism is international crime, pure and simple. It's unacceptable and it's unconscionable, and we've got to go after it the way you go after crime: tough, no holds barred. No concessions, no concessions under any circumstances. If you grant concessions to terrorists, you might as well forget about stopping it, because you're encouraging it, and we all know what happens when you do that. Bibles and birthday cakes and agreements to free Arab terrorists in Kuwaiti jails were outrageous kinds of policy that this administration has followed. You go after terrorists, and you use every single tool or weapon you can—undercover operations, sting operations, and if necessary, military strikes against terrorist bases.

QUESTION: Governor, you spoke earlier about combining public resources with private initiation to form a strategy of—

DUKAKIS: Private initiatives. This is not a fraternity we're running here.

QUESTION: Be that as it may, you want to combine these two items to form a strategy of nationwide economic growth.

DUKAKIS: Right.

QUESTION: Can you elaborate a little more specifically on the strategy of nationwide economic growth, specifically with regard to the role of the public and private sectors?

DUKAKIS: Sure.

QUESTION: And whether or not this strategy will involve a tax increase?

DUKAKIS: How many questions is that?

KALB: Three, I think.

DUKAKIS: Well, let me start with the first part and see if I can add a bit to the second. Yes, I think we need strong and aggressive economic leadership in the White House beginning in 1989. That means getting our fiscal house in order by making tough choices on spending, by putting in place and leading an aggressive strategy for economic growth and job creation, by going out and getting new revenue, beginning with the $110 billion in federal taxes owed that aren't being paid in this country. And I would go out and try to collect every dime I could of that money. I can't rule out new taxes; no serious candidate for the presidency should. That's where you begin and by getting interest rates down—every point reduction in interest saves you another $15 billion in the federal deficit. That's the first step.

But we have to do much more than that. You don't elect a president just to be a bookkeeper and a bill collector. We've got to invest in needed public infrastructure, in good schools and good skills, in technology, and in regional development. And I would do all of those things because that's the way to create economic growth. That's the way to get the rate of growth up. And that's the way to create good jobs for people in this country.

QUESTION: Would you raise taxes?

DUKAKIS: I might. But not until I had gone out and tried to collect every single dime I could of the $110 billion in taxes owed that aren't being paid in this country. Tax compliance is now at 81 percent in this country—81 percent. That's unacceptable. It's unconscionable. If we simply increase the rate of compliance by 5 percentage points, that's $35 billion in additional revenue annually, three times what they've been arguing about on Capitol Hill for the past month. That's where I'd begin.

QUESTION: Governor Dukakis, I'm a public school teacher from the state of Oregon, and I'd like to know what your priority would be as president in the area of funding public education? Particularly in the area of compensatory education for the disadvantaged and educational opportunities for the handicapped, both of which have been cut by the Reagan administration?

DUKAKIS: Well, I'm going to try to get those resources back, although I'm not going to kid you, and I don't think any serious candidate for the presidency can. The next president is not going to have billions and billions of dollars to spend in his first year or two as president. We're looking at massive federal budget deficits, and a major job in getting that deficit down. That's why my first and most important education priority as president would be good teaching and good teachers. And that is why I would create a national fund for teacher excellence. I've suggested a quarter of a billion dollars—that's about one-fifteenth of Star Wars—which would provide scholarships for young people willing to make a commitment to teaching, would revive the National Teacher Corps, would create a network of field centers of teaching and learning— so that veteran teachers like yourself could take a sabbatical, refresh, revive, do research, come back to teaching. That's where I'd begin.

Over time as we got our fiscal act together, I think we can begin to commit some resources to compensatory education, to education for the handicapped. But I would expect the states to participate in that. I think it's very important that state governments assume and carry out their responsibility for the education of their youngsters. So I would expect the states to be an important part of that.

QUESTION: This question is about human values. It happened before I arrived in this state, but I understand from a song I've heard that there was a gay individual perfectly qualified to have adopted a child, did so, and then lost the child solely because of his sexual preference, sexual affiliation. And I understood further from the song that you had appointed a blue ribbon commission to study the matter. I also went to Swarthmore, and what I'd like to know is, Is that the kind of values that you learned at Swarthmore?

DUKAKIS: Well, you got the story wrong to begin with, so let me begin with that. I'm somebody who abhors discrimination against anybody—on the basis of race or ethnicity, or sexual preference or gender—and that's why I'm working very hard right now to see if we can get a civil rights bill through my legislature which will prohibit discrimination on the basis of sexual preference. On the other hand, there is no civil right to be a foster parent, and this involved foster care and not adoption. We have adopted in this commonwealth a policy in which relatives and two-parent families with other children and prior parenting experience are preferred when we place youngsters in foster care. On the other hand, there are many situations in which there are not relatives or what I will call a traditional family with other youngsters. And so in those circumstances we will place a foster child in another setting. When I was presented with legislation by my legislature to absolutely prohibit the placement of foster children in gay or lesbian households, I vetoed it.

QUESTION: Governor, I've heard that the best way to measure someone's character is to look at the people they admire. And I was just wondering if you were to choose three former presidents since the turn of this century that you most admire, who would they be? A brief sentence on why you chose each is enough.

DUKAKIS: Franklin Roosevelt, Harry Truman, and John Kennedy. FDR, because he had extraordinary confidence and leadership ability, was able to pick this country up when it was as down as it's ever been and move us forward—he inspired people to do that. Harry Truman told it like it was, didn't mince words, and was straight and honest with the American people, even though it got him into an awful lot of difficulty and political hot water. And John Kennedy was the inspiration for me and for literally millions of young people in the '50s and early '60s. And without that man and his inspiration, I suspect many of us would never have gone into political life in the first place. His career was all too short, but he was somebody who could reach out to young people and inspire and encourage us to go into public service in a way that I'm not sure any president ever has.

KALB: Our last questioner, Richard Zeckhauser, a professor of political economy here at the Kennedy School of Government. Professor?

ZECKHAUSER: I wanted to ask you about your strong and aggressive economic policy, and in particular, how strong and aggressive it might be. The studies that Marvin Kalb cited, which were somewhat skeptical of the contribution of the Dukakis administration, did give you credit or blame for reallocating industry in Massachusetts, and I'm wondering what you think the federal government's role is in reallocating industry across the United States and also in identifying successful and unsuccessful industry? I only have one question, but I have the second part of it, which is to what extent the Massachusetts miracle is replicable, if you believe as many of us in this room do that part of our success is drawing extraordinary people from around the country? I think the people who have spoken tonight have identified themselves as being from around the country, drawing in a disproportionate share of federal money, which is what our outstanding congressional delegation and our outstanding governor have managed to do, and our universities and high-tech industry, which is also unique, and not everybody can borrow from everybody else. Thank you.

DUKAKIS: Where do you want me to begin? How much time do I have? Well, let me say this, Dick. There's no question that there's a confluence of extraordinary resources and talent in this state. But let's remember it was here in 1975, and we were "taxachusetts" and "the new Appalachia." So something must have happened to change it, and I would suggest to you that it was aggressive economic leadership and the investment of public resources in combination with private initiative that made the difference. That's what we've got to do nationally. We've got to take public resources and invest them in needed public infrastructure, in good schools, and in good training for our workers in technology so that we can create research centers, centers that spawn new industry and new technologies, not just in Massachusetts and in California, but all over the country in association with some great research universities and investment in regional development. And I mean aggressive regional development in those regions and states that are hurting and hurting badly. Now that doesn't involve in my mind a reallocation. But it does involve creating incentives so that expanding companies will expand into these regions that need jobs and need employment, with some help from the federal government in partnership with state governments. I wouldn't let state governments off the hook for one minute. I would expect them to step up to the plate and put some resources in there as well. But it's that kind of investment in regional development which I think can make a difference. If we do those things, I think we'll have a strong and vibrant economy that creates good jobs for the people of this country.

KALB: I have a frivolous final question in 30 seconds. I found out today that ballroom dancing is the most popular show on public television. Do you dance?

DUKAKIS: Yes.

KALB: You do? When was the last time you took your wife ballroom dancing? I think you're—

DUKAKIS: I think the last time we danced together was at our son's wedding in August. But let me say this, if I'm successful, we're going to do some Greek dancing in the East Room of the White House.

Candidates '88

A CONVERSATION WITH
PAUL SIMON

Photo by Martha Stewart

About the Candidate

In a lot of ways, Paul Simon is like the hero of a Frank Capra movie. Picture the Simon of today: the glasses, the bow tie, the kindly, earnest face. Now dissolve to the 19-year-old Simon of forty years ago, a skinny, gawky kid who has just dropped out of a small Nebraska college to buy a near-bankrupt newspaper in Troy, Illinois, with a few bucks scraped together from loans and savings. Installing himself as editor, the kid sets out to change the world. He bangs out fiery editorials in the style of his hero, the legendary William Allen White of the Emporia, Kansas, *Gazette*. Braving bomb threats, he crusades against local gambling and corruption, persuades Governor Adlai Stevenson to send in the state troopers, and, at 21, testifies on national television before Senator Estes Kefauver's crime commission. Soon he takes on the local political machine and wins a seat in the state legislature, where he shocks his colleagues by exposing widespread bribery among them in an article for *Harper's* magazine. He goes on to the state senate, the lieutenant governorship, the U.S. House of Representatives, and the U.S. Senate. All the while, he keeps knocking out books with titles like *You Want to Change the World, So Change It* on his trusty manual typewriter. Finally, in 1988, he finds himself running for president of the United States.

Of course, that's not the whole story. Simon is also a political realist who learned how to survive in the rough and tumble of Illinois politics—so much so that he lost a bid for the gubernatorial nomination in 1972 because voters thought he was too close to Richard Daley, the boss of Chicago. But no one ever questioned his decency or integrity, and in 1988 he ran for president as a traditional, non-neo-anything Democrat. He invoked the names of Roosevelt, Truman, and Humphrey, advocated large-scale New Deal-type programs, and defended the old faith of "a government that cares."

Simon enjoyed a quick surge in the polls. Some wags insisted voters were confusing him with Art Garfunkel's ex-singing partner. But there was no denying the appeal of his big-hearted message or the reverse glamour of his Trumanesque countenance.

At the time of his appearance on "Candidates '88," Simon was beginning to run into heavy weather on the budget issue. He was having a hard time explaining how he proposed to fund the new programs he advocated and still balance the budget, and all within three years. And he was having to fight on every front: Jackson on the left, Dukakis on the north, Gephardt in the midwest, Gore in the south. Though he would win his home state's primary handily, the squeeze would eventually prove too much for him and his poorly financed campaign.

H.H.

The Interview

KALB: Senator, let's start on your economic plans—get right down to business. One of your colleagues, Dick Gephardt, said recently that your plans add up to Reaganomics with a bow tie, and even a number of your aides with whom I've talked in the last couple of days say that it's about time for you to begin to spell out some of the specifics. What we have so far is a long list of very good things, but do you feel that you can actually implement that kind of program and within three years get this gigantic budget deficit down to zero.

SIMON: We can. First, if I may just talk in general about the premise of your question, because one of the ways that Ronald Reagan has affected this country is not only in what has happened to the budget and in our priorities, but also in our thinking. We now have a mind-set out there that says we can't do all kinds of things. And I don't accept that mind-set. Some of my opponents are so frightened that they may be labeled a big spender that they're unwilling to make the investments that this nation ought to make. We're not going to do what we need to do as a nation just drifting into the future. We have to seize and create our own future, our own destiny.

Now if I may get to the specifics, I can break it into two categories. One, how do you move on a balanced budget? I've said at the end of my third year, barring a recession, that we're going to get it down to zero. The present projection is between $50 and $100 billion deficit for that third fiscal year. You can, without impairing the defense of this country, reduce outlays by the end of the third year in the area of defense by $20 billion. Just these last few days, Secretary of Defense Carlucci has been talking about a $30 billion cut—that's over a period of years.

Second, you can move in very specific ways to encourage employment in this country, moving on the trade deficit. I think you could get the trade deficit down by one-third. That alone would add about a million and a half jobs—and you don't do that just by wishing it happens. You do it by number one, putting one person in charge of trade. We now have 18 different agencies that handle trade. It is no wonder that Japan or any other country isn't listening to us because we don't have anybody in charge of the shop.

And if I may digress just to give you a good illustration from Illinois, Caterpillar signed a contract for almost a billion dollars, as I recall, with the Soviet Union for earth-moving equipment for the trans-Siberian pipeline. One of the 18 agencies involved is the

Defense Department. They vetoed the contract. The Soviets then went to France and Japan to buy the earth-moving equipment. Who lost out? It wasn't the Soviet Union. It wasn't France. It wasn't Japan. It was the United States of America—needlessly. And the pipeline was built ahead of time.

Anyway I'm digressing, but I think a series of very concrete steps can reduce that trade deficit. Through further employment you can also do some things to see that the capital of this country is used, not for corporations to gobble each other up, but for research to increase productivity, to create jobs. I think you can create an additional million and a half jobs. That reduces unemployment a million and a half—1.5 percent. Each 1 percent you reduce unemployment, you save $30 billion on the deficit. That 1.5 percent would be $45 billion—that's 20 plus 45 is $65 billion. I think that if you make clear you're getting hold of things so you don't have monetary and fiscal policy in conflict, you'll see at the end of the two-year period a drop in interest rates of at least 2 percent. The prime rate in the United States is 8.75 percent. The prime rate in Japan is 2.5 percent. That should bring it at the end of the third year—since each 1 percent you reduce interest, you save $24 billion a year—ultimately to $30 billion. That should provide the money for balancing the budget and if it does not, as a last resort I'm willing to increase taxes to see that it's done. But I'm committed to stop our borrowing from our children and grandchildren and future generations.

KALB: You have been describing ways in which you might be able to try to get the budget deficit down, but a lot of your domestic programs are obviously going to cost a lot of money. I would like, with your assistance, to just tick off a number of these programs and ask you, on the basis of your current estimates, how much each one of those programs is going to cost. So we have some feel for the specifics, include the detail as well as the generality—for example, your job training program. You yourself have estimated in the first year it's going to cost between 3 and 5 billion dollars and the second year possibly as much as $8 billion. Tell us about the third, fourth, and fifth years. How much is this program going to cost?

SIMON: First, let me say there are three priorities in spending that have to fit within the $1 trillion that is now part of the federal budget—a thousand billion dollars. The first year, as you indicated, the jobs program would cost $3 billion, I think, at the most. Five billion dollars in gross. You save some on welfare and on other things. Then in the out years, how much we spend will depend on our revenue. I'm not going to have just endless programs, but I think we have to reverse that. Again this is part of the mind-set. We have to also ask ourselves, What does it cost this nation not to have a jobs program that deals with the whole problem of the underclass in our society? We never ask about those kinds of problems. What does it cost in teenage pregnancies? What's the cost of our failure to invest in people, to teach them how to read and write and lift them, as my jobs program does? The jobs program, education, and long-term care for seniors, those are the three priorities. And the last one has to have a self-financing mechanism.

KALB: I want to do it specifically, though, step by step. The expanded college student loan program that you've talked about— how much money is that going to cost?

SIMON: I've not talked about an expanded student loan program, but rather a shift from loans to grants, and that's going to have to be gradual, and I can't assign a specific dollar term to it. But the interesting thing is the present program, the loan program. We have shifted from loans comprising 46 percent of college assistance eight years ago to 80 percent now. And that is very, very costly.

KALB: How much is the child care program going to cost that you'd like to institute?

SIMON: I can't tell you, but that will be part of a jobs program. Again, there will have to be priorities. The child care plan can be tied in with the education programs.

KALB: You've talked about an all-out attack on adult illiteracy, also related, but how much will that cost?

SIMON: Right now we're spending $5 million on the library program and $2 million on the Vista program, a little college work study. If we were to expand that to, let's just use a figure of $500 million—a huge amount for that kind of program—it would pay off so quickly. With 23 million functionally illiterate adult Americans, what does it cost not to do it?

KALB: You have also said you wanted a Simon administration to move quickly on water protection, acid rain, the ozone layer. Those are big-ticket items that will cost a lot money. How much money can you tell the American people those are going to cost?

SIMON: They are not big-ticket items in terms of cost in the federal treasury. Superfund is not a treasury cost. It's a very fine program. I'm one of the cosponsors if it. Take acid rain, for example. The program will be worked out so that, whatever the end result, a small fee will be attached in some way to the utility industry to pay for the acid rain program. But we have to move on it. Again, what does it cost not to move on acid rain?

KALB: That's a fair enough question, but you'll admit it's rhetorical. But for the purposes of our interview, I'd like us to try to be, if it is at all possible, specific on the costs of these programs. In a gathering age of austerity, which certainly faces this country, how are you going to pay for all of those additional government-funded programs and at the same time knock down the budget deficit to zero in three years and only then consider, as you said a moment ago, raising taxes. How would you do that?

SIMON: Let me first talk about where we're wasting money right now. In fiscal year 1980 we spent—I'm talking about the federal government—$83 billion for interest on the federal debt. This fiscal year we will spend $203 billion for interest, an increase of $120 billion. What do we get for it? Nothing. And all of a sudden I come along and say let's spend 3 to 5 billion dollars on a jobs program. Let's spend a few billion more for education. And I'm labeled the big spender. The reality is, we can do these things, but many of these things are going to need a self-financing mechanism.

KALB: What do you mean by self-financing?

SIMON: Let's take long-term care. We cannot take long-term care out of the budget. We have to face the problem. The long-term care thing is going to explode on us very, very shortly. By the end of the century one out of six Americans will be over the age of 65. We'll have almost 6.5 million Americans over the age of 85. We have to work out a system to pay for that, and that may mean an additional 1 percent on social security. There are other proposals. I have said that immediately after it is clear that I'm the nominee, I'm going to appoint a committee to look at this. I hope that committee will report back before the election, in any event by January 1, but I'm not going to approve any long-term care program unless there's a mechanism for financing with it.

KALB: What did you mean when you said 1 percent of social security? A 1 percent cut on the amount going out to people getting social security?

SIMON: Correct. One percent on employer, one percent on employee. That is one possibility.

KALB: What would that add up to?

SIMON: I can't give you the figure just offhand.

KALB: That's enough about economics. Let's move on to politics. Some recent polls have suggested that your rocket ship perhaps has begun to level off just a bit, and in those polls the candidate, interestingly, who comes in at first place is none of the above. Now why is it that from this group of six Democrats, not one has yet emerged to capture the popular imagination?

SIMON: I think largely because we're unknown. We still are. Even after being on this program, Marvin, I'll still be relatively unknown. You had a comparable situation in 1976, when virtually no one was known and then Jimmy Carter emerged after the Iowa caucuses. But it is interesting that in the state of Iowa none of the above leads the pack, because I think the people in Iowa have seen enough of us that they're making choices.

KALB: It is still, nevertheless, Senator, a serious problem, because some of the Democrats whom you know—Bob Strauss, Chuck Robb, Bob Graham of Florida—are now talking among themselves and other Democrats as well, looking beyond the six now running and trying to get a seventh, eighth, ninth who might come in and will be, in their view, electable. One, do you think that is a fair thing for these other Democrats to do to those candidates who are now running?

SIMON: It doesn't bother me. But frankly, in 1976 exactly the same thing was happening. People were gathering, saying that we had to get a different candidate from those who were out here.

KALB: Do you yourself, at this point, see a Cuomo or a Nunn or a Bradley emerging at the very last minute and saying, "Hey, friends, I'm available. Take me"?

SIMON: I can't discount it totally, but I would be very surprised.

KALB: Do you think you are going to get Governor Cuomo's support?

SIMON: I can't answer that. He's said some generous things about me and has even been kind enough to say it looks like Paul Simon is going to be very strong in New York, and, of course, I concur in his judgment.

KALB: You have also said some very kind things about him. You've said that he is superbly qualified for any government position: "We need your leadership." Leadership for what? For the presidency?

SIMON: Leadership to move around the country. There have been people, not you, but others—journalists—who say that if he's really not interested in the presidency, he shouldn't be speaking out on the issues, that he shouldn't be running around the country.

I say we need that voice. There's no question he's one of the most articulate spokespersons in this nation, and, for the people who really understand the issues, he has one other quality that I think is important—Mario Cuomo cares. I want a government that cares. I want a government that's willing to fight for people, not a government that is responsive only to the whims and the wishes of the rich and the powerful.

KALB: We've heard a great deal in this campaign, Senator, about the word and the issue of character. Why do you think it is such an important issue in this campaign?

SIMON: I think it's an important issue in every campaign—for a variety of reasons. That we've had headlines about various candidates in both the Democratic and Republican party is probably more of an issue. I think what has happened with the Iran-Contra thing also makes it more of an issue. But I would add as a former journalist, who still writes occasionally, that I am concerned that we don't go too far off on that.

KALB: Meaning what?

SIMON: Too far in the direction of probing to the point where we're not examining the issues as you and I are today. Let me give you a very practical example. When the birth date of the first child of one of the Republican candidates makes the front pages of every newspaper in the nation, I'm not sure that's the real kind of issue that we ought to be looking at. I think the important issue is what the candidates are saying about the future of a child born today. That's what we really ought to be looking at.

KALB: It's interesting, Senator, because a couple of evenings ago Senator Kennedy, your colleague, was in this forum and launched a rather polite but, nevertheless, clear-cut criticism of the press and the way in which it is covering this campaign, implying very strongly that there is in the press coverage a kind of trivialization of serious political issues in this country. Do you agree with the senator from Massachusetts?

SIMON: There is some truth to that. And if I may take two minutes to tell you a story about when I was—

KALB: Do it in a little less.

SIMON: Okay. I was in the state legislature in Illinois and Senator Douglas called me one day and asked me to introduce a resolution calling on him to make the corn tassel the national flower. Since I had great respect for Paul Douglas, I agreed to do it and got to thinking about it all day. That night I called him, and I said, "Paul, are you sure you want me to introduce a resolution calling on you to make the corn tassel the national flower?" And he laughed and he said, "Just remember this, Paul, the substantial things you do in politics don't get very much coverage. You introduce it. I'll introduce it at the national level. It will be in every newspaper in Illinois. It will be defeated, but no one will be angry with any of us." And he said, "You will have done something to stay alive politically." It was a very interesting insight both into politics and into journalism.

KALB: That seems to be the lesson only of survival, not necessarily of leadership. For example, you were participating along with 11 other candidates the other night in Washington in a debate, and in two hours on NBC you and the other 11 were supposed to have set forth your views. The American people were supposed to have learned from that process. Did you get a chance, in your own view, to set forth your views, and do you think the American people learned from that process?

SIMON: I think the American people learned from the process, and let me give you a good example. This whole question of the economic package: How do you move to balance the budget and also invest in the future as we have to? I had to answer that in one minute. I met with my staff, and we finally decided it is just impossible to answer that one question in one minute. So we decided to provide the evidence and say what we want to do, but really duck the question. I think it was probably a mistake, but it is very—

KALB: A mistake to duck the question?

SIMON: A mistake to duck the question.

KALB: But how could you do it if you don't have the time?

SIMON: Well, I could have started answering it, and then Tom Brokaw could have cut me off.

KALB: Do you feel that these debates—you run from one to another all across the country—are good things or things that you simply feel you must do?

SIMON: They are good if they're limited in number. We have too many of them.

KALB: What can you do about it?

SIMON: I suppose I could decline. But when the other candidates accept, it makes it very, very difficult.

KALB: So that you're locked into one of these cycles that even you as a candidate can't quite break out of?

SIMON: It is very difficult. Now, I have not attended a few because of other commitments. I much prefer this kind of a format, where you really can probe, in at least a little more depth, what a candidate believes.

KALB: Well, so do I. Do you feel that the whole process is front-loaded too much on Iowa and New Hampshire?

SIMON: I do not. I think there is something very good about two states where you have to go into someone's living room, where you really can't just use the glitzy television multimillion-dollar approach and move in. It's so the candidate like Paul Simon, who's not nearly as well financed as at least one other candidate and a couple of others, really has a chance. Frankly, my voting record is such that as you tick off the major contributing financial interests, my voting record is not a good one for getting political campaign financing. It's great for the people of this country. But in Iowa and New Hampshire I have a chance.

KALB: Now you said, "If I can win both those states, that would just about do it." Now that quote really fascinated me. These two states represent a very small fraction of the percentage of Americans who will vote, even in the primary process. And yet by your own yardstick and your own calculations, if you can win those two states, that would just about do it. What is so fair about that kind of system if that would just about do it in only two states?

SIMON: I think—and I'm not absolutely sure on this—that if you'll check with the reporter who wrote that, he asked "If you win those two states, would that just about do it?" And I said, "It might." And that's how the quotation came out.

KALB: If I'm taking it out of context, I apologize. But is the point still valid?

SIMON: But the point still has some validity. I don't think it would just about do it, but it would give you a huge leg up on the ladder. There's no question about it. Now there are things about Iowa and New Hampshire that are not typical of the nation in terms of percentage of blacks and Hispanics and in a variety of other ways. But you are tested in small states, where people really have a chance to get to know you, and that, I think, is a very healthy thing. Now the test goes beyond that, and you can still stumble well beyond New Hampshire.

KALB: You are a senator, and in addition to being a politician, a writer. You have written 11 books, and one very cynical reporter I talked to the other day said you've written more books than most of your candidates on the other side have read. That's a terrible thing to say. But if there is a 12th book in the works, would it be about this campaign?

SIMON: The 12th book in the works will be my eight years in the White House!

KALB: Okay, what is the best book—I ask you this because your wife says that you don't read fiction—that you've read?

SIMON: That I have written or read?

KALB: Read. I know you think all 11 are the best.

SIMON: In terms of a best book that I have read, I guess the book that really moved me—I was about 11 or 12 years old— was *Black Boy* by Richard Wright. Not as famous as his book *Native Son*, but while my father had been active in civil rights and everything, it just stirred me as nothing has ever stirred me that I have read before or since.

KALB: Because?

SIMON: For some reason it hit me at the right age at the right time. And one other interesting little side bar on that: Richard Wright, I learned years later, became a writer through a WPA writer's project. A federal jobs project brought him out and enriched the nation and enriched me.

KALB: Senator, none of your books is about foreign affairs. So in the time that I have left, let's talk about that. In your view, would a Simon administration devote itself primarily to the achievement of arms control agreements with the Soviet Union?

SIMON: Well, I think that has to be a major item on the agenda. But I think we have to also recognize that if there is an unthinkable World War III, it is unlikely to happen as World War II started, with one Super Power attacking another. It is much more likely to happen as World War I did, with some incident somewhere. So you have to use the tools of diplomacy in Central America, in the Middle East, in the Persian Gulf—wherever—to prevent an eruption. I think that it also has to be very much on the foreign policy agenda.

KALB: Robert McNamara, former secretary of defense for Presidents Kennedy and Johnson, said here at Harvard a couple of weeks ago that, in his view, nuclear weapons simply cannot be used as a first-strike weapon—in his view, just can't be used—no matter what the circumstance would be. Do you share that?

SIMON: I don't think anyone can go quite that far, but I think you can go almost that far. But the reality is, if there would be, say, a conventional strike on the part of the Soviets into Central Europe, nuclear weapons would be used. If the United States or West Germany or somebody invaded the Soviet Union, nuclear weapons would be used. But I would add, I think we have ensured to the point where that kind of a frontal assault is very, very unlikely.

KALB: But just to be clear, in the event that the Soviet Union, because of its superior conventional strength in Europe, were to break through and move into West Berlin, move toward Paris, would a Simon administration—you as president—be prepared to use nuclear weapons?

SIMON: I don't think any president can exclude that possibility. But I think what you have to do is to prevent even that possibility from occurring through greater understanding and through, on our side, a buildup of the conventional forces, moving away from excessive reliance on nuclear weapons.

KALB: On that issue of conventional forces, we know that the President and General Secretary Gorbachev have already agreed on a treaty to ban medium- and short-range missiles. Senator Byrd has just said that he thinks the next step should not be an effort on the part of the two Super Powers to try to get a treaty on long-term, long-range offensive and strategic defense but, instead, to go for a treaty on conventional weapons. Do you agree with that?

SIMON: I would like to see whether it's a formal treaty or not. I'm not sure a formal treaty is necessary. I would like to see some withdrawal of conventional forces on both sides. I think that would be a healthy and stabilizing thing.

KALB: But you have talked about a withdrawal under a Simon administration, a withdrawal of American forces from Western Europe, and I want to be clear whether you had in mind a unilateral withdrawal or a withdrawal that would be pegged to an agreement with the Soviet Union.

SIMON: I think you have to negotiate this kind of thing with our allies in Western Europe and with the Soviets. I do think that we now spend 6.7 percent of our GNP on defense. Our friends in Western Europe spend 3.3 percent. At one point that kind of an imbalance made sense. About 40 to 45 percent of our expenditure on defense is for the defense of Western Europe. I think it is only reasonable that our friends in Western Europe pick up more of the tab. And I think in some way, between the Soviets and our NATO allies and the United States, we are going to have to move toward some lesser U.S. role in Western Europe.

KALB: I want to ask you a question. Do you mean that you foresee the possibility that in 5 years, 10 years down the road, the United States could begin to pull away from its total defense through the NATO alliance of Western Europe?

SIMON: I think our commitment to defend Western Europe has to remain, and that has to be strong and no one should question that.

KALB: Within NATO?

SIMON: Within NATO, that is correct. But I think we also have to ask very serious questions: in view of our economy, in view of the substantial improved economies in Western Europe, whether the present imbalance in investment really makes sense. And then I think we can take some steps such as Henry Kissinger has suggested of having the military commander in Western Europe be a Western European. I don't think it has to be an American. I think we can take some steps not to totally disengage—I think that would send the wrong signal—but to say to our friends, "You have to assume more of the burden."

KALB: One final question from me: Why do you feel that, out of all the candidates running today, Paul Simon is the best equipped, the best knowledgeable, the best man to sit opposite Mikhail Gorbachev?

SIMON: I think it is a question of not only sitting with Gorbachev, but of the whole spectrum. And here the differences between the candidates are not cataclysmic, but there are differences in degree. Number one, I bring more experience in government than any of the other candidates, particularly experience in foreign affairs and in dealing with the economy.

Number two, I really have a commitment to make the kind of investments we have to make. I don't shy away from using the tools of government. We're not going to move on the question of urban education, for example, unless there really is strong federal government leadership. I was in Louisiana the other day, where the dropout rate is 46.8 percent. The dropout rate in Japan is 2 percent. Are we just going to drift into the future and not make investments that change that? I think we have to do that. So I'm willing to use the tools of government.

Third, I think if you look at the long history, I've been willing to stand up and do the tough things.

And then, fourth, I believe I have demonstrated a strong commitment to both defending this country and to seizing and creating opportunities to move on the arms race.

KALB: Senator, we've reached that blessed point in the program where I stop asking the questions and we go into the audience. Let us start the questioning now from the floor with Francis Bator, the Ford Foundation professor of international political economy at the Kennedy School of Government. Professor Bator.

SIMON: I am really relieved.

BATOR: It's a great pleasure, Senator Simon, to welcome an old-fashioned liberal. I hope that's not the kiss of death in 1988. In any event, a liberal with no prefix. But in one particular, you pose for someone like myself a puzzle. Having spent about 40 years studying budget rules for the government for an economy like ours, I've come to agree with most—not all—most of my economist colleagues that a balanced budget rule for the federal government, even with a lot of loopholes, is a very bad rule; that countercyclical shifts in the budget position of the federal government play an absolutely critical role in moderating fluctuations, swings in output and employment, and the real economy. Take 1981, 1982—good deficits—they saved us from a very bad recession—also '74, '75. There's no argument that deficits of '84, '87 have been very bad deficits, but one doesn't want to prescribe penicillin just because once a patient swallowed a whole bottle in one sitting, as it were. My puzzle, Senator, how is it possible that a sensible, level-headed fellow like Paul Simon advocates a rule that is as foolish, even dangerous, as a balanced budget amendment in the federal Constitution?

SIMON: Okay.

KALB: Senator, that's an easy one.

SIMON: First, it's interesting that Thomas Jefferson in 1796 wrote a letter in which he said, "If I could just add one amendment to the Constitution, it would be to require a balanced budget." But he wanted a rigid one. I do not favor a rigid one. What I have favored is one that says you have to have a 60 percent vote for precisely the kinds of situations you've talked about.

We cannot continue to have interest just mushroom. The fastest growing item in the budget is interest. We have done the politically easy thing. When I was first elected to the state legislature in Illinois, a man wrote to me from South Roxana, Illinois—had 13 points to his letter. The first 12 were increased services he wanted from government. The 13th point was to cut taxes. We have adopted his program. And you just can't keep that up. And so you have people who are, I think, generally of a progressive persuasion. Someone like George McGovern, who's not a radical right winger as I recall, favors having this kind of a requirement.

The other thing that is happening that is almost unnoticed is not only are we squeezing out our ability through increased interest payments to respond to education, health care, and other things, there is a massive redistribution of wealth that takes place. Who pays the $203 billion this year? By and large, people of limited income. Who gets the $203 billion? By and large, people who are more fortunate economically. So we compound the problems of something that's happening quietly in our society. It doesn't make the headlines, but eventually it will erupt in real problems. That is, there is a shrinking middle class—few people moving up, more people moving down, and that interest payment compounds that.

QUESTION: Senator Simon, I think it's widely recognized that some of the social investments made in the '60s and '70s were often poorly managed, sometimes poorly conceived, and yielded poor returns. How do you intend to ensure that your programs will yield the intended returns?

SIMON: Well, there are programs that were not massively successful, though I think that most historians now looking back at that period have come to the conclusion that there were very wise investments. And I have seen a lot of programs that really have worked. I helped to create something called 94-142, which mandated that all handicapped young people in our country will have a chance at public schools. I remember the opposition we got on that. That has turned out to be a tremendous help to hundreds of thousands of people. We must pay attention to our problems, for example, 23 million functionally illiterate adult Americans. Do we face up to that problem and do something about it, or do we continue to just drift and say, "Oh, no, no. We can't do anything about it. I may be labeled a big spender if I want to do something about it." Let's tackle our problems. Let's shape our own destiny. We can do it.

QUESTION: Senator Simon, have any of your Senate colleagues endorsed your candidacy, and if so, who are they?

SIMON: My colleague in Illinois, Senator Dixon, has. A number of colleagues, if you wish to check, are quietly being of assistance but have not publicly endorsed me. I think there will be some endorsements before too long, but I haven't frankly pushed for a lot of endorsements that way. A number of House members have endorsed me. But I'm really trying to get out there in Iowa and reach the people, rather than spending a lot of time jawboning with my colleagues on endorsements. But I think you will find some endorsements coming along before very long.

QUESTION: Senator Simon, according to a *New York Times* op-ed piece, you were a cosponsor of a Senate bill to force the closing of the Palestinian Information Office in D.C. This is run by an American citizen and reportedly has violated no laws. Could

stand up firmly for human rights. I think simply to abandon the government of Duarte would be a real mistake.

KALB: I'd like now to call on Jill Neptune, the vice-chair of the student advisory committee of the Institute of Politics, where the senator, by the way, was a fellow.

NEPTUNE: Welcome back.

SIMON: Thank you. I think I am the only former fellow, the only alumnus of the institute, who's ever been a candidate for president. That certainly qualifies me.

NEPTUNE: I don't know. A lot of attention is right now focused on Washington and the upcoming summit. And I was wondering, if you were president today, what your agenda would be for the summit when you were meeting with Gorbachev on the arms race and beyond and other issues you'd like to see addressed? In a related question, do you think these summits are useful? You've kind of promoted yourself as the nonmedia candidate, the non-blow-dried, the nonpackaged—are the summits really real opportunities for breaking ground or are they strictly photo opportunities?

SIMON: No. I think they are important, and I recognize they can be used for photo opportunities. Richard Nixon, with whom I don't always agree, said the president of the United States and the leader of the Soviet Union ought to get together at least once a year. I couldn't agree more. As far as the agenda, I would hope it would be beyond arms control. I think one of the things the president of the United States ought to be very clear about is on human rights, whether it's El Salvador somebody just asked about, or South Africa, or the Soviet Union. I have worked on the problems of divided spouses and some of the refuseniks and just incredible problems these people face. And I don't do it from the viewpoint that we're absolutely perfect on everything. We have problems in this country. No question about it. But I think we ought to push the Soviets there. And then finally, as president, if Mr. Gorbachev is there on January 21, 1989, I'm going to say to him, "If you're still willing to stop all nuclear warhead testing, we'll stop all nuclear warhead testing." It's verifiable. That really moves us a substantial step away from the arms race.

QUESTION: Senator, do you support a comprehensive family policy for our country, and if so, what specifics would that policy include, and what leadership would you bring to the issue that would get it on the agenda?

SIMON: Well, when you say a comprehensive family policy, I don't know exactly what you would include. But clearly I have said we have to move on the jobs front. And the public sector jobs programs that I advocate would be of particular help to women and female-headed households who are disproportionately among the poor, and those homes really are disadvantaged.

Second, my stress on education clearly would be a great help to the families of this nation. I think there are a series of things we can do that really would help families in this nation and one of those, incidentally, is being here on the campus. I think we ought to gradually shift away from our loan reliance to more grants so that people, once they get out of college, are not overwhelmed with loans. They can do the things that we think are part of the American dream.

QUESTION: Senator Simon, through much of the 20th century, American prosperity has been fueled by the strength of our manufacturing sector of the economy. Now it seems that it's somewhat in a state of decline, in part due to high wages and part due to poor research investments by management. How, as president, would you try to revitalize the manufacturing sector of the American economy?

SIMON: I agree with 90 percent of the assumptions in your question, and I think it's absolutely vital that we do so. We have accepted this myth that we are becoming an information society, a service society, and that we can have prosperity with that. That just isn't going to happen. Silicon Valley in California has lost 30,000 jobs in the last few years because the information base follows the manufacturing base. The reason for it is not, however, high wages. The average worker in Japan today, for example, makes more money than the average worker in the United States. The reason is policies. Take that atrocious tax bill that passed last year—I'm one of three people to vote against it. That tax bill, among other things, reduced the amount that a corporation can deduct for research. Absolutely as shortsighted as anything we can do. Anyone who believes we can become a more productive, a more competitive nation by cutting back on research, I'll sell a bridge in Brooklyn. You know, it shouldn't be done. We have to encourage the manufacturing sector, and I think it has to be done with presidential leadership—jawboning to some extent. I also think it requires some changes of the tax law.

QUESTION: Senator, in spite of what some people say and statistics that try to be representative of this fact, the state of Massachusetts really is suffering from crime. How can a president lead a nation in the battle against what is "the enemy within" and provide citizens a safe home?

SIMON: Dramatic changes are not possible, and you should not expect that whether Paul Simon or anyone else is elected president. But I think there are things that we can do. And what we know, for example, is that those who are high school dropouts are much more likely to get involved in crime.

I was at a breakfast in New York City the other day. The dropout rate in New York City among Hispanics is 61 percent, among blacks, 57 percent. We have to give people an opportunity to lift themselves, a real opportunity for a better education. And that's going to ultimately help on crime.

The jobs bill would give people an opportunity to work, an option other than crime, and I think it will help. And then there are other very practical things—the drug program. We need something more than public relations slogans. We need interdiction. We also need, for example, seminars for teachers so they can tell when someone may have a drug problem. Those are the kind of practical things we have to do.

KALB: Senator, our final questioner is Mary Jo Bane, a professor of public policy here at the Kennedy School and director of the Center for Health and Human Resources Policy.

BANE: Senator Simon, when you answered Marvin Kalb's first question about the costs of your domestic proposals, you implied that with regard to the guaranteed jobs program, we needed to make those investments partly because they would help deal with the problems of what people have called "the underclass," with teen pregnancy, and so on. The model for the jobs program, though, seems to be the WPA model from the 1930s, which was designed for relatively well-trained, experienced people building bridges and so on. Can you help me understand how a jobs program now could deal with the serious problems in the cities of people who have not been part of the labor market, are not very well trained and so on? How do the states make that work? How do they do it in conjunction with their welfare programs? How do you see that happening?

SIMON: First, I'm going to send you a copy of my latest book called—

BANE: I've read it.

SIMON: In last Sunday's *New York Times*, it was very interesting that William Wilson, who has written the book *The Disadvantaged Society*, and who is getting a lot of attention right now, said, "The only piece of legislation that really deals effectively with this whole problem of the disadvantaged society is the bill by Senator Simon." We move in into any community and we say to people if you've been out of work five weeks, then we will give you a job 32 hours a week at the minimum wage. Projects selected by local people, and then there's a screening process. If you can't read and write, we're going to get you into a program. If you can't speak the English language, we'll get you into a class. If you have no marketable skills, we'll try and help you, so that we invest in our people and lift them. We finally face a choice, ultimately of paying people for doing nothing or paying people for doing something. I'm conservative. I want to pay people for doing something.

KALB: Senator, in about 15 seconds left, why did you wear a red bow tie?

SIMON: Because I heard you were going to wear a red tie, Marvin.

Candidates '88

A CONVERSATION WITH
PAT ROBERTSON

Photo by Martha Stewart

About the Candidate

Pat Robertson was often called the Republican Jesse Jackson, and indeed there were some striking parallels. Both were ordained Baptist ministers, though Robertson had resigned from the ministry when he announced for president. Both staked out ideological positions at the edge of their respective parties' mainstreams. Both commanded support of an especially fervent kind. Both brought tens of thousands of new people into the political process. Both entered the presidential race laterally, via leadership in social movements as opposed to holding political office. Both hoped to be convention kingmakers even if the nomination itself eluded them. And both were in it for the long haul, promising to play a role in national politics for many years to come.

Substantively, of course, the two could not have been more different. And while Jackson had been involved in national, albeit nonelectoral, political activity for decades, Robertson was brand-new to it. There was another big difference: Robertson's religiosity formed the explicit basis of his political appeal.

The presidential candidacy of Marion G. Robertson, 58, was made possible by the reawakening of charismatic fundamentalist Christianity in America and the accompanying explosive growth of television evangelism. He himself was a TV evangelist for more than 25 years; his program, "The 700 Club," which pioneered in adapting the talk show format to religious purposes, made his face and voice familiar to millions. Robertson prefers to be known as a businessman, arguing that this more accurately describes the founder and chief executive of an enterprise, the Christian Broadcasting Network (CBN), which grew from nothing to a payroll of 4,000 employees and an annual budget of $200 million. But if CBN is a business, it is an unusual one: 80 percent of its revenues come from tax-deductible contributions given in response to religious appeals on "The 700 Club."

Though weaned on politics, Robertson rebelled against following in the footsteps of his father, conservative Democratic senator A. Willis Robertson of Virginia. After college at Washington & Lee, a stint in the Marine Corps, and Yale Law School, he drifted to New York and worked rather aimlessly in various business ventures. His conversion to born-again Christianity came in 1958. Thirty years later—albeit by a highly circuitous route—he was a far more famous politician than his father ever was.

Robertson's candidacy tapped a deep vein of resentment with what many of his followers saw as the amorality of secular society. Unlike the other two "movement" conservatives in the race, Jack

Kemp and Pete du Pont, Robertson put his strongest stress on social issues such as school prayer and abortion. And although he outlasted those two rivals, his surprising second-place finish in the Iowa caucuses, ahead of everybody except Bob Dole, would turn out to be the high-water mark of his campaign.

Robertson had a hard time shaking off the electronic paper trail he had left during his years at CBN. His claims to have diverted a hurricane through prayer, his predictions that the battle of Armageddon would engulf the world by 1982, and his insistence that only believing Christians and Jews were fit to hold public office all came back to haunt him—on "Candidates '88," among other places.

H.H.

The Interview

KALB: Mr. Robertson, let us start with U.S.-Soviet relations. This has been a big week in Washington.

ROBERTSON: Yes, it has.

KALB: President Reagan and Mr. Gorbachev have signed a treaty eliminating a whole class of nuclear weapons, the medium- and short-range missiles in Europe and elsewhere. And according to the latest poll, more than 70 percent of the American people feel we are now entering a new era in U.S.-Soviet relations, a new era of cooperation.

With that as a preamble, a couple of quick questions. You have described the President as a Neville Chamberlain. Do you believe he has sold out the interests of this country to Gorbachev?

ROBERTSON: I would like to clarify that one. I was asked by ABC television to comment on a transcript in the *New York Times*. And I said that the words I read seemed to sound more like Neville Chamberlain in that interview than Ronald Reagan in 1980.

But having said that, I'm cautiously optimistic about the treaty. My underlying concern has to do with decoupling our NATO allies from American military power and the overwhelming Soviet conventional superiority. I think I would like to see the Senate put some kind of condition subsequent on the treaty that indeed we would move forward with what's called mutually balanced forced reduction in terms of conventional arms. I think that's the essential problem I have.

KALB: So you do not feel that the President in what he did last week sold out the interests of this country?

ROBERTSON: I still don't trust the Soviets.

KALB: Well, do you think the President does?

ROBERTSON: He has gotten what seems to be a pretty good treaty. The *Wall Street Journal* had an article—editorial—a couple of days ago with a count that indicated they could be hiding some SS-20s up in the Urals or someplace. But the experts, at least in our government, say it's a good treaty.

KALB: Are you prepared to take the word of experts on that?

ROBERTSON: I still have some internal doubts, Marvin. The internal doubts have to do with Soviet human rights violations, their invasion of Afghanistan, some of their aggressive actions against other nations.

KALB: Do you feel that the American people are right or wrong in believing overwhelmingly, as they apparently do according to the polls, that we are indeed entering a new era of cooperation with the Russians?

ROBERTSON: I think we're in the midst of a classic Soviet peace offensive. That's been described in the past. Anyone who is the protege of the former head of the KGB makes me just a little bit nervous. I don't care how sweetly he smiles and what kind of furs his wife wears.

Nevertheless, there's still that nagging doubt that these people really aren't sincere. Let them let the people out of the Gulag and let the Jewish refuseniks start going to Israel in large numbers, and I'll begin to be a little bit more sanguine about the chance for peace.

KALB: Have you ever in the past supported an arms control agreement with the Soviet Union?

ROBERTSON: Of those I've seen so far, the main one that I had to comment on was SALT II, and of course the Senate rejected that. That was fatally flawed, and the Soviets have violated it.

KALB: I don't think they rejected it. They never quite got to a vote.

ROBERTSON: Well, it would have been voted down, I believe. That's a technicality. But they would have rejected it, I believe.

KALB: What about SALT I in 1972? Did you approve of that?

ROBERTSON: I didn't comment on it at the time.

KALB: What about now? Do you feel that as you look back that the SALT I treaty, the ABM treaty, the SALT II treaties were treaties that you as president could have supported?

ROBERTSON: Well, the Soviets have violated SALT I from all I can gather. They have been violating the ABM treaty. This Krasnoyarsk radar, for example, is felt by many experts to be in violation of the ABM. And what we have witnessed over these years is a mammoth buildup of Soviet capability, nuclear submarines, conventional weapons, and very sophisticated nuclear forces. So instead of being in parity, we are considerably below their capabilities, and that worries me.

KALB: In an interview a couple of weeks ago, perhaps not even two weeks ago, with the network anchormen, the President said, in citicizing a number of people who were criticizing him, that they felt a nuclear war between the United States and the Soviet Union was inevitable. Do you feel that a nuclear war is inevitable?

ROBERTSON: I feel just the opposite. I don't think that the

Soviets will ever begin a nuclear war against America, and I don't think we'll ever start one against them.

KALB: Why do you say that?

ROBERTSON: I think we both recognize the terrible dangers to both of our populations that would come from nuclear war. What I'm more concerned about is the type of blackmail that could come from overwhelming superiority. I think the nuclear balance has kept us from at least a world war in the years since World War II, and although I hate nuclear terror, nevertheless it has restrained the Super Powers. I hope we can keep some kind of balance so that we will still be restrained in the future.

KALB: Mr. Robertson, you have been quoted in the past as saying the struggle as you saw it between the U.S. and the USSR was between a Christian America and a satanic Soviet Union. Is that something you still feel?

ROBERTSON: I can't recall those exact words. That doesn't sound exactly like me. But I do know the Soviet Union is based on atheism and we are a theistic people in the Judeo-Christian tradition here in America. I'm with Abraham Lincoln if I can paraphrase: I don't think the world can forever be half-slave and half-free. I think ultimately we must come down on the side of freedom. Lincoln said that if you familiarize yourself with the chains of bondage, you prepare your own limbs to wear them. And I just cannot get comfortable with the genocide of the Cambodians or the rape of Afghanistan or some of the other Soviet aggressive acts, especially against dissenters in their own nation.

KALB: But then what would you as president do about things like Afghanistan?

ROBERTSON: First of all, I would step up the propaganda war. I think we need to call what is being done what it is. I think we have to build hope in captive peoples that one day there's a chance for freedom.

KALB: Hasn't President Reagan been doing that?

ROBERTSON: Well, I can do more. You asked what I would do. I would continue that and add to it. The second thing I would do is to give aid and assistance to those brave men and women who are fighting for freedom in Afghanistan. I was over on the border of Afghanistan and talked to some of the Mujahadeen leaders. They are wonderful people. And a few Stinger missiles have seemingly brought them a great deal of relief. As a matter of fact, the Soviets are having a tremendous loss there. I don't think that we should let up the pressure. And I would favor helping Unita and Ranamo, and also the freedom fighters in Nicaragua.

KALB: But isn't the President of the United States doing exactly what you say you would do?

ROBERTSON: I'm not criticizing him. I would continue it.

KALB: You would continue?

ROBERTSON: Absolutely.

KALB: Okay, in the Middle East—now here I know that I'm quoting you exactly because I've read it several times—you cited Chapter 38 of Ezekiel as your guide to what would happen in the Middle East, and you have said there will be "an invasion of Israel by Russia, Iran, Ethiopia, and Libya. When the smoke clears Soviet Russia will be reduced to a fourth-rate power and Israel will be the wonder of the world. This is what the Bible tells us will happen, and it will happen." Do you still believe that?

ROBERTSON: Well, I'm a person who believes the Bible, and you will excuse me for a certain measure of pessimism. I said that in about 1979 under the Jimmy Carter administration, and I was extremely pessimistic about the state of world affairs.

KALB: It was also in '82.

ROBERTSON: I have seen some correlation of forces in the Middle East. Syria is a Soviet client state. I think that Iran, if things continue on the present course, will probably fall into the Soviet hegemony. And Libya has been a client of the Soviets, and these powers don't like Israel. And sooner or later, I think there will be a clash over there. I wish it weren't true. I'm not going to help it. But we must realize that Israel is the last bastion of democracy in that Middle Eastern caldron, and the Soviets have been attempting mischief in there for a number of years. That's why, when I was talking about Shimon Peres, I wasn't too enthusiastic about the thought of a Security Council supervising a Middle East peace. I don't want the Soviets back in there. And Prime Minister Shamir was of the opinion I share that it should be bilateral talks between Israel and her neighbors. I would like, frankly, as president, to call a peace conference in Washington with Israel, with Egypt, with Jordan, and with Syria to see if they could work out their differences, hopefully to keep the Soviets out of the Middle East.

KALB: And you really think Syria would show up, or even Jordan?

ROBERTSON: I think Jordan would if King Hussein could be protected from being assassinated. And I don't know about Hafez

Assad. I would think sooner or later he would recognize he cannot overwhelm Israel militarily, and that the ray of peace would be best for him. I'm an optimist in those things.

KALB: I'm trying to understand indirectly the way in which the Bible may influence your decisions. I don't think that has slipped past you. And what I wanted to know with reference to a specific issue like the budget deficit, for example: Again you've quoted the 25th Chapter of Leviticus that every 50 years God declares a year a jubilee year, and He would cancel out debts between the people. Now if you were elected president, would you simply cancel all debts?

ROBERTSON: Marvin, you're going to win the election on this one. I assure you there are more debtors in this country than anything else.

KALB: Would you cancel the debts?

ROBERTSON: The president obviously can't cancel debts, but Russian economist Nikolai Kondratev, famed for the Kondratieff cycle, points out what happens in our Western civilization is that every 54 to 56 years there's a long wave cycle dealing with debt accumulation, and that's the largest number one single economic problem we're facing. There's $10 trillion in America. Ten trillion dollars around the world. A large portion of that debt is uncollectible. Now we do cancel it, but we do it with different means. We could hyperinflate it as the Germans did, and bankrupt the middle class, or we can put the economy through a wringer of a terrible depression and foreclosures and anguish, or we could say, let's be realistic about this, let's write some debts down to current market value of the underlying assets. Let's realize that Third World debts to banana republics will never be paid, so why keep holding them on the balance sheet and adding nonexistent interest to noncollectible loans?

KALB: So that of the couple of trillion dollars that the U.S. is in debt, how much of that, if you can be specific, would you simply declare null and void?

ROBERTSON: That can't be done. We have to honor the debts that we have, but I certainly think as a nation we should do something about paying it off. Our net savings as a nation is 2.8 percent, the private sector saves about 8 percent, and the government is negative 5 percent, so we come out at less than 3 percent. Our saving rate is unconscionable right now. We're piling debt on top of debt, and there's going to be an awful crash unless we have some rational means. The Jews had a rational way of doing it. The

Israelis, about 15 years out of the cycle, began to slow the thing down, and there was an easy soft landing. That's all I'd like to see.

KALB: How would you specifically handle the enormous budget deficit? Would you, for example, impose taxes on consumption?

ROBERTSON: I think the way to do it, first of all, is to begin a series of budget cuts. The politicians, frankly, aren't playing square with the American people. Did you see that little legerdemain the Democrats pulled a couple of weeks ago? They said they'd save $900 million for the American people, and the way they'd do it is not to give themselves a big raise as they planned. They gave themselves their third raise of the year, $2,700, and said they wouldn't add $900 million to raises for the rest of the federal employees. That's nonsense. That isn't a saving. That's an illusion. I think we can get real savings of $100 million for fiscal year 1990.

KALB: One hundred million dollars?

ROBERTSON: One hundred billion, excuse me. And in 1991—fiscal year 1991—I would go for a balanced budget. And I think we could do it by cutting spending as opposed to raising at least the marginal tax rates.

KALB: Then let me ask you specifically about raising taxes on specific consumption, and you just say yes or no. On a gasoline tax?

ROBERTSON: I am not in favor of that because it would hurt the poor. And I think it's one of those things that would cause disruption to many, many people.

KALB: What about a cigarette tax?

ROBERTSON: Well, I think that's a user fee. I think half of the hospital beds—I was told by a doctor friend of mine—are occupied by people with smoking-related illnesses. I don't see why we couldn't have a little user fee for those who use cigarettes to help pay for their health expenses.

KALB: What about alcohol?

ROBERTSON: Same thing.

KALB: One of the criticisms about Pat Robertson, which might not even be justified but I raise anyway, is that on your specific economic plans for getting that budget deficit down to zero by 1991, you really haven't been all that specific. So I have a question so that people understand. Is it that you really have no specific plans on these issues? Or is it that the specific plans involve such bitter medicine for the American people to have to swallow and take, you don't feel in the campaign you want to give them and lay it out that way?

ROBERTSON: I told the *Des Moines Register* that any candidate who gets too specific about budget cuts will remain perpetually a candidate, and that's obviously true. But I'll be specific right here on this program if we've got a few minutes. Of course, we don't have to break for commercials, so I'll lay out a few of them. Number one, the Heritage Foundation did a superb study and brought forth about $111 billion in easily attainable spending cuts or savings. One thing that they proposed that might be a little controversial but has some appeal is to index our bonds with an index situation. It wouldn't be necessary to pay what's known as an inflation premium. They estimate that could save as much as $11 billion a year. If the federal employees and the military personnel were paid wages comparable to the private sector, and had retirement benefits comparable to the private sector, we would save $8 billion a year. If we were to privatize the postal service, for example, either sell it or give it to the employees, we would save about $2 billion a year. I could go down the list, but it's that kind of thing.

KALB: You've also said that you would privatize social security. If you were to become president of the U.S., would you act on that immediately in a significant way?

ROBERTSON: Well, the young people, especially, for example, students and young adults in this audience, need to understand that by the year 2015 social security will be bankrupt and there will be no money to pay them. And what I want to see is the beginning of a private system so their retirement won't be subject to the vagaries of the political process in the year 2020 when the baby boom generation goes to retirement. But I'm talking about taking care of the elderly. We absolutely have to guarantee retirement to the elderly—that's a given in politics. But I would like a gradual privatization of benefits so that people could begin paying maybe a quarter of their social security payments into what would amount to a compulsory private tax-sheltered IRA program. Forty years down the road it would be totally privatized. We could do that gently. It would be a great boon to the insurance companies, a great boon to the banks, to the stock market, to the financial intermediaries of our country.

KALB: Mr. Robertson, I want to switch subjects.

ROBERTSON: All right.

KALB: You have spent most of your adult life as a reverend, a

Baptist minister. You're now running for president, and that started on October 1st in a public, declared fashion.

ROBERTSON: That week I resigned my ordination.

KALB: But I do want to talk to you about God, which is obviously a word and a concept fairly awesome.

ROBERTSON: Yes, it is.

KALB: You have said in the past that you have actually talked to God. I just want to be clear. Is that correct?

ROBERTSON: I pray. And prayer itself is conversation between a creature and the Creator, and I think it's a two-way conversation.

KALB: Do you have a two-way conversation in that you feel you actually hear a voice that comes back to you?

ROBERTSON: I think there's a question of a peace in a person's heart. My wife and I are so close, it isn't necessary for us to verbalize. Many times we just have great empathy with one another. We understand what each other is feeling or thinking. And I think in the spiritual realm, the relationship with a believer and his or her God is much the same way. There's an intimacy that comes with somebody who's known somebody for a long time. I told a *Los Angeles Times* reporter, "Could you imagine a guy working for IBM for 30 years, and his supervisor never once talked to him? I've been working for God all these years, and sooner or later, yes, he communicates what he wants me to do."

KALB: But you have said you have heard the voice of God, and I quote, "level and conversational." And I'm trying to understand whether what you're saying is that simply in your mind you hear a voice, or do you literally? Is there a voice that another person could share? Is it just something that goes from God's lips into your ears?

ROBERTSON: If I could quote the psalmist David, he uses the term *deep*, calls unto deep, and it's the kind of thing in a person's inner consciousness he feels he's communicating with his Creator. It's not something which is commonplace, but it certainly is written about in the Bible.

KALB: It is written about in the Bible, certainly. And Abraham had his discussions with God.

ROBERTSON: And Moses.

KALB: And Moses in detail. I just wanted to know whether you are one of those who has had that kind of conversation with God.

ROBERTSON: I think it's something that's available to all believers. I talked to the son of the man who translated—at least brought about—modern-day Hebrew. And he said his father heard a voice. He saw a light. There was this thing that happened. Out of that he went to Israel to begin to do this monumental work. But at one point in time he felt he had been touched by God.

KALB: Do you feel you've been touched by God?

ROBERTSON: Absolutely. And there's millions and millions of others who have too.

KALB: You said when you made your decision to run, "I made this decision in response to the clear and distinct prompting of the Lord's spirit. I know this is His will for my life." How do you know that?

ROBERTSON: There's peace. The apostle Paul said, "Let the peace of God be an umpire in your heart." And I think when a person has peace, if he has lived the type of life that I've lived for 30 years, he knows that peace, and the peace was there that this was the right thing to do. It's been a very costly decision. I walked away from an organization that I spent 25 years building, and a very satisfying life, and gave up a salary and a job. You know, it was quite a sacrifice. And you don't do things like that lightly.

KALB: Do you feel that if you were to become president—I don't mean to even belittle the concept here—that God would be with you, for example, in the cabinet room when there are major decisions of state that have to be reached?

ROBERTSON: I would certainly hope so. Randal Brook, who played the role of Annie in the Broadway show, said, "I would rather have a president who believed in a higher power than a person who thought he was the higher power."

KALB: Do you have a feeling—do you believe—that God is a loving and caring God who looks out for every single human being?

ROBERTSON: Absolutely. He is very caring and very compassionate, very forgiving and very understanding.

KALB: How do you explain the holocaust within that context?

ROBERTSON: The only way I can explain it is there are other forces at work in the world besides the force of good, and I remember William Shirer's book about the Third Reich, which I'm sure you've read. He used the term "demonic" to describe Adolf Hitler. He said he was demonized. Somebody else might say he was insane. However you want to look at it, it was a hideous monstrosity that in no way could be attributed to God, but it certainly could be attributed to the enemies of God.

KALB: You've spoken a great deal since you have declared your candidacy about the sanctity of the family, and I'd like to talk a little bit about your own, not basing anything upon second- or third-hand sources but your own autobiography, *Shout It from the Rooftops*. You described that moment when you felt born again: You met a Dutchman named Cornelius Vanderbragen, and he convinced you to go from swinger to saint. You went home and told your wife, "I'm saved, saved." And according to your own autobiography, she answered, "Pat, you're drunk. Both of us are going to have to cut down on our drinking. Just because you've lost your mind to become a religious nut doesn't mean I have to go crazy too." Now is that really what she was saying?

ROBERTSON: She didn't say it quite so strongly. But when I poured a bottle of Ballantine scotch down the drain, she thought something strange had happened. But in any event she soon felt it would be the best way to go. It took about a year.

KALB: If she felt that, let me get into that next period, because again from your book, when your wife was taking care of your baby son and she was already six months pregnant you announced you were leaving and going to a religious retreat in Canada. Again, I'm quoting your wife's reaction from your own autobiography: "I think you're sick. It's just not normal for a man to walk out on his wife and leave her with a small child when she's expecting a baby at any minute while he goes off in the woods to talk to God. God doesn't tell people to do things like that, at least my God doesn't." But you left anyway. Why did you do that?

ROBERTSON: It was one month's time. I was in business in New York, and I was up to my hips, if you will, in the Wall Street type of life, trying to pursue a dollar and to be a success in business. And I was making a very definite transition at that time in my life, and I needed to be with some people to have a little bit of teaching, a group of college students at a place called Campus in the Woods in Canada, and it was just something that had to be done. It had to be done for me, to get me into a new life. And everything was fine. Everything was fine at home. There wasn't any problem. And as I say, at this point I have four beautiful well-adjusted tremendous children.

KALB: No question about that.

ROBERTSON: That 30 days was a key time in my life. It had to be done. There are times a man has to do things.

KALB: But she asked you, she begged you, in fact, to come back. She said she needed you. I put this within the context of your current statement about the sanctity of the family.

ROBERTSON: Absolutely.

KALB: So why did you do it?

ROBERTSON: A husband doesn't always have to do everything his wife asks him to do. There is some give and take in marriage, and we don't totally give up our personality just because we get married.

KALB: With your own organizational abilities in the political sphere right now, you've certainly put the fear of God, if I can borrow an expression, into your Republican colleagues for the nomination. But, according to a very late poll, 55 percent of Iowa Republicans and 61 percent of New Hampshire Republicans have given you an unfavorable rating. My question for you is, Do you think that is because many Americans are still concerned about vesting their future and their fortune, their country, in the hands of a person they regard as a religious figure rather than a politician?

ROBERTSON: After the debates, I think the first of the debates we had together with Bill Buckley in Houston, my negative ratings in New Hampshire dropped 12 percent. We found in focus testing that it takes about five minutes for a hostile group listening to me talk on issues to shift from very negative to, at least, "I'll give him a second chance or look," and maybe over to positive. I haven't really done any of the so-called image-building on television dealing with issues, so people just don't know who I am. When they listen and hear what I'm saying, then they change perceptively and dramatically. I've been filtered through the media, and to say the media is fair or favorable to my candidacy would be one of the overstatements of the year.

KALB: Do you think it's fair?

ROBERTSON: No, it hasn't been fair. It hasn't been favorable. A program like this is wonderful because we can talk unedited, uncut, and the people can see and judge on the basis of issues what I have to say. But until that happens it's a straw man they're dealing with. They think I'm someone else, and I don't blame them if all they had to do is read some of these newspaper reports.

KALB: Joseph Brodsky, the winner of the Nobel prize in literature, just this past week said, "There is no doubt in my mind that should we have been choosing our leaders on the basis of their reading experience and not their political programs, there would be much less grief on earth." Do you yourself read a good bit?

ROBERTSON: I read a considerable amount. I estimate that last year I read 25 books. When I was doing a TV talk show, I had an author on almost every day, and I had to read continuously, but

I read a number of periodicals, publications. I'm not reading as many newspapers as I used to, but I do read the *London Economist*, and I read a number of economic papers.

KALB: But on books, what is the last major book that you feel you've read?

ROBERTSON: I've read a number of them on politics, which don't count.

KALB: They count.

ROBERTSON: Well, I read them from the Left to the Right. But I think Manchester's book *The Last Line on Winston Churchill* was one of the most key. I read a major book on Saudi Arabia called *The Kingdom*. But even Hafez Assad—what was his name? Abdul Assis—is an excellent book. But I think the one on Churchill is a standout.

KALB: Which is the last one that you've read that you feel really has something that you'd like to tell your children, "You've got to read this to grow up"?

ROBERTSON: Paul Johnson's book called *Modern Times*. It was an enormous thing, and it took forever to get it finished. But I did finally finish. It was an excellent book, and I would recommend that to anybody watching this show.

KALB: Mr. Robertson, we've reached that blessed part of the program where I stop asking the questions, and we go into the audience. Let us start with Sonya Michel, who teaches here at Harvard and has a particular interest in the role of women in our society.

MICHEL: I want to return to this issue of the family that Mr. Kalb started with and ask you about several of the policies you've mentioned in terms of the family. The first is your plan for a tax incentive to enable women to return to the home. If you could possibly convince American women who now hold jobs to return to the home, something I'm rather dubious about, how could this country possibly afford to pay—to compensate—families for the income they would lose if women give up their jobs, and wouldn't this interfere with your stated goal of reducing the deficit? Second, you've called for the ending of welfare programs to AFDC mothers—welfare payments. Aren't those payments there precisely to enable women to stay at home with their children, and wouldn't you be undermining the very goals you've set out? And how could both low-income or no-income women benefit from a tax incentive program?

KALB: Take any one of the three.

ROBERTSON: Some of my positions have been somewhat misstated, if you'll excuse my saying so. But on average, working women, many of whom have to work for minimum wage, get a take home net income of about $1,800 a year after they have paid taxes, child care support, necessary clothing, transportation, food, et cetera. It's minimal. They say the super-moms of the early 1980s have become the burned-out moms of the late 1980s, and I would like to give people an opportunity to be wives and mothers if they wish by using the tax incentives. But I've said repeatedly—as a matter of fact, every time I've said this—that I believe as a nation we must make available career opportunities for women who wish to have worthwhile careers.

And I'm absolutely committed to the proposition that if women do equal work with men, they should be paid equal pay with men without question as a national goal. And I'll tell you, I don't know what I would do without the women involved in my campaign. The head of our Michigan operation is a woman. The head of our Iowa operation is a woman. The head of our communications is a woman. The head of our voter ID and turn-out is a woman, and I could go right down the line. We probably have more women in high positions in my presidential campaign than any other candidate has in either party. So I am totally committed to making places available for outstanding women who wish careers. So I don't want to cut back on any payments.

Now you mentioned Aid to Families with Dependent Children. Regretfully, some of those programs have been an incentive to people who, in order to get out of an intolerable situation as a young girl, would have a baby and would have an option to get an apartment or stay at home or get married. And I think some of the options should be taken away. I don't think we should have anything that breaks up family units. And we shouldn't have anything that encourages births out of wedlock. That's essentially all I'm saying. But never would I want to restrict poor women with children from getting assistance. I want to do everything I can to help them.

QUESTION: Reverend Robertson, you have been quoted as saying you look forward to the day when children in public schools can pray again. I'd like to know what religious prayers you'd like them to pray, and what about the other religions that are there in the school?

ROBERTSON: I'm more concerned about a return to the moral values that we had in our school system when education was great. I was reading a very excellent article by Rabbi Haberman last night in the *Policy Review,* and he mentioned that the bulwark we have against tyranny in this country is our firm belief in God and our firm belief in some standard of authority above government. Otherwise, dictators can do as they please. There needs to be some ultimate recourse to which we can go. And I'm afraid that we're not teaching people that in our schools. I would like to see some return to a transmission of the moral values of our society. The prayer part is not nearly as important as the moral part, that we come to a moral framework in our education. And I think we're not doing that now, and that's the thing that has concerned me.

But surely the Supreme Court overruled an Alabama statute that permitted the children a moment of silence. They could have prayed to any God they wanted to in any form they wanted to, and the Supreme Court wouldn't even let them be quiet at the beginning of school. So I think that is reductio ad absurdum. As Daniel Moynihan has said, the Supreme Court decisions dealing with the establishment clause are an intellectual scandal, and I tend to agree with that.

QUESTION: As a United Methodist minister myself, I'm interested in how you as a pastor understand your goals as a politician. Reverend Jackson phrases his political aspirations in terms of God's desire for social justice. And it seems in what you've just said that you phrase your desire for political ends in terms of God's own morality, or your Christian fundamentalist concept of what is God's morality. As president, what sorts of morality would you like to see legislated?

ROBERTSON: I wouldn't want any morality legislated. I don't think that's the appropriate role of government. What I would like to see is some commonsense policies. It isn't a question of being left wing or right wing. It's a question of being smart or stupid. Some of the things we're doing are just dumb. Going bankrupt is dumb. I mean, to rob the patrimony of your unborn children is immoral in my estimation. I think failing to meet the needs of the poor and the really downtrodden in a society is wrong. I'm a conservative insofar as I believe in certain fundamental principles, but I'm also a conservative with a human, compassionate face.

Through the organization I founded in the private sector, I have helped feed, clothe, and house about 25 million poor Americans in the last 10 years and in the last three years have helped teach 123,000 people to read and write, primarily in the inner cities, without taking any money from the federal government at all. The question in my mind is, Do we allow the churches and other mediating organizations in our society, private enterprise, and private individuals to take a substantial burden of the task of helping people in our society, or do we put it all in Washington and centralize power and turn this country into a welfare state? I would rather have it at the lowest level of government—at the state level, at the local level, and in the private sector. And it's just a question of how you can accomplish things most expeditiously, not whether or not you do them.

QUESTION: You avoid the subject of homosexuality, and the subject of abortion, and the subject of the rights of battered women within a family.

ROBERTSON: What are you talking about?

QUESTION: These are also moral issues.

ROBERTSON: I have done any number of programs about battered wives. I've had them on my program to talk about it. I think it's shameful. Why would I want to avoid something that's my specialty?

QUESTION: It's just interesting to me what you choose to lift up as moral.

ROBERTSON: You think homosexuality is—I don't understand the question. I missed it totally.

KALB: Mr. Robertson, I'm going to ask you once again to please shorten up the answers.

ROBERTSON: Forgive me.

QUESTION: Mr. Robertson, totalitarian states often use schools to indoctrinate children with their own ideologies. How is your plan to bring your own version of God and morality into our schools different from this? And shouldn't schools in a democracy teach children the skills needed to decide for themselves between different views instead of telling them what to believe?

ROBERTSON: You think the schools today are doing a good job of giving the children a choice of what to believe?

QUESTION: Could you answer my question, please?

ROBERTSON: I'm answering your question with a question. Do you think they're doing a good job?

QUESTION: I'm not sure.

ROBERTSON: May I suggest that you read a book called *Molly's Pilgrim?* It's written by a Jewish author who indicated that the word *God* was expunged from her manuscript by Harcourt Brace because they would not permit the term *God* to be used in a textbook in the public school system. And I would also recommend to you the reading of Professor Paul Vitz's excellent study on the social science textbooks used in America in about 70 percent of the schools. And you'll find there that the words *marriage* and *wedding* and *wife* and *husband* do not appear once. There is no primary reference to religion in any of those books whatsoever, and Joan of Arc is portrayed as the first leader of the feminist movement. Now, if that's a fair treatment, I don't know. But that's what's being taught in the school today. Read Professor Vitz, Ph.D., NYU. It's an excellent study.

KALB: I'd like now to recognize Kris Kobach, a member of the student advisory committee of the Institute of Politics.

KOBACH: You've stated that one of your primary ways in which you would make these budget cuts would be in eliminating bureaucratic waste. Reagan tried the same thing in '83 and '84 with the Grace Commission, and met with little success. And academics like James Q. Wilson have said that in order to meaningfully reduce waste you have to create more rules and procedures, i.e., more red tape, which is self-defeating. Given these constraints, where specifically would you find enough waste to balance the budget, and how would you cut it out?

ROBERTSON: Well, I've mentioned three or four in an earlier discussion here with Marvin Kalb. We will never cut the budget and get rid of the waste until we get a Congress with enough guts to stand up to special interest groups. As long as we have the special interest groups with their money, with their PACs, with their enormous political power, the general average Joe in the general population doesn't stand a chance. I read an article in *USA Today* earlier this past week, "Congress Doesn't Have the Guts to Balance the Budget." And then there was a quote at the bottom from a congressman from California who said, "I love pork barrel, that's what gets me elected." Well, if we're going to have men or women whose only job is to get themselves reelected every two years, instead of people who care about the next generation, then we will continue this shocking thing. There's got to be enough outrage at the grassroots to say, "No more." And in order to do that, it will be necessary to overcome a huge entrenched bureaucracy. Can you do it? It will only be done at the precincts of America. It will never be done as long as power is concentrated in Washington. It's just that simple.

QUESTION: A couple of years ago on your "700 Club" program you stated that only Christians and Jews are really fit to hold office in the United States. I'm wondering why someone who is neither a Christian nor a Jew shouldn't be terrified by that somewhat un-American statement.

ROBERTSON: I'm not sure it's all that un-American, but I could rephrase it. The Constitution of the United States says there shall be no religious test for any office or position of trust in the United States, and I totally agree with that. And as president I'm sworn to uphold the Constitution, which means there can be no religious test for any office or position of trust.

QUESTION: You still said that no—

ROBERTSON: But what I said in a philosophical sense as a minister three or four years ago does not necessarily apply to somebody who's raised his hand and sworn on the Bible to uphold the Constitution. Now, if I could rephrase that statement to make it a little bit more understandable. Our institutions were crafted by people who had a theistic point of view. And it seems to me that we would best maintain them by electing those who agree with the underlying philosophical principles of the founding fathers, and that's essentially all I'm saying. And I felt that. But there's no way an elected official can do such a thing, because the Constitution says no religious tests, and I abide by the Constitution.

QUESTION: Dr. Robertson, if you were elected president, would you continue the current administration's policy of financing loans to communists in the Eastern bloc nations?

ROBERTSON: I think that would be one of the first things I would want to cut out. It seems to me it's somewhat counterproductive to spend $300 billion a year to defend America while at the same time our banks and financial institutions are shoveling out billions of dollars—it happens to be $120 billion now that the Eastern bloc countries owe the free world—to essentially prop up communist tyranny. I think it's immoral, I think it's wrong, and I think it ought to be stopped. And I might add—you mentioned the percentage—that it's about an 83 percent issue in America. The American people don't like it at all. They feel that somehow it makes no sense to defend against communism and to prop up communism with our money at the same time.

QUESTION: Mr. Robertson, some weeks ago the *New York Times* published a very long article comparing your candidacy to Jesse Jackson's. I'd like to ask you, in your view, are you or are you not the Jesse Jackson of the Republican party?

ROBERTSON: Well, I'm not for a number of reasons. First of all, Jesse Jackson represents a rather leftist view of American foreign policy, although he's ameliorated some of his views. When he went to Cuba, he said, "Long live Castro. Long live Che Guevera. Long live the revolution." Now that does not accord with the consensus of the American people. The views that I hold are pretty much traditional mainstream America.

Furthermore, Jesse has never had the business experience I have. I've run a complex of companies that have yearly revenues of about $200 million. I started a fully accredited graduate university including five graduate schools and a law school. I've been involved in business dealings in maybe 20 some nations, and have done a number of things that he just hasn't done. And I think that the comparisons are going to cease when people begin to realize that the base supporting me is vastly larger than the group that is supporting him.

QUESTION: Mr. Robertson, as an American Hispanic Christian, I seriously question your commitment to peace and justice and to the diversity of America. My concern is focused on two things, and I'd like you to answer them. One is your "700 Club" 's international level of support of the most devastating counterinsurgency campaign to take place in Central America in Guatemala, and the second is the exhortation to your listeners of the "700 Club" to support the Contras.

KALB: Do you have a question, please?

QUESTION: Yes. My question is, How does that reflect a commitment to peace and justice if you were to be a foreign policy president?

ROBERTSON: It's an interesting thing that the places we find suffering in the world—with refugees and heartache—are those nations such as Cambodia, Ethiopia, and Nicaragua, where there has been communist tyranny. The organization that I founded helped the airlift of medicine and food to refugees in a number of Central American countries. I personally took about $1,200,000 worth of medicine to Guatemala, which was passed out through evangelical clinics to help poor people in that country. There were no funds, no medicine, and no food given to any vicious counterinsurgency movement.

But I would point out to you that had there not been a revolution in the United States of America, where people in this city, particularly Boston and in other cities in New England as well as the original colonies, were willing to stand up for freedom, we would not have had a nation. And I think America needs to have a commitment to freedom that is as strong as the eloquent statement of John F. Kennedy at his inauguration. And I cannot see that we can have a world, as I said before, that's half-slave and half-free. I, personally, as president or as an individual, am on the side of freedom, period.

QUESTION: Mr. Robertson, what do you see as the fundamental source of friction in the American-Soviet rivalry? Is it nuclear weapons? Classic great power struggle? Ideology? Or any combination?

ROBERTSON: Well, according to Alexander Solzhenitsyn, the nexus of the Soviet system is a belief that the state is all-powerful and that individuals are merely pawns within the state. The genius of the American system is that we believe people have God-given rights and that the rights of the citizens are superior to the rights of government, that government is our servant, not our master. The Soviet system believes the exact opposite, that government is the master and people exist essentially for the pleasure of the government. And that is, in my estimation, the great struggle between freedom and slavery. And that's why there's a clash, the ideologies.

QUESTION: There are reports that there are still POWs in Vietnam. Would you please address the concerns of the families that are involved?

ROBERTSON: One of my reporters, Gary Lane, has probably done the most exhaustive study on that subject. He is convinced that there are indeed Americans still in Laos and that we are abandoning them. I don't know because I don't have any firsthand information. But I know Captain Red McDaniel, a great American hero who was a POW for many years, is convinced that there are people there. Regretfully, this is the kind of thing we've swept under the rug, because in order to get them out it will require a commitment of will that our leaders perhaps don't think we have.

But I think if brave Americans have gone into a war situation to fight for their country, whether or not that war was a good one or a bad one—and I'm not in favor of the war—I think it was a mistake—once they're there and once they're captured, we must go in and get them out. And I don't think there's any other choice.

Now, we should do so diplomatically. I don't think we should even consider initiating some kind of war, but we can't sweep it under the rug. And I think that's what's been done from what I can gather—although I have good friends on the other side who say, "Don't believe it. There are none left." So the debate rages. And I frankly don't have firsthand knowledge to give you an answer. But assuming they're there, we owe them a commitment as a nation to free them.

KALB: We are quickly running out of time, and our final questioner is Professor Harvey Cox, who has been teaching religion here at Harvard for many years.

ROBERTSON: A very distinguished gentleman.

COX: You were talking to Ben Kenchelo a few years ago, Pat, and he asked you this on your television show. Does the Bible specifically tell us what's going to happen in the future? And you responded, "Yes, Ben, it specifically and clearly, and unequivocally says that Russia will attack Israel, and that God will then destroy Russia through earthquakes and volcanoes." That was three years ago that you said that. Then you wrote a book a couple of years ago called *Answers to 200 of Life's Most Probing Questions.* That was published in 1984.

ROBERTSON: Machiavelli said, "Mine enemy would write a book."

QUESTION: Since you have no record of voting, we have to read your books and your statements and ask you about them if you're running for president. In that book you said in 1984, "We are getting very close to the time when God is going to say that the human race has gone far enough. He may be ready to step in and terminate this phase of human activity." What I want to know is, as president, would you continue to operate on the premise that the Bible predicts that Russia will attack Israel and that God will destroy Russia by earthquakes and that the human race is getting very close to the time when God is going to terminate it? And if so, how would that influence your foreign policy?

ROBERTSON: I don't think I ever said the human race would be terminated. There is in the Bible a hope for one day a millennium, a time of peace. A time when men will live together as brothers. A time when they will put down their weapons of war, and the swords will be made into plowshares, and the spears into pruning hooks, and when nature will be at peace, and we will stop having our military academies. They won't even study war anymore. That's the termination of the phase of fighting, killing, and hatred that we have now that would usher in an era of peace. And I devoutly hope such a thing will happen.

The other seems to be somewhat clear—the blueprint in the latter days that a country that fits the description of Russia might well invade Israel. But it's not something that foreign policy from America should be involved in. We do what we can to promote peace. And I would do everything as president to bring about peace. I'll work as hard as I can, but the rest is in God's hands, not mine.

KALB: What is the final last word—in your opinion, what is the best word to describe Pat Robertson if we wind it up with that?

ROBERTSON: Mr. President.

Candidates '88

A CONVERSATION WITH
ALBERT GORE

Photo by Martha Stewart

About the Candidate

From the moment he entered the presidential race, Albert Gore, Jr., never missed a chance to point out the parallels between 1988 and a previous election—one that took place when he was just 11 years old. In 1960, a popular president, the oldest man ever to serve in the White House up until that time, was nearing the end of his second term. The outgoing vice president was the Republican favorite. And on the Democratic side, a vigorous young senator sought his party's nomination, hoping to become the youngest elected president in the nation's history.

But the list of parallels between Al Gore and John F. Kennedy did not stop there. Like Kennedy, Gore was the heir to a Democratic family dynasty. Like Kennedy, he went to an elite private school and to Harvard College, served in his generation's war, married a beautiful woman, and put in time as a reporter before being elected to the House and then to the Senate. He even had the striking blue eyes and the shock of dark hair. And Al Gore, only 39 when the election year dawned, was fully three years younger than Jack Kennedy had been at the corresponding point in his career.

Yet Gore was not particularly successful in turning on, to use a bit of generational slang, his fellow baby boomers. This was the result partly of his wife Tipper's crusade against dirty rock songs and partly of his own rather buttoned-down style (in a memorable jibe, Michael Kinsley called him "an old person's idea of a young person"). But mostly it was the result of his campaign's strategic decision to position him as a moderate-to-hawkish centrist who could recapture the South for the Democratic party—and vice versa. In the wake of Super Tuesday, that decision would look brilliant indeed. But it would leave Gore with a message—or the lack of one—that would be a difficult sell in the industrial North, New York, and California, where the nomination would most likely be wrapped up.

There was no doubt about Gore's talent and intelligence. Though an indifferent speaker, he was often brilliant in debate. In his 11 years of service on Capitol Hill, he had established a reputation as a diligent legislator, honing the investigative skills he had acquired as a reporter for the *Nashville Tennessean*. Some snickered at his efforts to spur action on the deteriorating ozone layer, but the laughter stopped when the dimensions of the problem loomed larger. He made himself one of the Senate's leading experts on nuclear arms control, mastering the technicalities and pushing for a mobile, single-warhead "Midgetman" missile that would be more stabilizing and less threatening than the MX. Whatever his political fate in 1988, he fairly radiated potential.

H.H.

The Interview

KALB: Let's start with Gary Hart, get that over with and go on to Al Gore.

GORE: Suits me.

KALB: What is your reaction to the political resurrection of Gary Hart? Do you consider it a bad political joke or a serious political challenge?

GORE: Well, I think that the electorate is going to react more or less as you had started your introduction of this subject. It's going to deal with it and get it over with and then move on to the serious part of the campaign.

KALB: Get it over with—meaning what?

GORE: What I mean by that, I think there's going to be a lot of media attention for a few weeks, and in the public opinion polls there will be a flurry of activity in his behalf. But the campaign is at an interesting stage right now. The public opinion polls still reflect primarily name recognition. But the campaign for the hearts and minds of the opinion leaders in every community across America is really very far advanced at this point. And that contest will eventually be reflected, not only in the polls, but more importantly in the outcome of primaries and caucuses. And he is not going to be a significant factor in that contest.

KALB: Gary Hart says that he is the candidate with ideas, implying that the other six of you have none. Is he being fair? Is he just playing to the gallery? What's your reaction?

GORE: Oh, I think that's probably on the outer boundary of what's considered normally excessive campaign rhetoric.

KALB: A number of people, to carry it perhaps one step further, have said his getting back into the race is an act of selfishness and arrogance. Do you share that?

GORE: Well, I'm not going to try to guess his motivations or put my judgment in place of his or to guess why he is doing this. It's his personal decision, and I really don't think that after it's all said and done he's going to end up having much impact on the race. He was a candidate and supposedly the front-runner at the time I announced my candidacy last spring, and when he got out of the contest it did not have a measurable impact on my campaign, and I doubt that his reentry is going to have a significant impact after this media flurry dies down.

KALB: Okay, the next time there's a debate will you be a good southern gentleman and offer him the seventh chair at the debate?

GORE: I haven't been a sponsor or host of any of the debates thus far.

KALB: You don't mind him sitting there with you, though?

GORE: Well, the people who put on the debates invite the candidates, and I presume that he will be involved in the debates from here on out if he chooses to accept the invitation.

KALB: Let's discuss the effect for a moment of the Hart reentry on the Democratic party and its prospects for next year. James Reston, writing in the *New York Times* today, stated, "The only possible explanation of the Democrats' campaign for the presidency is that somehow it's being run by the Republicans. The reappearance of Gary Hart goes on and has been helpful in only one respect. He has created such a mess in his party that it will either have to wake up or give up for another four years." Do you see any sign of the waking up, presuming you're not going to give up?

GORE: Well, I think the waking up in the Democratic party began some time ago. I think that the movement to create Super Tuesday represented part of a waking up on the part of many leaders in the party to give more of a say to people at the grassroots level throughout the country, and I think that that contest on March 8, when almost 40 percent of the delegates will be selected, represents the eye of a needle. Some candidates are going to make it through the eye of that needle and some will not. I think that when it's all said and done, the Democratic party is going to come out stronger as a result of this long contest. And I think it's pretty normal, if you go back and look at presidential campaigns in the past, 10 months before the voting to have people react to events of the moment and project them forward all the way until election day when, in fact, this campaign has evolved a long way already. It's going to evolve more, and there's going to be a winner of this contest who's going to be strengthened by having gone through this process.

KALB: Now, is the winner, in your mind, going to be one of the six original?

GORE: Well, I have one in mind.

KALB: Is the winner going to be one of the six, could it be the seventh, or could it be one of the Democrats lurking on the sidelines right now—Cuomo, Nunn, Bradley, and even raised the other day, Tom Foley, congressman from Washington.

GORE: He's certainly well respected. I don't think that it's likely to be someone not in the race at this point. You know, every four years there is talk about a brokered convention, and people who follow the process closely just seem to yearn for that kind of event. But when was the last time we had a second ballot at a Democratic convention? It's been a long time.

KALB: Senator, don't you think the reason that there is even that talk of a brokered convention is that right now no one of the six has really "caught fire"? It is even possible for a seventh to come back in, and within three days, according to today's polls, two major national ones, have him at the very top with all of you sort of slipping back even further, suggesting either that the six are not catching fire, having sort of slipped by somehow, or maybe it's all premature. Maybe we're too young in the campaign.

GORE: I think it is premature. And as I said earlier, I think we're at this funny stage in the campaign where the polls reflect one thing and the real contest is somewhere else. We had a situation similar to this in the Democratic party in 1960 when there was a personally popular Republican president with a vice president trying to succeed him. The country seemed to be slowing down, but all the commentators said they had the stature on their side because the Democrats were not very well known. One of them appeared young, in fact and, as a matter of fact, happened to be a Harvard graduate. We went in that year, just to extend the parallel, if I remember, from the oldest president ever to serve as of that time, to the youngest president ever elected as of that time, by sheer coincidence.

KALB: You got that line. Senator, let's deal with your strategy and leave the Hart incident or event for the time being. Your strategy seems to be that you are giving up on Iowa. You jokingly said that you're going to come in a strong sixth in Iowa, and maybe now a seventh, I don't know. But—

GORE: My goal is to carry Iowa in the general election. I'm serious about that. In order to do that you have to take an approach very different from the one needed to carry—

KALB: You have certainly taken a different approach regarding Iowa, there's no question about that. But your strategy is to do reasonably well then in New Hampshire, South Dakota, and Wyoming so that you build up a little bit of momentum so that when you get into the big 14 southern and border states, the March 9th Super Tuesday—

GORE: March 8th. There are actually 20, and a third of them are outside the South. It is becoming almost a national primary.

KALB: I'm describing your strategy. But as you enter the

March 8th primary, you would like to have sufficient momentum so that you can then do what on that day, win in the South? Do you expect to do that?

GORE: Yes, I hope to do extremely well on Super Tuesday, not only in the South, but in many of the other states that are selecting delegates outside of the South on Super Tuesday. And I hope to exceed my expectation level in states following Iowa that precede the South. But really all these horse race questions are ones that a lot of others deal with more than I do. I try to focus on the challenges facing the country, articulating a vision of America's future that I think is compelling enough to bring our country together, and talk about the leadership I think that we need.

KALB: We'll get to all of those things, but I want to get through the strategy first. Do you feel that you will carry more southern states than Jesse Jackson, for example?

GORE: Well, I've already overtaken him in a number of southern states, and the trends in all of the others are that he is either stalled or declining slowly and we are gaining rapidly in every single one of them. Now, if that trend continues, then I think the result will be extremely favorable.

KALB: What do you make of the recent statement by the Democratic Leadership Council, which is led by such people as Senator Nunn and former Governor Robb, that the Democrats from the South who switched in 1980 and '84 and voted for Ronald Reagan but then came back to the Democratic party and voted for the Senate—in fact, turned the Senate over to the Democrats last year—next year, when it comes to the presidential campaign, will go back to voting for a Republican.

GORE: Oh, I disagree with that.

KALB: You disagree with that?

GORE: First of all, I don't think they said that. I think they said that could happen unless we have a nominee who speaks to the traditional values and approaches of the Democratic party. And one of the things I've been trying to do in my campaign is to talk about social justice, economic progress, and a strong American role in the world. I think that's important, and in fact, that same organization did a poll specifically of that group of voters you've cited which showed that I had moved very rapidly into first place with by far the highest positive ratings among that group and that, as the nominee, I would offer by far the best chance to carry areas like the South and states like Iowa, for example, that are nominally Democratic but go Republican unless we have a nominee who can appeal to independently thinking voters, who are frequently more moderate than those who dominate the caucuses, for example.

KALB: Senator, aside from the importance of the South in your own political calculations, a major theme in your campaign has been that the U.S. is now moving into a new post–World War II era and that the U.S., therefore, requires new post–World War II leadership. The word *leadership,* which was used earlier, is one that comes up very frequently. In a recent speech of yours that ran 20 minutes, you used the word 19 times. Now, I would like you to help me understand what you mean by leadership. How do you define it?

GORE: Well, let's look at those two eras that you referred to. One was created in 1945 and is now ending. We must create a new era because the current era is showing strains and stresses. In 1945, Omar Bradley, one of our victorious generals, said the United States has matured to world leadership. It's time we steered by the stars and not by the lights of each passing ship. At this point we are no longer the bankers of the world. I was in California recently and noted that there are only nine banks there with assets of more than $5 billion. There are 23 branch offices of Japanese banks with assets well in excess of that figure.

KALB: But define leadership for us.

GORE: Well, I think leadership, to use General Bradley's phrase, must be involved not with tinkering around the edges with a few budget cuts here and a few tax increases there. It has to involve the articulation of a vision of America's future that's clear enough and compelling enough to inspire us to work together in moving toward that vision. It must be from a president who understands where the expertise is in this country, who can inspire the best and brightest to come in and help make the administration a success, and lead this country forward. Leadership with experience in the Congress, from someone who, for example, has a personal equation with every committee and subcommittee chairman in both the House and the Senate, capable of producing a consensus among leaders on the great challenges of our time.

KALB: Senator, those are very good and nice words, and very large thoughts.

GORE: You asked for a definition of leadership.

KALB: Yeah, and you're providing it. And I would like to ask you as well whether you feel that at age 39 you're ready to provide that kind of large leadership.

GORE: Yes, I do. I'll be 41 just two months after the inauguration, with about two years difference between my age and that of John Kennedy when he assumed office, and less than that compared to Teddy Roosevelt when he became president. And I will have had more experience in the House and Senate than a majority of candidates on either side of this contest. Moreover, I think that experience is far more important than numerical age as Presidents Kennedy and Theodore Roosevelt have shown and as others have shown. I have dealt deeply with the issues that will be at the top of the agenda confronting the next president of the United States. So the answer to your question is yes.

KALB: One columnist, Michael Kinsley, says that "True leadership consists of telling people things they don't want to hear, making them mad and changing their minds." What have you been telling the American people that has gotten them mad? What have you been telling them that has changed their minds?

GORE: Coming from a state with 100,000 tobacco farmers, it was not easy to tell them that 350,000 people die unnecessarily because of smoking each year, and then leading the fight for the toughest possible health warnings and measures where smoking is concerned. It was not particularly popular with members of my own political party to say that as we entered strategic arms negotiations with the Soviet Union, it would be best to have some minimal bipartisanship in support of a negotiating position that was calculated to elicit a favorable response from the Soviets. And some of the weapons systems that I supported as part of that strategy became extremely unpopular. I have the lashes of several Mary McGrory columns to prove it. But, in fact, many of those people who were very cynical about some of the unpopular things that I said on strategic arms control are now pretty surprised that we have concluded an INF treaty and may be on the verge of a significant breakthrough on strategic arms control. In fact, I think the next president of the United States is going to have to accomplish that latter far more important objective. And I think it's critical to have a president with experience in arms control, the U.S.-Soviet relationship, and foreign policy in general in order to take advantage of what could be an historic opportunity for accomplishing the very transition that is so essential if we're going to move from that post–1945 era to a new era wherein we can concentrate on the human agenda, rather than continue to see the world as a whole spend one trillion dollars a year on new ways to kill people.

KALB: Senator, you have said recently—and this is still within the framework of trying to get more of your ideas about leadership—and I quote, "I know exactly what needs to be done and I am impatient to do it." Now the problems before the next president, it seems to me anyway, are so enormous, speaking of deficit, budget deficits, and trade imbalances and the arms control issues that you've talked about, that don't you approach even the possibility of being president of the United States with some humility?

GORE: Oh, of course. And I think anyone who contemplates the awesome challenges confronting the next president would have to do so. That quotation was in the context of a speech about nuclear arms control. I do, in fact, believe there is a formula that has reached the stage of near consensus in the dialogue between thinkers both in the United States and in the Soviet Union. I advanced a set of ideas several years ago. In fact, I talked with you on another program some years ago at the very beginning of my participation in this effort. It's interesting to note that the Soviet Union has just published a comprehensive study on what the ideal strategic balance ought to be. It's just been translated into English, and they conclude that the ideal balance would be 500 to 600 single warhead mobile missiles on both sides. A surprising congruence with the so-called Scowcroft Commission. A group of strategic thinkers that advocated views—

KALB: Back in '83?

GORE: Yes. They picked up and advocated views that I had articulated to you and others before the Scowcroft Commission was ever appointed.

KALB: Now, you have described yourself as a raging moderate. It's a wonderful term. I assume you mean that you would be tough on defense, and yet at the same time prudent and cautious on domestic issues. You've also been very—

GORE: And passionate about it.

KALB: And passionate. You've also been very tough in criticizing the people who are running for the Democratic nomination. You have said that you are in the race with people who are advocates of retreat, complacency, and doubt. Now that's pretty tough stuff. And the last person I remember who would utter something like that was probably Jean Kirkpatrick referring to the 1984 Democrats from San Francisco. Who are you talking about among your colleagues who's advocating retreat, complacency, and doubt? Are you talking about Dukakis?

GORE: What I said specifically was that the politics of retreat, complacency, and doubt may appeal to some, but they don't appeal to me.

KALB: Who are you talking about?

GORE: In fact, I have said before that I think all of the other candidates in the race have at times succumbed to the temptation to respond to a constituency within the Democratic party which has existed since the end of the Vietnam War, and which takes views, for example, that we should retreat from our mission in the Persian Gulf, which although it began because of a mistake, nevertheless is in our best interests as a nation in my view.

KALB: Are they really advocating retreat? They're talking about going to the U.N. They're not talking about pulling out, they're all talking—

GORE: I beg your pardon. Some have advocated removing the flags from the tankers.

KALB: True.

GORE: The U.N. has to have the unanimous vote of the Security Council in order to act, doesn't it? And if China or the Soviet Union objects, then we would substitute for our current successful policy, a policy of stalemate as we pull back from our mission in the Gulf to keep the sea lanes open to a body of water containing 70 percent of the free world's oil reserves, tilting the balance in the Iran-Iraq War toward Iran, unleashing the prospect of Shiite fundamentalism spreading into Kuwait and Saudi Arabia throughout the gulf, threatening the security of Israel and the United States' best interests in the Middle-East, and causing a major geopolitical upheaval. Now, I'm happy to say that because of the speeches I've made and because of the debates on foreign policy, I've noticed that some of the other candidates are recalibrating some of their statements on foreign policy and defense policy. Some have even done so with respect to the Persian Gulf. I'm still waiting for them to do that on policies like a total ban on the flight testing of ballistic missiles, which I think would be a very serious mistake.

KALB: Where are you tough and where are they advocates of retreat on Nicaragua and the Contras? You are not in support of giving any military aid to the Contras, are you?

GORE: No, I'm not. As a Vietnam veteran, I think one of the lessons of that war is that the outcome of any guerrilla war is going to depend in large part on the attitudes of the people who live where that war takes place. And regardless of their attitudes towards the Sandinistas, the Nicaraguan people are not affording much support to the Contras, perhaps because they associate them with the old Somoza regime, rightly or wrongly. And so I think the Arias plan is a far preferable approach; I think we should back it wholeheartedly. Now, I have supported an initiative by the Democratic leadership in the Congress over the opposition of the Reagan administration to give nonmilitary maintenance aid to begin the process of resettlement of the Contras if, in fact, the Arias plan is successful. They're going to be resettled either in Nicaragua or in Florida, and I think that it's better to take the approach of the Arias plan, and I do support it.

KALB: Senator, I think what I'm trying to understand is, are you trying to sound tough? For the most part, given a couple of exceptions—and you have ticked off some sophisticated nuances on the Persian Gulf—basically you share the view of most of the other Democratic candidates.

GORE: Well, I don't think that our allies in that region or around the world would see it as a sophisticated nuance if we pulled out of the Persian Gulf.

KALB: But I don't think any of the Democrats are trying to pull out.

GORE: Well, I think if you advocate taking the flags off the tankers.

KALB: Senator, we didn't have flags on the tankers up until six months ago, and yet the United States and the Carter administration, Republican administrations before, always said that the United States will do what has to be done to keep the lanes open.

GORE: And that is the tradition that I'm advocating. I think the Democratic party used to have a consensus on the fact that our nation must play a strong role in the world. I think that during and after the Vietnam War a certain neo-isolationist impulse understandably became a part of our national dialogue but has not yet been put in proper perspective in the Democratic party. And what I'm saying is, we've got to put that in perspective, we've got to learn the correct lessons from Vietnam, but avoid learning the wrong lessons from Vietnam. One of the wrong lessons was best summed up in an earlier era by Mark Twain, when he said, "A cat burned on a stove won't sit on a hot stove again, but won't sit on a cold one either."

KALB: Moving right along, when you were here as a senior you did your thesis on "The Impact of Television on the Conduct of the Presidency, 1947 and 1969."

GORE: Purely a coincidence.

KALB: Purely a coincidence. Do you think right now that television is a crucial element in the campaign?

GORE: Of course.

KALB: Absolutely. And is it—

GORE: In fact, it's one of the reasons I accepted your invitation to come here.

KALB: I thought it was my personality. All right, do you feel that it is really a good thing for an Al Gore to be young and to look like Superman and—

GORE: Come on.

KALB: That's a really good thing for a candidate these days. I mean, supposing you wore glasses and had a lot of wrinkles around your eyes—

GORE: Lived in a telephone booth—

KALB: Lived in a— That's right. You couldn't then run?

GORE: No, I think that's absolutely wrong. I think that television has a big impact on politics—no question about it. I think it has a big impact on the nature of the presidency as well. And I think that anyone who leads this country has to think long and hard about the ability to communicate with the American people over television, either to get elected or to govern well. But I don't think that necessarily translates so easily into image and process. I think television does give the people an unobstructed ability to explore for substance and to have a direct relationship with the candidates who are running and with the president who's attempting to govern. And, so I think that substance is still, by far and away, the most important element.

KALB: A question about youth. Again, according to some of the reporters who have been covering you, and Hendrik Hertzberg, who's a resident fellow here at the Press-Politics Center and wrote a piece recently for *The New Republic*—I'm sure you've read it: "Gore has been totally unable to capitalize on his youth. The question is why, the answer is Tipper and her crusade against dirty rock 'n roll." Now, Tipper is your wife's nickname, and we're delighted to have her here with us. Is that accurate?

GORE: I think Hendrik's even here, too, somewhere.

KALB: Is the explanation correct, first of all, that among young people in the United States, were you expecting more of them to come onto a Gore bandwagon than you have found?

GORE: Well, first of all, let me say that I think that paragraph you quoted is preposterous.

KALB: Okay.

GORE: I think there's no substance to that whatsoever. Now,

as for the enthusiasm of young people in the presidential campaign, I remember when I was a student at this institution in the great movement for Gene McCarthy and Bobby Kennedy. I don't think any of that really started until the election year. And the idea that students, a full year before the election takes place, are going to march in divisions out to the early primary states before the voters are paying any attention to what's going on is just plain wrong. In fact—

KALB: I remember in 1968 with McCarthy, the kiddie campaign was underway by February, January, March of that year.

GORE: That's what I'm saying. We're still in December and the analysis you talked about was well in advance of that. I think on January 1 you're going to see a different mood in the campaign. Where my campaign is concerned, there are already students for Gore organizations on campuses all across this country. I'm going to be spending a lot of time asking young people to be involved in my campaign. In fact, I see some in your audience here today, and I hope to gain some recruits. But we are getting a lot of enthusiasm and excitement.

KALB: On this rock 'n roll issue and Mrs. Gore's effort to try to get rid of, soften up, whatever the right term is, some of the dirty lyrics, do you feel that her emphasis has in any way hurt your campaign?

GORE: Oh, no, I do not. First of all, let me respond to one of the premises in your question.

KALB: Go ahead.

GORE: Her effort is not to get companies to soften up their material. Her effort is to ask the entertainment industry to use its own standards to evaluate its own products in recognition of a trend that has been speeding up whereby younger and younger children are exposed to increasingly explicit material. Now, without advocating any change in that material, she is asking them to assist parents in their evaluation of what they think might be appropriate for their young children. You know, we have a voluntary system of that kind in the movie industry—and parents have found it very helpful. We have four young children, and I have found it very helpful as a parent. Eighty percent of the industry has agreed to the voluntary system she has asked for. It involves no government role whatsoever. And some of the leading civil libertarians in this country have publicly praised her approach and have said it does not raise any questions of censorship. If I could say one other thing on this. Is it only legitimate for conservatives or Republicans to raise a question about what Tipper calls the stripmining of our culture? The fact that the average child sees 18,000 murders on television by the time he or she graduates from high school? About the effect on very young children of messages that glorify brutality against women and violence throughout the society? Let me just finish briefly because I have come to feel strongly about this. I am very proud of what she has done. I think we as a society ought to ask questions about how we raise children in this culture and pay more attention to elevating the awareness of all of us about the messages that young children get.

KALB: The answer to your question is no, it doesn't have to be just Republicans. I would like to say, by the way, that just looking at Mrs. Gore, I'm sure that she would be an asset to any candidate. Anyway, we have reached that point, we have reached that point where—

GORE: I'm just glad she's not running.

KALB: Where I stop asking the questions and the audience begins. Our first questioner is Graham Allison. I know the senator knows him because he was the senator's section leader back in the 60s.

GORE: Before he became famous.

ALLISON: I will pick up an arms control question since Marvin didn't ask so much about that—specifically about the similarities and differences between the INF Treaty signed by President Reagan at the summit, and the SALT II Treaty which President Carter signed, but which was never ratified by the Senate. Now, four of the six Republican contenders for the presidential nomination oppose Senate ratification of the INF Treaty as they opposed Senate ratification of the SALT II Treaty, and some of the arguments sound familiar. In contrast President Reagan, who said the SALT II Treaty was fatally flawed, says the INF Treaty advances America's security interests. So who's consistent on this? President Reagan or the four Republicans who say don't ratify INF?

GORE: The four Republicans are consistently wrong on both issues. It's outrageous that a majority of the Republican candidates for the nomination would not support a president of their own party during a summit meeting when our nation was exploring the possibility of a very significant breakthrough on the far more important question of strategic arms control. The SALT II Treaty should have been ratified. President Reagan, in spite of his vitriolic rhetoric during the campaign when he was first elected, came to observe most of the provisions of the SALT II Treaty after assuming office. This new treaty, the INF Treaty, is a good one. Just a couple of brief points. The Russians will have to destroy more than four weapons for every one that we have to destroy. We get on-site

verification for the first time, which is a very important psychological and political breakthrough and has some real advantages for
verification itself. Our allies, the French and British, are exempted
from the treaty and will be able to have a virtual monopoly on
intermediate-range weapons. And it does not lead, after all, to the
denuclearization of Europe. We'll retain 4,600 nuclear warheads in
Europe. It's a good treaty. It ought to be supported. Now, it does
only cover 3 percent of the warheads and none targeted on the
United States, and because of the administration's repudiation of
SALT II, ironically, the Soviets, if they wished, could proliferate
strategic weapons and target them on exactly the same targets in
Europe. So it's very important for us to go to the next step,
strategic arms control, and remove this obsession with SDI or Star
Wars that has thus far on our side, at least, frustrated the ability to
gain that breakthrough. If we have a president of the United States
in January 1989 who understands arms control, has experience on
the subject, is willing to negotiate from a position of strength, and
is willing to pursue what could be a historic chance for a breakthrough, we could really see an important transition in this world.

QUESTION: Senator, on average, a woman earns 69 cents for
every man's dollar in this country. What role do you see for the
federal government in correcting this inequity?

GORE: Well, I support the Equal Rights Amendment. I'm a
cosponsor of the Equal Rights Amendment. Beyond that I'm one
of a much smaller group in Congress who has supported the
leading measure on pay equity that is now pending in the Congress. It is limited in scope because it only involves federal
employment and really only involves a ground-breaking study in
that regard. I have to say that when I had hearings on this subject
I wondered about the difficulties involved, but the more I learned
about it, the more I found that it really is outrageous to have the
kinds of discrepancies that are so prevalent in our society. Our
challenge, and often the challenge of leadership, is to change the
way people think about ourselves, about our country, and about
our future. And we must accelerate the maturing of our society
and civilization in so many areas. This is one. Tipper and I have
three daughters in addition to our son. I have long been committed
to this task. My mother was one of the first two women to graduate
from Vanderbilt Law School back in the '30s. And I've been raised
with an appreciation of breaking new ground and changing the way
our society appreciates the role of women.

QUESTION: Senator Gore, under the Reagan administration
the U.S. policy toward Central America has taken an increasingly

bloody turn. Yet Congress continues to support funding for the
Contras, not in the form of resettlement aid as you support, but
direct aid to the Contras, and continues to send military aid
unconditionally to the governments of Central America that are
known for human rights abuses. As president, what are three
specific steps that you would take to ensure the development of a
mutually beneficial relationship between the Central Americans
and the United States?

GORE: Number one, I would put our nation four square
behind the Arias plan. I had a long private discussion with President Arias when he was on his way to Oslo to receive the Nobel
prize. He is a visionary leader in our hemisphere, a young man,
incidentally, who has advocated a possibly successful plan, and I
would put our nation behind it so that it would be successful.
That's number one. Number two, I would have direct discussions
with Gorbachev on a subject that he evidently raised in a Rose
Garden stroll with President Reagan, to which President Reagan
apparently did not respond to in a forthcoming way. And that is
about the level of Soviet aid to the Sandinistas. And incidentally,
the information about this alleged plan to vastly expand the
Sandinista army is really outrageous. And President Arias has
rightly criticized the Sandinistas bitterly for that announcement. It
undermines his plan. Third, I would embark on a new program of
economic development in Latin America.

We have to understand that the seeds of communism include
not only armed revolution, but poverty and injustice and hunger,
and political injustice and bitterness. We must have economic
prosperity that we stimulate in this hemisphere and partnership
with our allies.

QUESTION: This year, only 6,000 individuals will be allowed
to emigrate from the Soviet Union compared to 49,000 during the
Brezhnev period, and during this recent visit Gorbachev was
rather vitriolic in his statements regarding emigration. As president how would you persuade Gorbachev to comply with the
human rights aspects of the Helsinki Agreement?

GORE: I thought that Gorbachev's statements during the Tom
Brokaw interview were really appalling on the question of Jewish
emigration. His approach is shockingly similar to that of his
predecessors. I was the only candidate for the Democratic nomination to attend that large march in Washington two Sundays ago
on this subject. We took our whole family there; I'm very strongly
committed to it. On two trips to Moscow, Tipper and I have met
with the refusenik community at length. Now, there are two kinds

of so-called linkage. We should make it clear to the Soviet Union that any time we talk about arms control or bilateral issues, the subject of emigration is going to be on the agenda, and we should also make it clear that progress in other aspects of our relationship will be affected by progress on the issue of human rights and Jewish emigration. That's the proper kind of linkage as opposed to stopping everything until we're totally satisfied. But we must have a president who's deeply committed to it and who is willing to go toe to toe with the leader of the Soviet Union on this subject.

QUESTION: Many people in Massachusetts and the rest of the country are concerned with the plight of Salvadorans and Guatemalan refugees in this country. As you know, the new immigration law gives amnesty to those people who arrived here prior to 1982. However, the civil wars in these countries got increasingly worse after 1982. Therefore, most of these people don't apply for amnesty. In Congress right now there's a bill called the Moakley-DeConcini bill S332 which would grant extended voluntary departure status or temporary safe haven for Salvadorans and this is desperately needed. I want to know if the senator, who is a supporter of Moakley-DeConcini, would be a cosponsor, and I'd like to know what his policy would be in terms of other countries in the world that violate human rights of their peoples.

GORE: I strongly support it. I have done so on every occasion that it has come up and I will continue to. I thought I was a cosponsor. Whether I will be, yes. I support it very strongly on humanitarian grounds. I think it's an important measure.

QUESTION: Senator, I'd like to ask your opinion of the recent U.S.-Canadian free trade agreement. First of all, do you support the deal? And second, do you feel it sets any precedence for U.S. trade policy regarding Japan, Mexico, and other nations?

GORE: I do. Number one, I support it very strongly. There are political problems with it, both in our nation and in Canada.

There's going to be a difficult ratification battle in Canada, evidently, and I hope they will have the vision and foresight to ratify it as I hope we will. I think it is an important measure. I come from a little town of 2,000 people called Carthage, Tennessee, and that was the hometown of Cordell Hall, the father of reciprocal free trade. I think it's awfully important to avoid protectionism, have leadership capable of removing unfair barriers, but move toward fair and free trade. Now, in the past, bilateralism—that is, one-on-one negotiations between our country and one other country—has been viewed as another form of protectionism because of the prevailing wisdom that multilateral negotiations represent the best way to proceed. But the current round of trade negotiations begun in Punta del Esta are expected to take at least seven to eight years before there's any resolution. Other nations have refused to put items like services on the agenda, and I think the time has come when we have to make a choice. Are we going to allow a building up of protectionist sentiments around the world or are we going to take a new approach? I think the kind of bilateral approach toward opening up trade, which we saw with the negotiations with Canada, could and should be used in our negotiations with other nations. We have the largest market and the biggest purchasing power of any nation in the world. The time has come for us to use that power in negotiations toward free trade. So I favor using it as a precedent, yes.

KALB: The next question by Mike Zubrensky, associated with the Institute of Politics here at the Kennedy School.

ZUBRENSKY: I'd like to pursue the raging moderate theme that Mr. Kalb brought up before. As a congressman, you've received a very liberal rating by the ADA year in and year out. Yet as a presidential candidate, you've railed against your Democratic opponents for being weak on defense and you've lambasted the caucus process in Iowa as being too liberal. The question is, When the voters go to the polls next year, which version of Al Gore will they be endorsing?

GORE: Ah, hardball, there. First of all, I've never used the phrase "weak on defense." And I've never attacked the caucuses as too liberal. I think they are too vulnerable to narrow interest pressures because 97 percent of the people in that state do not participate in the caucuses. Only 3 percent do. I have not changed a single position during this campaign. My record is that of a moderate. I have taken that approach. Really, I chose that label "raging moderate" in the first place—

KALB: It's a great line.

GORE: When people come to you, they always want to know, "are you liberal, conservative?" They want to pigeonhole you right away, and in fact, these labels have far less significance than they once did, and I finally, in frustration said, "If you've got to have a label, I'll choose the label raging moderate." But in fact, that's the approach I've taken during my what will be 12 years in the House and Senate. I have not moved at all. I have seen some movement on the part of other campaigns, and I've resisted those pressures.

QUESTION: Senator, my question is about dissent. Earlier in your campaign you criticized the other Democratic candidates for a sense of false unity and cast out your dissenting view. And you were also on campus here in the late '60s when the students dissented in sometimes vociferous and violent ways. My question is, Did you participate in those protests? If so, how? And if not, why not? And if you're elected president, how would you like those who dissent from your views to express themselves?

GORE: First of all, earlier in the campaign some voices were raised in behalf of total unity even before the nomination was settled, and the view was expressed that disagreements in debates might be damaging to the party. I think that's what debates are for and I said so, and I welcome more of those debates. Now, back to during the time of the Vietnam War when I was a student—yes, I did participate in protesting the war. There were quite a few rallies and mass meetings where speeches were made, and I attended many of those and felt myself in solidarity with those who felt the war was a serious mistake. I think it was a serious mistake, and I was opposed to it.

KALB: And yet, Senator, you volunteered.

GORE: I did. For two reasons. First of all, if my draft board had been in a large city like Boston or Washington or New York or Los Angeles, it might have seemed like an abstract proposition. But I come from a town of 2,000 people, and it was no secret who was on the draft board, and there was a quota each month, and that the oldest went first. And if I found some way not to go, and there were plenty of ways not to go, then I knew that one of my friends would have to go in my place, and I felt that I had a duty to serve. The second related reason, which was not a cause but was a factor, was that my father was an articulate, eloquent opponent of the Vietnam War policy in the Senate Foreign Relations Committee. And he was running for reelection and to the extent that my personal decision had any impact on it, even marginal, ironically the best way I could oppose the war was by going to it and being a part of it, which I did. The last part of his question was how would I want those who dissent to my policies as president to express themselves? Quietly, quietly.

QUESTION: Senator Gore, the Congress has labored and seems to have brought forth a budget compromise which doesn't satisfy very many people. There's probably a paucity of leadership on both the congressional and presidential side. I'd like to hear your views on how you view this serious problem, and as president, what would you do to lead, perhaps the American people, to a lowering of general expectations and a realization that sacrifice has to be shared by many groups?

GORE: We've got to have a realization that sacrifice will be necessary, and we must have a president who's willing to fight for the average working men and women as those sacrifices are allocated in this country. Secondly, we've got to have a realization that the challenge is not to suddenly balance the budget in one, two, or three years. But to reestablish confidence in our ability to exercise some control over fiscal policy and our economic destiny. Third, we must recognize that it is essentially a political challenge. And we must have presidential leadership from a president personally involved, who brings the Congress together and begins a series of consensus-building meetings that will not end until we have an approach that can gain the support of a majority in the House and Senate. And that's going to mean cutting spending, and not just on the military side, but wasteful spending intentionally overlooked by this administration even as they've cut too deeply in other areas. It involves a recognition that we will have to continue making investments in areas like education to build for a competitive America in the future, and we've got to have additional revenue. Now, if enhanced tax collection, which congressional Democrats have been arguing for for years and loophole closures don't suffice, then new taxes will have to be a part of the agenda. But I don't think you start building that consensus with another list of nonnegotiable demands, and I don't think you lead off by proposing new taxes, no matter what.

KALB: Senator, our final questioner is the Reverend Peter Gomes, Chaplain of the Memorial Church here at Harvard.

GOMES: Mr. Gore, the assumption behind conversations of this sort generally is what you will do if elected and what you will do to vindicate the trust of the people who presumably are smart enough to elect you. But you and I have taken a study of at least the last nine elections in the country, and the country has seen fit in the last nine, in six of them to return the Republican party to the White House, and in only three of them to return your party, so there is a chance that neither you nor your party will achieve the ambition of the White House in the next election. So my question is, On that remote possibility, what plans do you have, what role would you see for yourself as a participant in either the reconstruction of or the reconciliation of the Democratic party in the light of yet another repudiation at the hands of the people for the White House? What role would you see for yourself?

GORE: What a depressing hypothetical you propose there.

GOMES: I'm a Presbyterian.

GORE: You know what Mark Twain said about Presbyterians. He went out to Silver City, Nevada, and he wrote back that there was drinking in the streets, gambling, open prostitution. He said "It was no place for a Presbyterian, and I did not long remain one." The possibility you raise is, of course, one we must contemplate, but the future is not something we predict in a crystal ball. It's something we make with our dreams, with our minds, with our hands, and with each other. And if the Democratic party is going to create a victory in the election of November 1988, we must learn from that past you have described, and understand the need for a nominee who, number one and most importantly, can offer visionary leadership for this country capable of steering by the stars and not by the lights of each passing ship, and number two, a nominee who can carry areas like the South and appeal to independent voters in every region of this country, and rebuild the Democratic coalition that gave the Democratic party a string of victories throughout most of this century. That means a commitment to social justice, economic progress, and a strong American role in the world. I believe that I can offer that kind of leadership and the best chance for the Democratic party to win the election. And so I'd like to close in the remaining seconds by asking for the support of those who are here. I believe that I can make a difference. I want to win this contest with your help, and I ask for your participation and involvement.

Candidates '88

A CONVERSATION WITH
JACK KEMP

Photo by Martha Stewart

185

About the Candidate

Of all the claimants to the mantle of Ronald Reagan as leader of the conservative wing of the Republican party, no one could make a better case for himself than Jack Kemp. The 52-year-old congressman from upstate New York was the co-author of the Kemp-Roth tax plan, which was the basis for the 1981 tax cut that was Reagan's proudest domestic achievement. He was the favored candidate of *National Review,* Reagan's favorite magazine. He had more friends and contacts in the conservative movement than anyone else. And he was no newcomer: He had supported Reagan not only in 1980 and 1984 but also in 1968 and 1976. And during off-season breaks from his job as all-pro quarterback for the Buffalo Bills, Kemp had even worked for then-Governor Reagan as a staff aide in Sacramento.

Yet the conservatives never quite managed to close ranks behind Kemp. Perhaps it was because he articulated their hopes but not their fears. Kemp was fervently optimistic, relentlessly upbeat. As a spokesman for the liberating power of the free market, he was unsurpassed. But some red-meat right-wingers found his brand of conservatism antiseptic and academic. When he talked earnestly about the need to return to the gold standard, their eyes glazed over. And when it came time to give voice to the resentments many of them felt—against liberals, against welfare cheats, against gays, against feminists, against the press—Kemp fell silent. He was too nice, and too sunny, a guy.

In addition, Kemp had an affinity for groups that do not vote in large numbers in Republican primaries. The blue-collar congressional district in which he had won nine elections was heavily Democratic, with generous dollops of East European ethnic groups—a suburbanized version of Archie Bunker's neighborhood. Although Kemp's record of opposition to spending on programs for the poor is as consistent as Jesse Helms's, he is a vocal supporter of the social security program—and he is a vocal advocate of the proposition that the Republican party should reach out to black Americans and to the economically disadvantaged.

Kemp's style, if not his politics, was Kennedyesque. (He was the original inspiration for the character of Congressman Bob Forehead, fictional leader of the "Kennedy look-alike caucus" in Mark Alan Stamety's comic strip, "Washingtoon.") The rigors of campaigning seemed to agree with him: He remained as fit and handsome as he had been back in his football days. At the time of his "Candidates '88" interview he was in the fight of his life, contending with Pat Robertson for the support of social conservatives and Pete du Pont (who had been endorsed by New Hampshire's biggest newspaper, the *Manchester Union Leader*) for the backing of economic libertarians. Ultimately Jack Kemp would be forced out of the race, but not before vowing that he would be heard from again.

H.H.

The Interview

KALB: The Reagan revolution—is it alive?

KEMP: Very much so. I think right from the start it was a political revolution. It was a way of looking at our country and the world in terms of its possibilities, not in terms of its limits. To talk about the Reagan revolution is to recall the days that we were told we were entering an era of limits, an era in which we were told we should reduce our sights, that our children might grow up with perpetual energy and food and other types of shortages. The Reagan revolution, to a large extent, suggested we could grow without inflation, something our economist friends said couldn't happen. We were told that there were shortages of everything, and I think—deregulating oil, reducing tax rates—we have grown out of some of these problems. We've got more to do.

KALB: But it's a revolution and not just an attitude of optimism, isn't it?

KEMP: I think it is a revolution in terms of politics as well as intellectually in terms of stimulating the economy here and around the world.

KALB: If it is a revolution based upon ideas, I don't think anybody is going to argue that of all the Republican candidates, you best personify those ideas. Why is it, therefore, that you run a distant third in all of the national polls among the Republicans?

KEMP: There's a couple of explanations for that. Number one, I've never run for president before. This is my first time. So I'm running against a couple of people who have been around this track two or three times.

KALB: And that's very important?

KEMP: Well, it is to a certain extent, sure. I'm running against a sitting vice president. We live in a marvelous democracy, where a member of the back benches of the House of Representatives can actually come out and actually compete with a sitting vice president for his own party's nomination. We think that by the time this race really gets started sometime in January that folks are going to take a lot closer look, not only at the front-runners, but at some of us who might not be considered front-runners. And I think ultimately the Republican party is going to want someone, Marvin, who can broaden the base, reach out to people of different colors and ethnic backgrounds, different socioeconomic backgrounds—I think by that time I'm going to be doing very well.

KALB: You touched on the idea that you were a congressman, and you put that as one of the wonders of democracy, and it certainly is. But the last time a congressman was able to go from the House of Representatives to the White House was more than a hundred years ago, when Garfield did it. Is it something that has to do with simply being a congressman?

KEMP: I don't think so. I don't think many of them have tried.

KALB: You remember when Morris Udall ran in 1976, he said he'd arrive in a town and somebody would walk over and say, "Hi, Senator," as though that was a better thing to be than a congressman.

KEMP: There is that bias to a certain extent in a lot of people's minds, But, clearly, if you start talking about rules, I think all rules for running for president are off given the small Democratic primary process in America. No longer will we pick our presidents in either party in back rooms, making deals between states. It's a very small "D" democratic and some would say radical process by which we pick our American presidents. Jimmy Carter came out of nowhere. Ronald Reagan was not considered to be the choice of the establishment, and I am not the choice of the establishment. But I'm a populist conservative and progressive conservative, and I think I have a good chance of getting the nomination.

KALB: Given all of those definitions, do you think one reason that you may be running third at this point is that the conservatives themselves cannot coalesce around a central figure? That they themselves are so fractured and divided, that they can't focus, and therefore you're all split?

KEMP: To a certain extent that might be, in your phrase, a weakness, but it might also be a strength. Everybody in our party talks a lot about the president, this president. The conservative movement was, in the past, split. It didn't unite around Ronald Reagan until he captured the New Hampshire primary. There were other conservatives in the race. And I think it's a sign of strength that the Republican party is dominated by a conservative philosophy on economics, foreign policy, and those values that we cherish in a Judeo-Christian society.

KALB: Congressman, a number of people who know you really quite well have said the following about you, and I just want to throw out a couple of quotes. The economist Arthur Laffer, with whom you have dealt: "I know Jack better than anyone, and he's not capable of being judicial, presidential." Conservative author Kevin Phillips: "Jack represents issues that peaked two to six years ago. His gospel is supply-side economics. His theme music is simply out of date." Is Jack Kemp out of date?

KEMP: If it's out of date to talk about growth and getting the world economy more prosperous and liberated from the high tax, high interest rates, high tariff policies of the world, I can't imagine why that would be out of date. If providing leadership on tax reform is out of date, it's hard for me to think the American people are going to think it's out of date. If talking about a strong policy of achieving peace in our day and for our children and our grandchildren through strength is out of date, then I think those values are out of date. I guess I'm suggesting that Arthur Laffer and Kevin Phillips, friends of mine who are supporting George Bush, may have a reason for saying those things. I'm sure you can find some folks who are supportive of Jack Kemp.

KALB: The next question I have right here. There are also many, many people who think you're terrific, absolutely terrific, a first-class guy, and ought to be president of the United States, and that you're one of the few guys who really deals with ideas and cares about ideas. And the *Wall Street Journal* said, "Kemp probably spends more time with genuine intellectuals than any other presidential candidate." Who are these genuine intellectuals you spend all this time with?

KEMP: Marvin Kalb.

KALB: And who else?

KEMP: You really want me to start naming names?

KALB: Well, a couple of people, sure.

KEMP: Irving Kristol of NYU. Professor Robert Mandell of Columbia, Jean Kirkpatrick. Those are the type of men and women that I'm very comfortable with, and think a lot of, and would have a strong role to play in a Kemp administration if I am fortunate enough to get the nomination of the Republican party.

KALB: Let's go back then and talk about the President, because I would like that to be somewhat of the theme through this. The President, in recent days and weeks, has signed a medium- and short-range missile agreement in Europe. That you disapprove of. He has recently signed a compromise budget package involving an increase in taxes and a decrease in defense spending. That you disapprove of, and I think you called a hoax. Has the President gone soft?

KEMP: I don't think the President has gone soft, and I think some of the language by the Right and criticism of the President have been demonstrably intemperate and I have not engaged in that type of language. I have not opposed outright the idea of reducing nuclear arms.

KALB: But you opposed this treaty.

KEMP: Let me make the point. My statements of criticism have been of the process by which once we got the Soviet Union to the table, where they need us, Marvin, a lot more than we need them. They need access to our markets, access to our technology, access to credit, access to exports, or to our markets at least. It seems to me we should have gotten more from the summit than we did. I think the Soviets ought to comply with their previous treaties. I think they ought to start keeping the Helsinki Human Rights Agreement with regard to the treatment of dissidents and Jews and Christians behind the Iron Curtain. I think they ought to get out of Afghanistan and Nicaragua. I would like to see a change in the behavior of the Soviet Union. I'm not against any arms control agreement that reduces offensive nuclear weapons. We have to. And we have to move to strategic defense systems, as far as I'm concerned. So I've been critical of the process, but I haven't disassociated myself from the idea of talking with, negotiating with, or even reducing arms with the Soviet Union.

KALB: I want to be very clear on the issue of the INF agreement.

KEMP: I think in linkage.

KALB: But do you support the treaty?

KEMP: I support the treaty if there's linkage to the behavior of the Soviet Union with regard to previous treaties, and with regard to their treatment of the Helsinki final act.

KALB: You opposed the treaty on any number of occasions.

KEMP: I have said in every debate and in every public forum, left or right, that I do not favor signing new agreements with the Soviet Union until they are required to comply with the previous agreements. I think it denigrates the treaty.

KALB: So you would not have signed this particular agreement as president?

KEMP: I would not sign the treaty until I had the assurance that they were going to comply with the previous treaty.

KALB: But they always say they comply with these treaties.

KEMP: Let me ask you a question. What good is it to verify a treaty if you find out they're cheating and you don't require there be a modification of the behavior? I favor a modification of the behavior of the Soviet Union by using whatever leverage we have at the table to require that they live up to their commitments. And I think most Americans would agree with that.

KALB: Perhaps. But I still want to hear clearly. You're sitting in the office, you're Ronald Reagan. Gorbachev is there. The agreement was on the table. Would you have signed it?

KEMP: Not without linking it to the behavior of the Soviet Union with regard to Helsinki, Afghanistan, Nicaragua, and the belief that I have and I think that is shared by most people, that we ought to move the world away from relying on offensive nuclear weapons to a reliance on defense, on strategic defense particularly, and technical defense for Europe and Israel.

KALB: So you would have signed that treaty if you had had a deal with Gorbachev that linked Soviet behavior to these other points we just made?

KEMP: Yes.

KALB: But absent that kind of agreement from Gorbachev, you would not have signed the agreement, correct?

KEMP: I would say hypothetically I would not have signed the agreement unless there had been an agreement that extended beyond just INF theater nuclear weapons.

KALB: But that's what they were signing.

KEMP: Well, I'm answering the question. I'm going on to say that I would have used that summit—where the Soviets, I think, desperately need access to Western markets, Western credit, Western technology, and where they need us more than we need them—to get more in return than just the removal of the Pershing missile from the European continent. The problem, if I can take it a step further, because it is important: We took out the Euromissile, the Pershing and the ground launch cruise missile from Europe, or we're going to. We've lost a capability. The Soviets have removed, or will remove, the SS-20 intermediate-range nuclear weapon. But they haven't lost any capability, because they're going to replace the medium-range SS-20 with what they have now, an SS-25. So they still have the capability of striking deep into the heartland of the continent of Europe, whereas our total nuclear deterrent to war in the continent, or on the continent with NATO, has been removed. We didn't get enough for it. That's my concern. So I hope that in the Senate there's a Scoop Jackson— who unfortunately died. I think he would have been someone who would have gone onto the floor of the Senate and added reservations to this treaty, not unlike what he did in 1971 or '72 under SALT I.

KALB: So if you were in the Senate, you would add reservations that would spell out the linkage that you're talking about.

KEMP: I'm very much a part of that process, and expect to be a part of that process.

KALB: I am hearing some of your views about the President, although they're muted, and I would like to hear your views on a number of other national leaders. I'll tick off the name, you give me a short thumbnail sketch of each one of these people. We're in a building named after John Kennedy.

KEMP: A great president. A great leader, because he gave hope. I disagreed with some of his policies, but certainly on the domestic economy and on international trade and on defending America's respect for international individual liberty and human rights, a truly great president and inspiring president.

KALB: George Bush.

KEMP: A great vice president. Terrific vice president. I think he'd make a great vice president someday.

KALB: Bob Dole.

KEMP: A great, great Senate majority leader. Good majority leader.

KALB: Richard Nixon.

KEMP: A flawed president who made some amazing break-throughs, but flawed. Bill Buckley once said, "The physician could not heal himself."

KALB: Oliver North.

KEMP: Ollie North is a patriot, definitely. He made mistakes and is paying for them dearly. He should not be sent to prison. The purpose of the Iran-Contra hearing was to get out the truth about the mistakes that were made, not to prosecute. That's the only point I've tried to make. Don't send this man behind bars.

KALB: The hearings were not to prosecute.

KEMP: The hearings were prosecutory, definitely.

KALB: Gary Hart.

KEMP: No comment. The people will judge.

KALB: Mike Dukakis.

KEMP: I really don't want to start judging the Democratic candidates. I think the people of New Hampshire, Iowa, and the primaries of Massachusetts and the rest of the country will make that judgment. It's unseemly for Republicans to comment on that.

KALB: I'll give you a Republican: Secretary of State George Shultz.

KEMP: Would make a great secretary of labor, not a great secretary of state.

KALB: Do you think he should be removed? You said that once before.

KEMP: I suggested it once, when he had opposed the Reagan doctrine of support for the freedom fighters, that he ought to step down. He called for the Soviets to get back into the Middle East talks. I didn't agree with that. I don't want the Soviet Union back into the Middle East. He's against SDI, and I'm for SDI. He's a decent, able, patriotic, fine man; I just disagree with him, and would think that Jean Kirkpatrick would make a better secretary of state than George Shultz. Somebody has to clean out the State Department and put in men and women—

KALB: Clean out the State Department of what?

KEMP: Clean out in the metaphorical sense of the word. Put men and women at the State Department who want to pursue policies that are pro growth for the world, pro democracy.

KALB: George Shultz is an economist, pro growth, very much so.

KEMP: Let me challenge you on that. The IMF, the World Bank, the U.S.A. I.D., and most people in economic positions of the State Department believe in austerity, sacrifice, pain, high taxes, devaluations of currencies. I don't know who's a greater threat to democracy in Central America, the IMF or the Sandinistas. That's how dangerous the IMF is and the policies they're pursuing in Central America.

KALB: I want to make one point, because there's a historical resonance running through my mind here. "Clean out the State Department" was a phrase used 30 years ago.

KEMP: I used it metaphorically.

KALB: You didn't mean there were communists lurking in bushes?

KEMP: Metaphorically. That's what the purpose of a campaign is, to elevate issues. And if I went to Washington, metaphorically, politically, I'd be cleaning out in the highest sense of the word.

KALB: They tell a joke about Jack Kemp—I'll try to get it straight. Up on the Hill some colleague of yours came to you and said, "Jack, we've got a terrible problem with teenage pregnancy." And you said, "Definitely. The answer and the solution is to cut taxes." It's a lousy joke, isn't it?

KEMP: It's brutal.

KALB: In your view, is the idea of cutting taxes, the supply-side economic theory, is that really still, right now, given the reality of our economy, the way to go?

KEMP: I have never pursued tax cuts for the sake of cutting taxes. I didn't run in '78 or '80. I'm not running in '88 as the Howard Jarvis of the tax reform movement, although I respect Prop. 13 and would have voted for it had I been a Californian. The purpose of cutting tax rates back in the '70s and '80s was to get the economy growing again, to strengthen the dollar, to encourage entrepreneurial capitalism as a solution to creating more jobs in America, and to that extent, I think it's worked. But my mother taught me a long time ago that the straw that breaks the camel's back is not the load of the straw, but the last or final straw. And right now the margin, this final straw, or the straw breaking the camel's back of the world economy is that there is no currency on this earth upon which you can depend over time to retain its value, and we must have a currency here and throughout the world that can be stabilized, can be honest, sound, predictable, and bring down interest rates for ourselves, for the Third World, for our trading partners, and to get the global economy beginning to grow again.

KALB: We had that didn't we, Congressman, with the dollar until recently it fell flat on its face?

KEMP: We actually had a currency that was as "good as gold," from 1944 to 1971, when Nixon devalued the dollar and took us out of the international monetary system that was organized at Bretton Woods. And since then, Marvin, I would make a case that inflation, interest rates, unemployment and debt, to a large extent, have been the result. And getting back to a sound, honest, stable dollar will not cure the world's problems, but it will give us low, long-term interest rates and it will help us help the Third World begin to buy something from Massachusetts or from Iowa, to pick two states, both primary states. But clearly, the world needs America to conduct monetary policy with an eye on getting our interest rates down. That would be helpful for this world. So right now that's the straw breaking the camel's back.

KALB: One of the things that happened—and I'm not saying cause and effect, although a lot of people think there is a cause and effect relationship—you had the massive tax cut in the early '80s. We have been living with massive budget deficits and trade deficits since that time. Do you believe, as many other people do, many other candidates who have sat in that seat, that the budget deficit is the single most important problem facing this country, and it must be addressed first and foremost by the next president? Would Jack Kemp do that?

KEMP: The budget deficit is a reflection of our problems, it is not necessarily the cause of the problem. Most candidates in both parties are telling us that the "big deficit" is causing the interest rates. Whereas I am saying the high interest rate policy of this country, of the Federal Reserve Board, is causing, in large part, the huge servicing of the debt, is causing the economy to be underemployed, is causing the farm economy to be flat, or at least to drop considerably from '81 to '86. So getting interest rates down is essential to young homeowners, it's essential to farmers, it is essential to Third World debtor nations, and it is essential, along with putting a lid on spending, to getting our budget into balance. So I think the answer to balancing the budget is not to raise taxes. It's to put a lid on spending. Give this President, or any president, Democrat or Republican, a line-item veto, but get our dollar stabilized so long-term interest rates will come down to the normal level of 4 or 5 percent. Housing would boom, U.S. auto sales would grow, our exports would rise. I'm not suggesting it's a cure-all. But it certainly would be a lot better for the farm economy, the commodity economy, and particularly in the Third World, that desperately wants to buy something from the United States, but right now they can't, because they're using all their earnings to finance the debt and pay off New York City banks.

KALB: You don't feel, to any degree or to any extent, that the supply-side economics theories of yours, Laffer, and other people in the late '70s applied by the President in 1981, '82, '83, are principally responsible for the massive budget deficit, the trade deficit, the fact that we have now become the largest debtor nation in the world?

KEMP: That's just nonsense. Marvin, it's embarrassing for such an intelligent newsman.

KALB: Two trillion dollars.

KEMP: It's single-entry bookkeeping—

KALB: Who's going to pay for it?

KEMP: Let me make the point. It's single-entry bookkeeping to talk about a deficit and not talk about the growth of this economy.

KALB: But most people keep one set of books.

KEMP: You mean assets aren't included?

KALB: Assets could be included.

KEMP: In order to be totally objective, as I know you desperately want to be, you have to go on to tell the people here at the JFK School that while the deficit is $140 billion or so, the gross national product under those tax cuts has grown from less than $2 trillion to $4.5. We're headed to $5 trillion. We have to get the deficit down, but not by raising taxes. The deficit, Marvin, is not a revenue problem, it's a spending problem. Revenues are rising and have risen 60 percent since Jack Kemp and Bill Roth and Ronald Reagan cut tax rates in '81. What has grown even more are our liberal Democratic friends in Congress, who have an insatiable appetite to spend people's money and redistribute wealth. So putting a lid on spending, getting interest rates and tax rates down clearly will bring our budget into balance. And we shouldn't panic and put this country through a recession by raising taxes or tariffs.

KALB: Congressman, the problem is, I heard that from the President in the '80 campaign, in the '84 campaign, everything you just said, and the deficits continue to go on. But we're obviously not going to resolve it. Let's do foreign policy.

KEMP: You've never heard it from somebody who believes it as strongly as I do.

KALB: I know you believe it. There's no question about that. Let me talk to you about foreign policy. President Reagan, in the last couple of days, certainly within the last week, has been sharply critical of the Israeli crackdown on the Palestinian rioters in the Gaza Strip, and the other day the U.S. abstained when it could have blocked a U.N. condemnation of Israel. Do you think the President was right or wrong?

KEMP: Well, as you said at the opening of the show, I'm a strong supporter of this President, but I would have had an ambassador to the United Nations in a Kemp administration who would have voted against the U.N. condemnation of Israel, and I would have had an ambassador who would have voted to condemn the Zionism as racism resolution. I think it's outrageous to pick on Israel in the U.N. They've got a very severe problem in the Gaza Strip and with the Palestinians. There's got to be a resolution. There's got to be a political one. We've got to be concerned about housing, education, and the economy. But just to condemn Israel in the U.N. as they do about once a week is a mistake. And we ought to oppose it wherever it raises its ugly head. And it's ugly.

KALB: The Contra issue: Nicaragua. You cosponsored legislation calling for $310 million in military aid to the Contras over the next 18 months. What I'm trying to understand is, in your mind, are you trying, by trying to get that kind of money, to induce the Sandinistas into a quicker, more fruitful kind of negotiation, or do you want to really knock them off, overthrow them?

KEMP: Well, I want to knock off a Marxist, Leninist idea. I think the best way to do that is to replace it with a good idea, a better thesis, which is democracy, freedom, private property, justice, equality of opportunity, capitalism, if you will.

KALB: So you would like the Contras to overthrow?

KEMP: I was on the Kissinger Commission, the bipartisan commission on Central America, and played, I think, a pretty key role, some people suggested. And I'm a strong supporter of building up democratic institutions in Central America, but I think it's important that we recall that the Sandinistas have violated, not only the pledge they made to the Organization of American States back in July of '79, but also the Arias proposal. So I think, frankly, the only pressure we have right now on the Sandinistas to keep any pledge for reform in Nicaragua is aid to the democratic resistance, and I hope it works. I think most men and women of goodwill don't want a Warsaw Pact country on the Isthmus of Central America, and that's about what we're going to get if Humberto Ortega is allowed to send his officer corps to Bulgaria for training. Goodness gracious, what are the Sandinistas doing having the PLO, Bulgaria, Czechoslovakia, and East Germany running their military? That's outrageous.

KALB: Move on to arms control. You have said, "The President believes in the total elimination of nuclear weapons," and every now and then I can see your eyes roll to the ceiling when you say something like that. Do you think the President is being terribly naive to believe that in this world, and that the security of the United States can be protected by the total elimination of nuclear weapons?

KEMP: I don't favor, at least in our lifetime, the total elimination of the nuclear deterrent.

KALB: What is the President talking about?

KEMP: The President has a wonderful streak of idealism and even utopianism. I think it is unrealistic to share SDI with the Soviet Union. I don't want them in the same space program as the United States of America. When they allow a vote in Leningrad and Moscow or in Poland, I would be much more willing to begin to talk about sharing technology with the Soviet Union. Right now it's important that we recognize something that Churchill said in '46, that had it not been for the nuclear deterrent, the Soviet Red Army would have marched from the banks of the Elbe River to the English Channel in about a week and a half. I believe in the nuclear deterrent, particularly at a time when the Soviets have overwhelming conventional capability. And it is utopian to think, at this time anyway, of beating swords into plowshares and spears into pruning hooks as the prophet Isaiah. We all pray for that day,

Marvin, and we should work for a better world, and a more peaceful world. And I'm not a hawk, I am a dove. But I'm a heavily armed dove, and I believe the best way to protect peace is through strength.

KALB: Columnist William Safire of the *New York Times* still thinks you're going to be the Republican nominee. And yet there are so many other conservatives around this country who write, who talk, who feel that somehow or another you're not authentic enough as a conservative, and that while you oppose abortion, you also oppose cutting social security, cutting food stamp programs, cutting Head Start. You have even said in a recent interview, "I don't believe in turning my back on the poor, the aged and minorities." So I suppose the question to you is, What kind of Republican are you if you don't want to turn your back on the poor and the minorities and the aged?

KEMP: Touché. I think Abraham Lincoln is my model. He was an emancipator, a liberator. He was a great believer in the Jeffersonian inalienable right of all people. Lincoln was a populist and a conservative and an American president that I think was really the lone star of the Republican party. He was loved by black Americans. He was loved by the people. He is my shining guide, if you will. Having said that, it seems to me you can be conservative and pro-people simultaneously, that keeping inflation down is pro-people. Creating more jobs through entrepreneurial capitalism is pro-people. Concern about liberating the world from poverty with democratic institutions and private property and free enterprise is pro-people. I don't think compassion is creating an economic desert in the United States of America—handing someone a glass of water and calling it compassion. Compassion should not be measured in America by how many people are on food stamps. Compassion should be measured by how few people need welfare, and so I consider myself to be compassionate in the sense of hoping to lift people up out of that social welfare system that is dragging them down.

KALB: Before we turn to the audience, I have one other issue I wanted to raise with you. It's the case of the Reverend Tim Lahaye. You appointed him as one of the cochairmen of your campaign. Then apparently you learned that this very conservative, influential evangelical leader had written that Roman Catholicism is a false religion, that Judaism yields to a secularist and atheistic spirit, and then you cut him loose. My question is, Why did you put him in there in the first place? Was it simply a search for support from the evangelicals?

KEMP: Well, I want support from evangelical Christians and Jews and Catholics. And I think there is no campaign that I can see in the Republican or Democratic party that has more. I've got 6,000 cochairmen and -women of the Kemp campaign. They're black and white and Hispanic and male and female.

KALB: Was it a mistake to put him in?

KEMP: He resigned, and I'm not going to jump on his grave. He made theological writings that, interpreted, are something that I don't think are part of any campaign. But I think he deserves the dignity to be able to resign. He supports me. I didn't endorse, I have not endorsed, his writings. So what good purpose is served in putting it back on the front burner? I don't think anybody thinks I'm anti-Catholic or anti-Semitic. In fact, I think I have a very strong record of civil and human and equal rights.

KALB: But the question I want to raise is: Charles Black, who is one of your top advisers, said that you're still accepting Lahaye's political support. In other words, even knowing what you know now belatedly about him, you're still prepared to accept it.

KEMP: He has assured me, and I take him at his word, that he believes in the Constitution of the United States of America, believes in the pluralism that is manifest in the First Amendment to the Constitution. He believes in Judeo-Christian values. And those theological writings have no place, he says, and I say, in a campaign, and he has resigned. So I accept that. Do I want the support of all men and women who support the Constitution, Judeo-Christian values, the First Amendment? You bet.

KALB: Do you want the support of somebody, do you want the support at the same time—

KEMP: I want the support of every man and woman in this country who believes in the Constitution, and—

KALB: And that Roman Catholicism is a false religion?

KEMP: I don't believe that.

KALB: I know you don't.

KEMP: I'm not going to let someone put me in that position because it is McCarthyism. You're putting me on the side of a view—

KALB: That's not McCarthyism.

KEMP: It is to me to say that I—

KALB: In 1984 we went through the campaign with Jesse Jackson, where he was asked to repudiate the Reverend Farrakhan.

KEMP: I repudiate anti-Catholicism. I repudiate anti-Semitism. I've repudiated ethnic and racial overtones, and there is no one in my campaign who doesn't, and if it ever raises its head, they will be gone tomorrow.

KALB: I know you do.

KEMP: I think that's enough for the American people and enough for Marvin Kalb.

KALB: Even enough for us. I'm not sure I understand that last point. We'll let it go.

KEMP: It answers your questions. I think it's enough.

KALB: But in any case we're at the point where these guys ask the questions. Our first question, Sara Sievers, a member of the student advisory committee, the Institute of Politics.

SIEVERS: Hi. Congressman Kemp, environmental groups gave your voting record the worst rating in the 99th Congress on environmental issues. Yet since announcing your candidacy for president, you've introduced acid rain legislation and sided with environmentalists on Seabrook. How do you explain your apparent change in these issues?

KEMP: Well, Seabrook and acid rain never came up. I'm a strong supporter of acid rain legislation. I think we should decontrol natural gas. I think that's a clean burning fuel that would be a better solution than just subsidizing giant nuclear power plants. But nonetheless, I think environmental records, as you know from looking at them, are based sometimes on rather distorted views. It was considered to be anti-environment to vote to do any exploration of the Alaskan wilderness. I think there are areas of Alaska that should be open to the exploration of those minerals upon which Western civilization depends for future sources of energy. They consider that anti-environment. I was a cosponsor of the Clean Water Act of Edmund Muskie. I did support the veto by the President because, unfortunately in this Congress, Sara, they add so much pork to any appropriation bill and there's no line item veto, so the only way the President could get some of that pork out of the Clean Water Act was to veto it. I supported it, but I'm a cosponsor of the act. I think in order to look at a legislative record, you've got to be a little bit more discriminating than listening to just one environmental voting index.

QUESTION: Congressman, I have a question about U.S. support for the concept of democracy around the world. In many areas of the world it seems to be the foreign policy of the United States to support governments that are friendly to the U.S. but which have histories of human rights abuses, and in many ways also lack anything that could be called genuine democratic processes. If elected, will your foreign policy continue the support for nations which are friendly to the U.S., in that they further the interests of U.S. business and national security, or would your first priority for them be that they cease violations of human rights as defined by the United Nations Charter and also that they implement full democratic procedures, much the same as we are currently demanding of the Nicaraguan government in the name of our alleged support for worldwide democracy.

KEMP: Thank you for the question. I think this country should treat countries that are friendly to the United States, that are authoritarian, with an eye on encouraging democracy, requiring democracy. I don't think we should just shut off our support for South Korea until they've achieved Jeffersonian democracy. I think this country has had a record of promoting democratic reforms, not only in South Korea, but in the Philippines. We should be harder on Chile, but we don't want to turn our back on the possibility that authoritarian governments can someday become democratic, as has happened in Latin America. There are several governments today, and I think even you would admit that El Salvador, once authoritarian, today is far more democratic than it was in even the early 1980s. So we need to encourage. We ought to probe. We ought to do everything we can, including using our foreign aid, to encourage democratic institutions in all countries, including South Africa. Should we totally turn our back on them and treat them as Marxist/Leninist states that are at odds with our country? No, I agree with Jean Kirkpatrick. We need to move authoritarian governments towards democracy, and we need to encourage democratic reforms in totalitarian states as well.

QUESTION: Congressman Kemp, on the campaign you've talked about the privatization of our public housing, in other words, selling the units to the individuals who are living there. Recently, in a Boston paper, this was called a radical idea. Do you really think this is a practical idea, and is it radical?

KEMP: I kind of like it that it's radical. Radical in Latin means getting back to roots, getting back to the foundation of our country. And I think converting from people renting a piece of property to the opportunity to own a piece of property is radical free enterprise, and I think we could empower the poor in many of our inner-city public housing projects if we gave them a stake in that piece of property. So I would, to the best of my ability, sell off some of the public housing projects at 20 to 25 percent of the market rate in order to give low-income public housing residents the first opportunity, probably in their life, to own a piece of property and empower them in terms of what it would mean for their future. I offered an amendment incidentally, and it was opposed on the floor of the House by some of my liberal Democratic friends because they said poor people wouldn't know what to do with their property. The elitists today are the ones who think that the poor are, by definition, poor forever, or don't know enough to get out of poverty. We need to give them the tools in which to get out of poverty—that means jobs, housing, opportunities for private ownership of private property. And I believe that we can unleash a radical free enterprise solution to some of these public housing projects which today are in dilapidated form.

QUESTION: Congressman Kemp, I have two questions concerning your proposed energy policies. First, what would you like to do with Shoreham and the Seabrook nuclear power plants, and more importantly, do you think that the industry that brought us Shoreham and Seabrook should be restructured and deregulated so that we can avoid similar problems in the future?

KEMP: That's not a bad premise to the question. I think there's going to be a radical restructuring of the nuclear power industry. I'm not opposed to nuclear power. I am opposed to subsidizing it. I'm not opposed to the idea of a nuclear power plant. I am opposed to opening it if it is not totally safe and within the guidelines that have been set up by the NRC for the type of an evacuation zone that a community would require. I think there's been some irresponsible conduct, particularly on the side of those who just want to close their eyes to the necessity of providing more power and electricity for the Northeast. I would not subsidize nuclear power. I would not abolish it. I don't favor subsidizing giant oil companies to produce fossil fuel energy at $70 a barrel. I basically believe in the marketplace, in deregulating natural gas and deregulating electricity. We need more power sources, we need more entrepreneurs willing to get into cogeneration, and I think we can find a solution to the source of energy for the Northeast that does not require us to open a plant that is, by definition at least up until now, incapable of designing an evacuation area that would, I think, be required by the community and both states.

QUESTION: Congressman, my question is about truth in advertising. As one of the chief architects of the 1981 tax cut, you advertise that as a measure that would so stimulate the economy that the net revenues to the U.S. treasury would actually increase to the point where we could balance the budget. And yet the history of the last six years has proved that to be slightly off, if not absurd, in that over the last seven years, even with over $300 billion in domestic tax cuts, we've had to borrow as much as we did in the previous 200 years of the country. Quite simply, what went wrong?

KEMP: That's quite a chunk to put forth. I'd like to just challenge a couple parts of your premise that I think are off the mark somewhat. First of all, I never said it would balance the budget by cutting taxes. I said we could begin to grow again without inflation. I said we could strengthen the dollar. I said we could create more jobs and create more small business opportunities for men and women in this country. And I would say even the most severe critics of the tax cut would give some credit to the idea of cutting taxes as a way of encouraging the creation of 14 million new jobs in four years, 750,000 new business starts. That's 50 percent higher than ever before in the history of the country. We're not going to hell in a hand basket. Frankly, we have to get the deficit down.

But, as I told Marvin Kalb earlier in response to his question along the same lines, revenues are not the problem. Revenues today in the United States of America, even after the huge tax cut of Kemp and Roth in 1981, are higher today by 60 percent than they were when we cut taxes. Revenues, as a percent of the national economy, are higher today than they were when we cut taxes. The problem is you have two things wrong: the insatiable appetite of the liberal wing of the Democratic party to redistribute wealth, and number two, spending has risen by 72 percent. Thirdly, I guess, would be the fact that we've had a central bank, a Federal Reserve Board that believes that too much growth causes inflation. And I'm out trying to get the engine of the economy growing.

And we've got a Federal Reserve Board that believes that if too many men and women are working, it causes inflation. So there's been a real tug of war in this administration between the growth wing of the Republican party and the austerity wing, and that's why I'm running for president: so I can make the next step, not only a low tax rate system for labor and capital, but a sound money, low-interest rate policy for America and the world. And we'll complete the next phase in the Kemp administration.

QUESTION: Just to add a footnote to that perhaps, for six of the years of the Reagan administration, the Senate was in the hands of Republicans, the White House was clearly in the hands of Republicans. You talk about a 70 percent growth in spending.

Again, that same question: What went wrong? If the Republican party, following your own ideas, ends up with this enormous, unprecedented—you'll have to admit that's a good use of the word—budget deficit, unprecedented trade deficit, unprecedented national debt, what, in fact, went wrong? Is it possible the ideas themselves were simply flawed?

KEMP: Thanks for the question. It's a legitimate one. First of all, it's not unprecedented. This year's deficit of the United States of America is 3.5 percent of the gross national product. When Harry Truman succeeded Franklin Roosevelt, the deficit coming out of World War II was 40 percent of the gross national product. We grew out of the deficit. The total national debt of America in 1945–46 was 140 percent of the gross national product. Today it's too high, but it's about 40 percent of the gross national product. I want to tell you something now. You've got to understand that our deficit, the thing that all the European countries are complaining about, is on average lower than the whole OECD countries combined. We've got to get out of this. But we shouldn't panic. We shouldn't raise taxes. We've got to get our interest rates down. We've got to put a lid on spending and give the president line-item veto. But to panic now, I think, would be to make a big mistake. And opponents, particularly Bob Dole, are running on bitter medicine for the American people. If we want bitter medicine, we could have elected Walter Mondale. We want the government to take a little medicine. We want the American people to be able to breathe a little bit with more jobs and a better growth, not only for America, but for the world.

QUESTION: The President you support has just signed a compromise that increases taxes.

KEMP: Well, look, unity in a party does not require unanimity. We don't have to march in lock step. I did not support a tax increase, and I don't think we ought to cut defense. I think we ought to do the things that I have alluded to.

QUESTION: Mr. Kemp, you speak of your strong support for human rights. How do you reconcile this claim with your statements that you wouldn't allow gays and lesbians to teach in public schools? How would you propose to go about removing gays and lesbians teaching in public schools?

KEMP: I didn't say that, with all due respect to your question. I do believe in human rights, and equal rights, and constitutional rights, and the civil rights of all people. I do. What I said was, where somebody stands up and promotes a cause as a lifestyle, a school board has the right to expect some example from their teachers in public service. So I said, as a father, on behalf of fathers and mothers and parents throughout America, that I thought a school board should have the determination over the conduct of their teachers—and I think it should be clear that no one wants any McCarthyism or probing into people's bedrooms. But where somebody advocates a lifestyle that is at odds with our Judeo-Christian values, it seems to me, as I said as a parent, without prying into their civil liberties, I would want the school board to have the final determination.

QUESTION: To advocate tolerance, you would say that's something you would disagree with, someone should be removed for doing that?

KEMP: Where they advocate a lifestyle that is at odds with community standards, yes. I hope I answered your question.

QUESTION: Representative Kemp, many of us are very much concerned about two concessions that Secretary Shultz has already made to the Soviets in the strategic arms reduction talks. One is that he has conceded that we will forego the defense of our country for at least seven years, which effectively means much longer, and secondly, he has agreed to allow them to keep at least one-half of their large first-strike missiles. Now, I think that is very inconsistent. What do you think?

KEMP: My problem with the process that we talked about a little bit earlier—the INF treaty process, the summit process—is that the State Department for years has been trying to get President Reagan to give up the Strategic Defense Initiative, and I don't think it should be a bargaining chip. I think it is morally justifiable in a Judeo-Christian society to defend yourself. We know from Gorbachev's interview with Tom Brokaw that they are going ahead with their own SDI. It seems to me it would be morally profound to move this country away from a reliance on offensive nuclear weapons of mass destruction, as a deterrent to war, to a doctrine of defense. And my complaint with George Shultz is that he wants to negotiate it at the summit talks. I don't. And I think we are about ready to sign a continuation of the ABM treaty, which the Congress will narrowly interpret, and it will end, effectively, the ability to deploy early the phased architecture of a strategic defense for ourselves, while we rush ahead to support it for Europe and Israel. I support it for Europe and Israel. I also support it for the United States of America.

QUESTION: You said you believe in promoting democracy around the world, but you also said that you would not condemn Israel's recent killing of over 20 Palestinians, including children, which was paid for with U.S. tax dollars. Don't you think there's a contradiction in promoting democracy on the one hand and paying for a military occupation on the other hand?

KEMP: I didn't say that I don't condemn killing. Let me just answer the question by repeating what I told Mr. Kalb at the beginning of the show. I think it is wrong to condemn Israel for a problem that has festered even before Israel was a state, even before Israel controlled the Gaza. It is wrong, in my view, to condemn Israel for a problem that is vexing to all of us and that we all want an answer to. I don't think condemning people is necessarily the solution to a political problem. And I want you to know that I hold out the hope that this country can get back to the type of moral climate, such as Camp David, when we brought Sadat and Begin together. I would hope that that same climate could be used in a Kemp administration, with all due respect to President Carter, that we bring people together rather than push them apart. But I just don't believe in mindlessly letting the U.N. condemn our friends. Israel is a democracy, and I want to support democracies where they exist. They're a true democracy and a true friend of the United States. Why should we bash them at the U.N.?

KALB: The next final question. Richard Haass teaches here at the Kennedy school.

HAASS: On Defense, I want to take one specific line of questioning. Caspar Weinberger has been criticized, as you know, for throwing an awful lot of dollars at defense and not really having his priorities straight and not really having a lot to show for it. For better or worse, a Kemp administration would not have that luxury. You could well have four years of no real growth in resources for defense. My question to you is, What would you do under those circumstances? What would be your priorities in terms of conventional forces, strategic forces, offense, defense?

KEMP: We're spending 28 percent of the federal budget on defense, so I would roughly keep it within that area. We're spending 6.5 percent of our gross national product on defense. The one answer, without cutting defense or throwing more dollars at the Pentagon, is to make the pie bigger, make the gross national product bigger. If we make this economy grow faster, as it did in the early '60s and as it did in the mid-80s, we'd have more money for defense, more money for housing, more money for roads and highways, more money for schools. Clearly, getting the economy growing again is a necessity. And finally we need a strong conventional capability. I would earnestly seek to move away from first-strike weaponry to strategic defense, and I think that would be good not only for us, but for the world. And my hope would be to tell the Soviets, "Keep your radar, you have your right to have your own SDI. We're going to do the same." And the world will be more peaceful and more progressive.

Candidates '88

A CONVERSATION WITH GARY HART

209

About the Candidate

Say this for Gary Hart: He certainly knew how to keep things interesting. In 1972 he was an obscure Denver lawyer who, as George McGovern's campaign manager, helped turn a long-shot antiwar candidacy into a revolution in the Democratic party whose aftershocks are still being felt. In 1984 Hart, by then a senator from Colorado and a presidential candidate, astounded the political world by derailing the Walter Mondale Express in New Hampshire and nearly snatching the nomination. And in 1988—well, calling the 1988 Hart campaign "interesting" is a bit like calling the Monkey Business a dinghy.

In the spring of 1987 Hart, 51, was the universally accepted front-runner for the Democratic nomination. He was the prophet of "generational" politics and of "new ideas," the clear leader in the polls, and a far more relaxed and effective candidate than he had been four years earlier. This time he was the one who looked "inevitable." Then came Donna Rice, the townhouse, the *Miami Herald*, the yacht, the pictures in the *National Enquirer*—a tidal wave of scandal, horror, and embarrassment that drowned the Hart campaign in a matter of days.

For many observers, what Hart would later delicately call "the events of last May" confirmed doubts about his character and judgment. Hart's defenders answered that Hart's personal life was his own business, and that beyond such trivialities as telling conflicting stories and changing his name, age, and signature, there was no evidence of duplicity or bad character in the long record of his public life. They had a point. But even they could not deny that he had been unconscionably reckless.

Months passed. Hart sulked in his house in Troublesome Gulch, Colorado. Then, on December 15, the day of the filing deadline for the New Hampshire primary, he rose like a Phoenix from the ashes of the fire he had set himself. His reentry into the race dominated the news for days, and for a brief moment it seemed possible his no-money, no-staff, lone-wolf guerrilla campaign just might catch on. Even after the long hiatus, his command of substantive issues was as full and clear as that of any of his rivals. But when he returned, so did the "questions" about his "character"—and, more devastatingly, the snickers. Fairly or unfairly, the best efforts of Hart, his wife, and his hardworking daughter Andrea could not erase the picture of him, indelibly fixed in the public mind, as the antihero of a tawdry drama of sexual and family intrigue.

Hart's appearance on "Candidates '88" (some would later say it was his finest hour) came at a time when he could still cherish a wild hope—a little past the midpoint of the month between his reentry and the January 15 Iowa debate in which he would put on a lackluster performance. In the wake of Super Tuesday he would withdraw for the second time in a year—without a delegate to his name but with his dignity in somewhat better repair than after the first time.

H.H.

The Interview

KALB: Mr. Hart, you have often been described as a political outsider, a loner. And since you reentered the race this time you seem to have taken a good deal of joy from the fact that you're a political underdog. When you did reenter you said, "I have the power of ideas and I can govern this country." I want to address those two things: your ideas and your capacity to govern the country.

And first the ideas which fall into three categories: economic restructuring, military reform, and strategic enlightened engagement, which I assume is a sophisticated way of saying, "How do we get along with the Russians a good bit better." Let us now assume you are president. I'd like you to apply your new ideas to some festering problems and some very major problems you would have to face—number one: arms control. Would you go for a 50 percent cutback in strategic nuclear weapons if you could?

HART: I think the next negotiating position of this government, and it would be my position as president, is to accept the Gorbachev challenge put forward in Iceland, which is massive reduction in overall arsenals in both ICBMs strategic systems, testing, and space systems, and as we have seen, progress in regional systems in Europe; and in effect, accept that agenda and go from there. What has held up that 50 percent reduction in overall strategic systems over the decade is the president's insistence on space testing or atmospheric testing of space systems. We don't need to do that. We can pursue those technologies without jeopardizing the possibility of genuine arms reduction. And I think the Iceland summit, as I said at the time, was an historic breakthrough, which the next president has to accept.

KALB: And you would then go ahead and try to get that 50 percent cutback in strategic weapons?

HART: I would not go beyond that. Frankly, I think a comprehensive test ban must be part of this nation's national security agenda. I have advocated what I call a Manhattan project, a joint venture with the Soviets for breakthroughs in verification technology, which has always held up our ability to reduce nuclear arms. And the possibility under Gorbachev exists that we can do that. I've also advocated a freeze on the production of nuclear materials, plutonium, and weapon's grade materials. And finally, I would add to that agenda a joint crisis monitoring capability to prevent accidental or miscalculated war.

KALB: On conventional forces in Europe, you have at least suggested over the last year or so that you might even increase the number of American forces in Western Europe if you had to. Under what circumstances would you increase?

HART: What I have advocated most specifically in a speech at Edinburgh University in '85 is application of the so-called military reform principles to NATO. To ourselves in Europe as well as our NATO partners, that means two or three things. It means over a period of time, through agreement with our military allies, a restructuring of the relative burden—I think in the 21st century. The United States ought to be prepared to pick up more of the air and sea defense of Europe, and our continental allies, doing relatively well economically, ought to pick up more of the land defense. I think we have to shift our tactic and our doctrine away from forward defense, which is a Maginot Line mentality, to maneuver warfare. And I think we have to increase the number of our reserve divisions. That does not necessarily mean an increase in expenditure or manpower. It may mean restructuring our military forces on the land as well as the continental forces of other nations in the smaller divisions, and having more reserve divisions available which can be put forward very quickly.

KALB: But not necessarily sent to Europe, but held back?

HART: Held back. Restructure the divisions which are there, change what is often called "the teeth to tail ratio," increase the number of combat units, combat forces, and reduce the number of support forces, and have the Europeans get more, prepare more ready reserve divisions themselves. The Dutch have already begun to do that.

KALB: Let's shift to the Middle-East, the PLO. Would you, as president, extend American diplomatic recognition to the PLO?

HART: No, I would not certainly at the present time. That has to be a result of overall negotiations in the region. After visiting there and visiting with the heads of state of Jordan, of Israel, and of Egypt in 1986 for about ten days, what I did come back believing was that we ought to pursue, so long as the Israeli government wants to, the idea of an international conference; and second, that we ought to have been much more active ourselves in pushing the peace process, including an economic development of the West Bank. King Hussein told me, as well as then Prime Minister Peres, that one of the things that's needed is to give the people on the West Bank a sense of greater economic opportunity to help them resist the temptation of terrorism.

KALB: The Arabs have said time and time again that for them the core problem in any kind of resolution in the Middle East is settling the Palestinian problem. Do you share that view—that this is the core problem?

HART: It is part of the core problem, it is not the core problem.

KALB: How would you define it?

HART: The core problem is to get the Arab confrontation states to accept Israel's existence as a matter of law and fact and move forward from that. Once that is done, then I think you can address other collateral issues, such as the Palestinian homeland and the rest.

KALB: Shift to South Korea. Would it be your view that there should be an increase or a decrease in the number of American forces now based in South Korea?

HART: I don't think there should be any change one way or the other. Again, that's based upon 12 years of experience on the Senate Armed Services Committee as well as a visit to Korea in late '86, on the way to Moscow. As a result of that, my strong feeling is that reduced tensions on the peninsula, that is, between South and North Korea, must be higher on our agenda than it has been. I spoke with Foreign Minister Shevardnadze in Moscow about whether the Soviets were prepared on that specific regional issue to use pressure on the North Koreans to relax their confrontation and their threat to the South Koreans. He was, I must say, somewhat taken aback by the question. I don't think he expected it, but he didn't rule out the possibility they could play a greater role there.

KALB: In the Philippines, there's a feeling of some considerable political instability on the part of Corazon Aquino's regime. If there were a military coup, not an unlikely prospect in the Philippines, and an anticommunist military government took over in the Philippines, would you do business with it?

HART: I think we'd have no choice but to do business with it, the same way we do business with the Soviets.

KALB: I mean, would you engage in the same kind of almost allied cooperation with the Philippines?

HART: No. Under my foreign policy, I think we then have to have an obligation that is political, economic, and moral to pressure that government, if that type of government should emerge, into democratic reforms—open elections as quickly as possible, free press, broad participation in the political process.

KALB: Wouldn't this be something that any president would really push for?

HART: We didn't so much under Reagan.

KALB: I mean beyond Aquino. Can you imagine any American president not recognizing the military government that might take over, and not at the same time saying that you people have to return to civilian rule?

HART: No. I think that's true.

KALB: On domestic issues—

HART: If I may say so, I think the real question is how to prevent that from happening. Again, this administration, as in the Middle East and elsewhere, has been much too passive. I think we all have to reward their final realization that the Marcos regime had to go and some last minute support for the Aquino revolution, if you will. But I think we're much too passive out there. And I think we are inviting some sort of upheaval if we don't have some new initiatives to give Mrs. Aquino a chance to get that economy on its feet.

KALB: Let's shift to our own economy. On the issue of taxes, would you raise them?

HART: I would raise revenues on the grounds that there's no other way we're going to get the deficits down and finance the investments in this economy.

KALB: What are the taxes?

HART: Oil import fees, which would raise anywhere from $12 to $18 billion a year, at least for the next three to five years, not only as a revenue-raising measure and a fiscal measure, but primarily as a national security measure. This country is getting dangerously reliant on foreign oil once again. The major papers of this country reported within the last three or four weeks that projected into the 1990s, this country could well end up by the middle of the next decade as reliant on foreign oil as we were in the early '70s. That is folly; it is nothing but folly in a security sense, political sense, and economic sense. Also, luxury taxes could raise 2 to 4 billion dollars. And user fees could raise 2 to 4 billion dollars. A continuation of the third bracket on upper-income individuals could be initiated.

KALB: A number of the people who have been here, sitting in this seat, other candidates, have said similar things. Gephardt, Jackson, and Simon certainly also favor the oil import tax. I was wondering if there is a particular quality that you would bring to raising revenues that is different from what they would be doing?

HART: Well, I don't think they've all been as straightforward or candid about the necessity. Here I would applaud Governor

Babbitt, who I think is willing to be your guest. He deserves a great deal of credit, I believe—and I've said this on other occasions—for his courage in stating the truth. This is not only an issue among the Democrats, it's also an issue with Republicans. None of the Republicans I'm aware of is willing to step in to the plate and tell the American people the truth: And that is you can't have lower deficits and a better education system and a cleaner environment and housing for the homeless and all the things we all want without additional revenues. It's a simple fact.

KALB: Would the budget deficit and the trade deficit be the top economic priorities of a Hart administration?

HART: Along with a third priority, which is investment, I said my campaign was based on three words: invest, reform, and engage. I would add a fourth, which is service. But the investment part is, I hope, a well-thought-out and well-documented program or policy, not only for public dollars, but for private dollars, to rebuild the basic foundation of this nation's economy: our manufacturing base, our energy production, our agricultural production, our education system first and foremost, including job training, and finally our research and laboratory base for new innovation.

KALB: Senator, I think that just about every candidate has said something awfully similar to that.

HART: I'm glad they're following my lead.

KALB: Perhaps they are. Perhaps they came upon it themselves. But is there something new that you're projecting in the area of the economy? Because if there is I'd like to hear it.

HART: Well, I think there is in several regards. One is the comprehensiveness of it, and the second is the detail of it. Not only in this booklet but in speeches and articles, I've tried to spell out in specific detail a 144 page trade bill, a 100 or 125 page infrastructure rebuilding bill, an education reform speech at Duke earlier this year that has 12 or 14 points—a bigger, broader view, I think, than traditionally politicians have had. We can either focus on the micropolicies or we can have broad-based, sweeping, comprehensive reform policies, and it's the latter that I've tried to feature.

KALB: Given everything that you've just said and putting it all together, how long would it take, in your view, to eliminate, to bring down substantially, the budget deficit?

HART: Well, combining those three objectives: reducing the budget deficit, a fiscal problem; reducing our trade deficit; and getting this nation's economy in the position where it can compete in the world marketplace in five to ten years. But a whole set of new policies have to be adopted. Let me say one other thing that I think may be different about my candidacy. What I've also tried to do is not just have an education policy or a military policy. I've tried to relate them, and you will find a careful reading of my foreign policy lectures at Georgetown a couple of years ago. The military reform effort for ten years is that they work together. The economics are the same thing. I don't think we can separate domestic and international economics anymore.

KALB: On the issue of how you would treat the problems of America's blacks. In the '84 campaign primaries that you won, you got 3 percent of the black vote. That doesn't suggest that you're really relating to them terribly well. What could you do as president to reach out to the blacks in this country?

HART: My principle opposition or competition in '84 was Walter Mondale, who had been vice president, protege of Hubert Humphrey, and very well known in the black community in this country for 15 or 20 years; and Reverend Jackson, a leading, if not the leading, black leader in America. So that's very tough competition. I did not emerge or burst on the scene, I guess, until after the New Hampshire primary in February. And then, as you know, it was a real roller coaster. I tried my very best at that time to put forward what I think is virtually—I shouldn't say perfect but close to perfect—civil rights record, not only for the 12 years in the Senate, but a deep personal commitment to the cause of civil rights and equality in this country that led me to support John and Robert Kennedy and George McGovern and others. And I was pleased earlier this year, when I was an active candidate, to see the polls beginning to acknowledge that I was getting my own record and personality across to the minority communities and had a much broader base of support in the black, Hispanic, and Asian communities in this country.

KALB: You still have Jesse Jackson as a very prominent candidate for the Democratic party. Do you think that you would be able, with your ideas, to reach out beyond Jackson's appeal to the blacks?

HART: Well, I think so, I certainly hope so, and I intend to make an effort in this regard. Part of it is familiarity. Part of it is a sense of feeling comfortable with that individual, knowing who that person is, having a sense of identity. And I think through campaigning, through information and education, I intend to make a very strong appeal to the minority communities across this country.

Candidates '88

KALB: I want to ask you about the possibility of a recession in this country. In November the leading economic indicators dropped 1.7 percent, which was the worst since the early '80s when the United States, in fact, did go into a recession, a rather deep one. How would you apply your ideas to head off a recession?

HART: Well, part of what must be done is what some of us have been advocating for some time. I argued a year or two ago that the unrealistically high value of the dollar was crushing American workers, making us uncompetitive. And that had to be part of not only a trade policy but a fiscal policy as well. Happily, that's begun to happen. It may be happening too much. One of the parts of both my economic and trade policies has been called a new Bretton Woods Conference: not only to bring the value of the dollar down against other foreign currencies, but to negotiate the so-called window, if you will, or margin of exchanges that are tolerable—not a fixed exchange rate, but a fluctuating one within a ceiling and a floor.

KALB: Has the dollar already dropped enough in your view?

HART: Oh, I think it has. It's got to stabilize. I don't think we can leave it to the so-called free markets to do that. That's why I think an international monetary conference must be part of that process. That would help. Investment in this nation's economy will help ward off inflation. We are a wasteful nation; we are a consumer nation. We must transform this country in the next decade from a consumer nation to a producing nation. Instead of spending our money, that requires investing our money, public dollars and private dollars.

KALB: Senator, in going over a number of your speeches on foreign policy and military reform, I think I have a pretty good idea on where you feel the United States has misused American military power. It is not clear to me where you feel American military power should be used. What is left to defend for the United States?

HART: A lot of things are left to defend.

KALB: Tick it off.

HART: Our existing post–World War II alliances and commitments, NATO principally, our commitment to the security of Japan and our allies in the Far East, Japan and the Philippines.

KALB: South Korea?

HART: South Korea, certainly. That would be part of the—

KALB: Taiwan?

HART: Under the terms of the Shanghai Accord, certainly. A

concern for security in the Western hemisphere which dates back
to the Monroe Doctrine—

KALB: Nicaragua, for example. Let me interrupt. If the Russians were to come through and deliver MIG fighters, missiles,
would you use American military power to wipe out that threat?

HART: Well, let's prevent it from happening by telling the
Nicaraguans—

KALB: But if it were there.

HART: Certainly, I think we must tell the Nicaraguans we will
not tolerate foreign military bases on their soil that jeopardize our
security or that of our allies. But let me point out one thing I think
I have done that perhaps other candidates have not done, that is
spell out conditions under which American military force should
be used generally. That's in the third Georgetown lecture and in
this policy book as well. There I set out six or seven criteria, and
part of those were incorporated in the '84 Democratic platform
and, curiously enough, adopted by Caspar Weinberger when he
was secretary of defense. That includes a clear sense of what our
objective is or our military mission. That includes an understanding about the command structure, so the civilians don't try to
supersede the military commanders once a decision has been
made. It includes exhaustion of political and diplomatic means. It
includes the inability of our allies to defend themselves. It most of
all includes a clear understanding on the part of the American
people as to the costs of the use of American military force, not
only in dollar terms, but in the terms of young American's lives
and that open debate by those American people as to whether
they want to support, on a continuing basis, American military
presence in any part of the world.

KALB: Senator, I said at the beginning of the interview that
I'd like to deal with two things: your ideas and then your capacity
to govern—because that comes right out of your phrase. Now you
may feel—perhaps even what some people sense is a touch of
arrogance—that you can govern this nation better than anybody
else. But before you have that opportunity, the American people
have to vote you in. So they have to feel comfortable with you and
with your positions. Now the polls are saying something very
strange. They are saying that Gary Hart is, among the Democrats,
the most popular and the most unpopular candidate at the very
same time. What does it say to you that the American people can
have this view at the same time, that you're at the top and at the
bottom?

HART: First of all, let me say I don't think you can run the presidency of the United States without—I wouldn't say arrogance—I would say audacity, a certain sense that you among, if not above, the others are best prepared to govern. If you don't have that, you shouldn't run for president. I think the question is whether it's under control, whether it's realistic, whether you have had a chance to size yourself up against the competition. And I recall very vividly as a much younger man in '71 asking George McGovern why he was running, and then in '75 asking Jimmy Carter. They both said the same thing: "Because I'm as good as the others." There is that touch of competitiveness. I think it's in your industry as well as many others. So I would say audacity rather than arrogance. I think the task of any candidate, perhaps particularly or uniquely me in this election, is to demonstrate qualities of character, of leadership, of courage, of independence, of integrity, that are necessary not only to put forward ideas and policies, but to inform, educate the American people, and form consensus through their elected officials for those policies. And my job in this campaign, as I said in New Hampshire, is to let the people decide, to convince them that I can do that.

KALB: Now, before we go any further, I want to sort of stop myself and ask you if there is anything that you yourself wish to volunteer to the American people on this occasion about the various womanizing charges that have been leveled against you this past—

HART: Only those that I've responded to fairly repeatedly in the past, including on national television. I have said that I was very sorry for the mistake that I made. I have said there is no way that anyone can respond to rumors and gossip, particularly in public life. I have confessed my errors and sins, if you will, in a way that I don't think any national leader has done in a long time. I've apologized to my family and just about everyone else. And there comes a point beyond that that people either accept or do not accept that.

KALB: Given what happened last May, why do you feel that the American people should trust you to be their president?

HART: That's a judgment they have to make. I have tried very hard over the course of a 50-year lifetime to live as straightforwardly and honestly as I can. We have a marriage that's lasted almost 30 years. We've raised two great kids. I don't think you can do that and be a very bad person. And I think I've served this country honorably and well for 12 years as a United States senator and run for president and been under a microscope. I never said I was perfect. When I announced in the spring, I said I'll make mistakes—that's because I'm a human being. I think we've got to have realistic standards for our leadership. I don't want to be held to any lower standard than our best presidents, but I don't want to be held to any higher standard either.

KALB: You said recently, and I want to read this quote to you: "I'm as qualified to govern this country as anybody in this race or anybody who has governed this country in the past 200 years."

HART: Did I say that?

KALB: You said it. You said it on MacNeil/Lehrer, and I can get you the date. Now what I want to know—

HART: That is arrogant and I take it back. Mr. Lehrer at the time was pressing me very hard.

KALB: It was through clinched teeth that you said it, but you said it. You've also said quite often, and you said a moment ago, that a principal goal of a president is to educate the American people and to lead them. And you've also said you'd like to spark youthful idealism in America as well. The question I have for you, Senator, is this: Can you lead the American people if, according to the polls, so many of them feel that you have lied to them and that you have conducted your personal life in a way that they don't like? So how can you—

HART: I don't want to quarrel about polls. I don't know which ones you're talking about or how the questions were framed. The fact of the matter is that if so many of them believe that, I won't be elected president. That's when I said, "Let the people decide." The people are the best judge of it, not the press, not the pundits, not the experts, not the party leadership. Let the people decide this. If they don't want me as their president, I won't be their president.

KALB: Don't you feel that a candidate—somebody who is going to be elected president and go before the American people—as you said before, has to be held up to a very high standard.

HART: Yes.

KALB: Can one lie?

HART: No, of course not. But on the other hand, one does have a right of privacy. And the American people don't have a right to know everything about our leaders' lives. That is an issue in this campaign, and I think the American people have to decide how far they want to go. It's not just Gary Hart, it's the caliber and quality of our leadership. Do we want to set up another barrier to participation in public life for young people when we already have an awful lot of deterrents there already?

KALB: What is the barrier that would be set up there?

HART: Well, I think an intrusion into people's personal lives that is unprecedented. Keep in mind, I've had an opportunity this summer to do a good deal of reading about accusations made against George Washington, Thomas Jefferson, Andrew Jackson, just about everybody. Keep in mind also that if you decide your leadership by polls, Harry Truman would probably not have been president. But a lot of people who at one time or another were fairly unpopular ended up getting in the White House or staying in the White House because people got things in perspective and decided what they thought was important.

KALB: Help me through the one part of it that I've never quite understood: When you told the *New York Times* on May 3rd, "Follow me around. I don't care. I'm serious. If anybody wants to put a tail on me, go ahead. They'd be very bored." The *Miami Herald* was not bored that weekend. It came out on May 3rd. The *Miami Herald* story came out on May 3rd. You talked to them two or three weeks before that. Judgment now: Why or how could you have put yourself in a position in the midst of a campaign that could have led to what, in fact, it did lead to?

HART: I will just repeat what I said before: It was a bad mistake. It was a damn fool mistake. I don't think it disqualifies me from governing this country. What I said to the press after weeks and weeks and weeks of trying to knock down, "How are you going to respond to rumors, questions?" was just to say "Follow me around in public." I wasn't doing anything in public that I was ashamed of or could be ashamed of. It didn't occur to me that people would start peeking in my windows and hiding in my bushes. We've never done that for 200 years in this country.

KALB: Let's move on. On November 11th of last year you did a speech at Yale which I considered absolutely remarkable because it dealt with the press and your views about the media and the way in which it covers the political process, and you spoke of a blurring of the distinction between the serious and the sensationalist press. I would like to ask you, because we're interested in that here, give me examples of the serious press and the sensationalist press in the U.S.

HART: I think we all know what those are.

KALB: You tell me.

HART: It's a difference between the *National Enquirer* and the *New York Times*. Where the distinction gets blurred is when a major network takes its lead story from the *National Enquirer*. That I think, is a little different from what we've usually had.

KALB: But the *New York Times* in the case that you're referring to also ran that story. It isn't that the *New York Times* did not run all of those stories.

HART: I understand. But I think you, given your background, and others that have been in political journalism for a long time would be hard pressed to deny that the standards of what is printed today are different from the standards of what were printed even ten years ago.

KALB: I agree. You've made the point time and time again in that speech and on other occasions as well: that the press is much more interested in sex than it is in serious, substantive issues. In effect, you were saying that sex sells and substance doesn't.

HART: Well, do you disagree with that?

KALB: No, but I asked you.

HART: Let me throw a caveat in here because it is being alleged I am running this campaign against the press. I am not saying anything bad against the press, I am answering your questions. This is not Gary Hart attacking the press. What the Yale speech said, you'll recall, was that we are all to blame to the degree we are not demanding and insisting on serious issues, the issues that govern our lives. It's not the press's fault. It's our fault. The consumers decide. We get the information we ask for. As I said at the time, somebody is buying the *National Enquirer*.

KALB: The American people who are going to vote.

HART: Precisely. So this is not my attack, if you will, on the press. What I was trying to do was to say we're trivializing our leadership, which was the essence of the speech. I tried to give ways in which that was happening, and I quoted, as a thesis for that argument, a very eminent historian, Barbara Tuchman, who made exactly that case. She said there's something wrong when we can all get more excited about a politician's personal life in a way that we never have before, but don't get excited when 250 young Americans are killed in Lebanon.

KALB: Senator, I think the issue there—and she was addressing this as well—had to do with judgment. And if a candidate gives the press the option of focusing on sex, then why should the American people give that candidate their trust and their vote?

HART: I don't think any candidate that I know of, including myself, gave that option. I certainly didn't intend to, and didn't want to. You have to go to extraordinary lengths if you're hiding in bushes and peeking in windows and intercepting telephone calls to find out something about a person. Let me give you—

KALB: Was the press intercepting calls?

HART: They told me they had. But in any case, I don't want to get into a quarrel about that. I was also told they were trying to put listening devices on my walls. They deny that happened, but a reliable source told me that. That was another issue I was trying to bring up in that speech. If you say it is now permissible to print anything, you have also said it is now permissible to find out anything any way you can. Now that's a privacy issue the American people ought to be worried about.

KALB: It is a privacy issue, there's no question about it. But don't you feel that since there is only one person who's going to have his or her finger on the button, there's something very special about that one person.

HART: Of course.

KALB: It isn't as though you can protect, once that person goes into the ring and says, "I want to be your president." You are also affirming that even he at that point—

HART: Or she.

KALB: Or she should have the right to say, "This far and no further."

HART: But that's what we've said for 200 years.

KALB: For 200 years we didn't have the kind of technology that we have today.

HART: So if we can find it out, then we should find it out. Is that it?

KALB: Yes, supposing that is addressed.

HART: Well, good-bye to an awful lot of future leaders in this country because I know firsthand that a lot of people won't put up with that because then you legitimize—

KALB: Let me ask you this.

HART: Let me say, the historic standard, Marvin, for 200 years has been that a leader's, a public person's private life was private until it affected their ability to govern. That was restated by a very eminent historian or columnist George Will in a recent edition of *Newsweek*. That we have had as a standard in this country for 200 years. You are saying because we can intercept conversations, we can use lenses to look in people's windows—

KALB: I am not saying anything about intercepting conversations. I did address the issue of the technology.

HART: That's what technology means.

KALB: The question again reverts to judgment calls made by the candidates themselves.

HART: I made a mistake. I have categorized it as a damn fool mistake. The question on the part of the American people is whether that mistake disqualifies me from leading the country. Only the American people can decide, and that's why I got back in this race.

KALB: I want to ask you—

HART: And it has, by the way, not disqualified leaders in the past.

KALB: Granted. I just want to ask you if, in your mind, you are capable of separating judgment into two categories?

HART: No.

KALB: There's a judgment that has to do with one's private life, there is judgment that might be addressed to nuclear weapons or the economy or something like that.

HART: Mr. Kalb, I have talked more about my private life than probably any living American—more than Ronald Reagan or anybody else. I have said and my wife has said that we have been separated. We have gone into the details of that. We have talked about it.

KALB: And sort of enough is enough.

HART: Well, for God's sake.

KALB: Let me just ask you—

HART: But the issue of judgment, if that's what you're after.

KALB: It's not just what I'm after, Senator. A lot of people—

HART: It must be judged over a lifetime. And I was under a microscope in 1984 when I ran for president for six months. We had reporters asking neighbors why we put fences around our backyard—for our dogs. Who paid for the fences? Who came to our parties? Were they loud parties? Was there drinking? It's not as if I just parachuted down onto earth. I've been around in public life for more than 15 years—

KALB: One more question on that.

HART: And judgment also has to do with whether you voted against the Reagan tax cuts in '81, whether you opposed the MX missile, whether you fought against Reaganomics, whether you fought against Contra aid. I have broken no laws, I have not lied to Congress, I have not deceived the public in this regard, and I have not shredded any papers, and no money changed hands. And we've got to get this thing in some kind of perspective.

KALB: Senator, let me ask you the last question on this issue. Why is it then that there is so much attention devoted to Gary Hart on this issue and really not much at all to any of the other candidates?

HART: Well, I don't know. I think it's a combination of a lot of things. I have run against the tide, I've overcome a lot of odds all the way through my political life. I worked for George McGovern. When I ran for the Senate, when I ran for reelection, when I ran for president, and I have not particularly because I wanted to. I've always been bucking the odds. I became a serious candidate in '84 against those odds. All of a sudden the question wasn't what are the ideas, but who is this guy? Then as the emerging front-runner that continuation of who is this guy in a way that is beyond, I think, our normal standard. I can't necessarily account for it.

KALB: Senator, we are at that blessed moment in the program where I stop asking questions and the audience begins.

HART: I thought this was fun.

KALB: Our first questioner is Kathryn Dominguez, an economist and one of the newer members of the Kennedy School faculty. Professor Dominguez.

DOMINGUEZ: Senator Hart, as you probably well know, a number of Latin American countries have recently announced a moratorium on their interest payments and debt to U.S. banks. You have been quoted as saying that good economic policy is good foreign policy. Given that, would you be in favor of intervening in the debt crisis? Or more specifically, do you think it would be politically feasible for the U.S. government to intervene on behalf of the debtor countries, given the potentially adverse effects such actions could have within the U.S.?

HART: I don't think we have any choice. I said, again referring to the Georgetown foreign policy lectures in June of '86, that first of all, international economics must become a primary foreign policy tool for the first time in our history. And second, using a specific instance of that, I talked about the Third World debt, and particularly, the 300 to 400 billion dollar Latin American debt—Mexico, Brazil, Argentina, and the others—and I said that the United States must no longer be acting as the primary collection agency for American private lenders or even international institutions.

What I did advocate was a government-led effort by all the lenders, both private and public, national and international, to restructure those debts over time—considering debt equity swaps which others have since begun to look at, notification of banks that they're not going to get their money back on the terms that they hoped they would five or ten years ago when those loans were made, and they were good loans, and at the same time requiring that debtor nations undertake some regulatory tax land reforms to get their economies back on their feet. Now, that's not just an altruistic and a right foreign policy of helping new democracies stabilize. It's also in our economic interest. Our trade deficit with Latin America, as you well know, is bigger in gross terms and percentage terms than our trade deficit with Japan, and the reason isn't because of Latin American protectionism. The reason is because they can't afford to buy our products. So that debt is crushing American workers. It's in our interest from a security point of view, a political point of view, and an economic point of view to restructure those debts. We have no choice.

QUESTION: A major concern that individuals engaged in basic medical research have is a continuance and growth of federal funding for these projects. What policy and program would you establish in your administration to ensure growth in these funds and a protection of these funds from across-the-board budget cuts and/or the transfer of these funds to military uses?

HART: First of all, I'm against across-the-board budget cuts. I think Gramm-Rudman is a fraud and very bad public policy. That's why, together with Senator Moynihan and others, I led the fight against it—and I think we got 23 or 24 votes in the Senate. Again, it wasn't the popular thing to do, but it's bad policy. It's terrible policy for a lot of reasons that we don't have time to go into. When I talk about investment, I try to be very specific. Senator Chiles of Florida and I, on the Budget Committee, put forward on behalf of our party in the Senate in 1986, an investment package. It's contained again in these documents, and I will elaborate on that in the coming days as to what I—

KALB: You carry that like a Bible.

HART: Well, I'm the only candidate for president who has put anything like this out, and I'm proud of it. It is the beef and it is a blueprint for this country's future. But I think every candidate for president ought to put forward a budget saying where the revenues will come from, where the cuts will come from, and also if you believe as I do that we have to invest more, where that investment will go. Where I have advocated investment is in education: American Defense Education Act, High Technology Act, In-Job Training, Job Training Partnership Act, and the ideals for investment in job training and job transition that I and others have put forward—and finally, in a research program in biotechnology in medical research, in energy research, and in environmental research that you can't guarantee against budget cuts, but certainly wouldn't be cut in any Hart administration under Gramm-Rudman or any other way.

QUESTION: If you are to become president, what would you do about the growing problems of poverty, specifically an increasing percentage of blacks and women living underneath the poverty line?

HART: We have to continue to finance those elements, both the New Deal and the Great Society, often shorthanded as the safety net, which had been cut very badly. Contrary to what Ronald Reagan has said under this administration for the past seven years, those programs are for the people who cannot help themselves. That turns out, unfortunately, to be a majority of people in what we call welfare—dependent children, single-parent households, usually women, and elderly people. All people who cannot hold jobs. Now Senator Moynihan has put forward a proposal for welfare reform which is addressed to those people including some of the women who are single heads of households. Some of the policy has been implemented by Governor Dukakis in this state, and transitions people from poverty and welfare and dependency into the job market. That requires a stable income base in terms of housing, nutrition, health, and the basic necessities of life in exchange for job training and job location. That seems to me the only policy of welfare reform that makes any sense: a solid safety net under those who cannot look after themselves, increased housing for the homeless, which is a scandal in this country, and attacking the root cause of the worst thing Ronald Reagan has done to this country, and that's increasing children in poverty.

QUESTION: In the wake of the Iran-Contra scandal, the people of this country are increasingly frustrated with the covert seizures of power which have been going on in the executive branch. The other candidates haven't really addressed this. What are you going to do to bring the CIA and the National Security Council back under the constitutional framework of checks and balances?

HART: It's a serious problem. The first thing that happened to me when I went to the United States Senate, three weeks after I got there in '75, was I was appointed to what was called the Church Committee. That was a shorthand word, the chairman being the late Senator Frank Church, for the Senate Select Committee to Investigate the Intelligence Community. We did that for two years and issued a comprehensive five-volume report calling for reforms in the intelligence community—CIA defense intelligence, National Security Agency, and all the others, including the Drug Enforcement Agency—that were partly implemented including the creation of an oversight capability in the Congress that meant something. The problem is that when Ronald Reagan came back into office that era of reform was reversed, under the late director Bill Casey. Given the kind of policies this administration pursued, we went back into the bad old business of covert operations, destabilization, and I wouldn't be surprised if five or ten years from now in another investigation, we will find out that there may have been assassination attempts carried out under this administration as we found out in the late '50s and early '60s. And then I served for a couple years on that first oversight committee.

All I can tell you is as president I would appoint a director of the CIA and a director of the entire intelligence community that would insist that no covert operation go forward without a piece of paper with my signature on it as president. And not one of those pieces of paper would be shredded. And if I authorized any covert operation, and that operation was approved by the Congress as is required by law in a timely manner, and it went sour or it went wrong, I would accept responsibility for it. Now that is the best guarantee you can have against rogue elephant operations in the intelligence community.

QUESTION: Senator Hart, the last two administrations have made major strides towards deregulating our energy industries. For example, gas prices have been decontrolled, natural gas pipelines are being converted to common carriers, and in the electric utility business, entrepreneurs are allowed to generate electricity on a deregulated basis. In your administration, what would you do to further these trends?

HART: I would further many of them. I have been, as I quote, a liberal democrat in favor of taking off price controls on energy, particularly newly discovered energy. That was not, again, a popular position in the 1970s, but it was a national security issue for me. How I would regulate energy, as I indicated, is to impose a $10 a barrel tariff on imported oil. Now that is an interference in the marketplace, and the justification for that philosophically is this: Markets cannot guarantee a hot lunch for a poor child, markets cannot guarantee this country will be sufficiently independent of foreign oil. That we don't have to go to war for it and lose young American lives unnecessarily, that's how I justify that interference in the marketplace. But I would go back to the energy independence policies of the 1970s that included not only specific deregulation of new supplies of oil, but also incentives for development of alternative renewable supplies and incentives most of all for conservation. The Reagan free market approach to energy is not working, and that's why we've got ships in the Persian Gulf today.

QUESTION: Mr. Senator, in 1986 you went to Jordan and spoke to King Hussein, and then you spoke to the Prime Minister of Israel. But you did not speak to the Palestinian people who are under occupation. So you don't know how painful it is to be under occupation. Now my question is this: Do you believe in a secular Palestinian state in which the people can live in peace and they don't have to throw any stones at the Israelis? And if that is the case, then I believe that you don't believe in the U.S. Constitution. Thank you very much.

HART: What I said and will continue to say is that until Israel's security and survival is guaranteed by not only the Palestinians but by the surrounding states, there probably won't be a resolution of the Palestinian homeland or statehood issue. When the Arab nations, or when the confrontation nations, or when the bordering nations are willing to make that basic guarantee and accept Israel's existence, then I think that opens the way for some resolution and frankly brings some pressure to bear on the Israelis to seriously negotiate that resolution. What we should not do as Americans is impose our own judgment or will on those negotiating partners. What we ought to be doing is to bring them together every way we can. The way I tried to do after visiting with King Hussein and after visiting with President Mubarek was to put forward an economic step for the West Bank that would have given greater hope and opportunity to the unemployed Palestinian youth.

QUESTION: Senator Hart, you've talked about economic restructuring. Yet the first item you mentioned in terms of balancing the budget is nothing short of trade protection. It's the oil import fee which is trade protection for the big oil companies. You've justified it on national security grounds, which is arguable. But what isn't arguable is that by having trade protections for the oil industry, you may start a new series of trade wars that would be damaging economically.

HART: Let me ask you this. If this is trade protection for the big oil companies. Why are they opposed to this fee?

QUESTION: Because some of them support it and some of them oppose it.

HART: No. All of them oppose it that I know of because they are net importers of oil. They are making more money off oil coming into this country that they're bringing in from the Persian Gulf than they are from drilling for oil in this country. And that's why the oil industry has always been against this. Even the independents were against it until the last year or two. Let me tell you, the oil industry in this country is powerful. If they wanted this, they could turn up more than 15 votes in the United States Senate, which is all we got the last time.

QUESTION: In the survey of international issues that opened this program, I noticed the omission of South Africa as an international issue. And it is my hope that in your new administration, in your new ideas approach to things, that you'll come up with some new ideas for South Africa. Could you elaborate on some of those new ideas and also put them into a broader human rights perspective?

HART: I wish I had some new approaches in South Africa. My ideas are like many other people's: new in the sense they're different from the Reagan administration's. I was among the leadership that advocated and fought for sanctions that were imposed over the resistance of this President and this administration— finally, and happily, and thankfully. Do they go far enough? Probably not. But I think we as Americans ought to take some leadership from what is an increasingly frustrated, if you will, peaceful and moderate leadership in South Africa—Bishop Tutu particularly. As to where, how we should go, there was, as you know, a debate in this country that sanctions were going to hurt the very people they were designed to help. I don't know the answer to that. But if leadership like Bishop Tutu says, "We need this, we are willing to pay the price for it as the people who will suffer for it, then we must do it. I think overall the one further thing that we can do and should do is organize our democratic allies to themselves bring greater pressure to bear on the South African apartheid government. We have not done that under Reagan. I would try to. Do I have some brilliant new insight in the area? I'm afraid I don't.

QUESTION: Senator, I notice the fourth point of the Gary Hart plan is an interesting word, service, and you haven't had a chance to elaborate on that. I've heard that the Gary Hart campaign is the only forum I've heard the term *national service* come out. So I would like to give you an opportunity to tell us what that is.

HART: Thank you. I have advocated the creation of a voluntary national service. There are people involved from my campaign that have undertaken to create that on a local basis here in the Boston area, and I applaud them and reward them. I think part of the reason they are supporting my candidacy is because of the sense that this campaign hopes to bring, particularly to young people, but not necessarily just one age group, that we owe something to this country. I don't think the country is prepared for a mandatory national service. But I think to give young people an opportunity to give something back to their country—for the same reasons that I got into politics, under John Kennedy—is something very important. I think we ought to have a literacy corps. I think young people getting guaranteed student loans should be required, if you will, in exchange for that, to give a few hours a week to help educate, teach a young person or adult how to read. The list goes on of things that people who receive something from the government ought to be prepared to give back to our country.

KALB: Senator, our final questioner is Professor Joseph Nye, an expert on arms control and director of our Center for Science and International Affairs.

NYE: Senator, you have spoken a number of times against the spread of nuclear weapons. There are now seven or eight countries that have nuclear weapons, but you have spoken mostly in generalities. I wonder what new ideas specifically you have about the spread of nuclear weapons to countries like Israel, South Africa, Pakistan?

HART: The one specific that I did mention in a rapid run-through of my arms control policy was a freeze on the production. An international freeze on the production of plutonium and weapons grade material is very hard to enforce. I understand the difficulties of that as you and other experts in the area know. But we ought to begin to try to take the lead. We have strengthened to a degree the international inspection capability of the International Atomic Inspection Agency. We can use that, I think, as a format to challenge other nations to join us in strict inspection of the weapons grade material that's being produced. We also ought to be exercising more political and diplomatic leadership in getting international nonproliferation agreements, which is very hard for us to do when we are encouraging other nations to develop a nuclear capability that can be made into a weapons or military capability. And that's why I have joined Senator Glenn and others in being very critical of this nation's policy with regard to Pakistan and other nations and proliferation. But I think it's one of the most serious problems we face. There were 140 tons of plutonium in the world as of four or five years ago. That's an awful lot of material to make weapons with. We've got to stop producing it. Freeze that production and we can take the lead.

QUESTION: How will you apply that to Israel and South Africa.

HART: Well, it's a problem, as you know. Once the horse is out of the barn, it's a little late to close the barn door. Here I think we have to insist to the degree we can—given the realities of national sovereignty on international inspection of power plants as to whether they are in fact being used to reprocess and putting the international spotlight on nations that refuse to disclose what their nuclear capability is. Further than that, there's not a military solution that I know of.

KALB: Senator, in about 15 seconds, which do you enjoy writing more: fiction or nonfiction?

HART: Depends on the circumstances. I've enjoyed writing novels, and I hope to do that again as president or beyond that.

Candidates '88

A CONVERSATION WITH
BRUCE BABBITT

Photo by Martha Stewart

About the Candidate

If there had been a special primary in which only political corre-
spondents could vote, Bruce Babbitt would have won going away.
Reporters liked him. They liked his candor, his intelligence, his
consistency, and his easygoing, deadpan humor. They thought he
deserved a break, and in a spurt of favorable newspaper and
magazine articles they tried to give him one. The voters, it would
later develop, thought differently. Babbitt would remark wryly
that if his campaign had done nothing else, at least it had exposed
the vaunted power of the press as a myth.

Babbitt's candidacy was like a civil war between style and
substance. Style was his weakness, substance his strength. He
regarded his television technique as abysmal; many who watched
him on the early TV debates could only agree. He tried hard to
improve. ("If they can teach Mr. Ed to talk on TV," he said
hopefully, "they can teach me.") And as his performance on
"Candidates '88"—which he would later describe as the high point
of his campaign—showed, he did improve. But his image of
nervousness, awkwardness, and twitchiness was too well established to be erased.

By contrast, Babbitt had a carefully developed and coherent
world view, with an impressive set of proposals for restoring
American economic competitiveness. He was the only candidate
with a fully thought out plan for seriously reducing the budget
deficit—including a 5 percent national sales tax, which he called a
"progressive national consumption tax." As he fought for his share
of attention in the crowd of candidates, he came to emphasize his
commitment to higher taxes as proof of courage and character. It
did win him attention. Whether it won him votes was questiona-
ble.

Babbitt, 49, came to the race with a record of solid accomplish-
ment in the two terms he had served as governor of Arizona. He
took one of the most hidebound and conservative states in the
union and more or less singlehandedly pushed its state government
into the 20th century, as even his Republican opponents in Phoenix
admitted. A leading advocate of what came to be known as neo-
liberal thinking within the Democratic party, he emphasized de-
centralizing solutions, fiscal responsibility, and public-private partnerships.

The scion of northern Arizona's most prominent family, Babbitt
graduated from Notre Dame and was preparing to become a
geologist when he came face to face with the poverty of the Third
World during a field trip to Bolivia in 1962. He switched to Harvard

Law School, participated in the civil rights movement and the antipoverty program, and got elected attorney general of Arizona. He became governor by accident when both the incumbent resigned and the lieutenant governor died. But he made the most of his good fortune, winning near-universal respect in the state for his political and policy skills. He won respect as a presidential candidate, too; and although he left the race after a dismal finish in New Hampshire, no one will be surprised if he eventually turns up in a high post in some future Democratic administration.

H.H.

The Interview

KALB: Governor, you believe so strongly in the need to raise taxes in order to lower the budget deficit—

BABBITT: What a way to start an interview.

KALB: —That you literally stood up for the idea during an NBC debate in December. I want to ask you two questions in reference to that, one having to do with taxes and one having to do with why you felt the need to stand up. But the taxes first: You are proposing a 5 percent national consumption tax, a kind of value-added tax, as it is referred to in Western Europe, or a national sales tax. Critics have already said that will place an unfair burden upon the poor. Aside from that point, why do you feel that this kind of tax is the best way of addressing the budget deficit?

BABBITT: Marvin, the important thing is the deficit. We've had a long run in this country of candidates who are ignoring the issue and obviously compromising our economic future. Now, a lot less important than the kind of tax is having the guts to say the word—say we have to cut expenditures and raise taxes. Why a consumption tax? It's a tax that's easily administered. It economically makes sense because it dampens down consumption rather than taking income. That's an incentive, I think, to savings and investment. Can you make it progressive? Yes. How do you do that? You can lower the bottom income tax bracket, you can exempt food or medicine, or you can mail rebates to those who don't pay income taxes. I would say it's a progressive consumption tax that makes economic sense, and it's part of the truth-telling that's necessary to address our economic future.

KALB: But, is it, in your view, the best way of addressing the budget deficit problem?

BABBITT: Yes, it is. Obviously there's no silver bullet, but I think candor compels that we admit the deficit does matter. It's the key to economic growth in the future, and the only way we're going to get at it is two things: cut expenditures and raise taxes. I believe a consumption tax is the best form of taxation.

KALB: Governor, let me ask you about another major proposal of yours that has to do with this means testing. You'd like to make certain that all the money earmarked for social programs in fact ends up with the poor, not in the middle or the upper classes. Two questions: How would you do it in the first place? How would that work? How would it be applied?

BABBITT: The concept of needs testing is a way of setting priorities—it's a kind of question. In a sense, it's the opposite of Gramm-Rudman, if I can start with Gramm-Rudman.

KALB: You don't approve of it?

BABBITT: It's a moral outrage to elect representatives who go to Washington and say, "Notwithstanding that we were elected to make some choices, we don't have the guts to do it, so cut everything across the board." AIDS research, your student loan, the important things will all get cut equally with military bands, Star Wars, presidential libraries, that sort of stuff. Now, there's got to be a moral principal behind budget cutting. The needs test asks simply, Is that program necessary? More importantly, is it focused on the basis of need, whether it's mortgage subsidies or entitlements, farm subsidies, whatever it is.

KALB: It's all for social spending, though. You're not talking about a needs test for a tank, for example.

BABBITT: Why not? Yeah, sure.

KALB: For any kind of government spending?

BABBITT: Sure. A needs test question for the Bradley fighting vehicle or for the MX missile might have prevented them from being built.

KALB: Is this something, Governor, that you feel can be administered by the executive branch of the government?

BABBITT: Absolutely. It's a question that the president must ask and answer. Now, the problem with this political debate is that it's a giant wasteland out there. Everybody is saying the deficit is important, but God forbid any one of them should be caught answering a specific. I'll tell you how to apply it—your second home down on the shore, for example.

KALB: Mine?

BABBITT: I can apply it to farm subsidies, to home purchases, you name it. The home purchase is a nice example. How many of you have second homes? Well, this is a Harvard audience. I would have expected more. But it's students. With subsidized home purchases through the mortgage interest deduction, it's a good idea for first homes, but why do we do it for second homes when there are homeless people that we are not helping at all?

KALB: How much money are you going to save in terms of taking care of that budget deficit by handling this particular item that you're focusing on?

BABBITT: You're telling me that's small potatoes.

KALB: In effect, yeah. What's the big potatoes that you're talking about? What's going to cut into the deficit?

BABBITT: Farm subsidies, I think, is a nice one—$30 billion. The problem is that the subsidies are going to the wrong people, they're going to corporations, to agribusinesses—$10 million subsidy checks, $10 million to one farm in California. Some farm, huh? Some family.

Obviously, the big fish are the entitlement programs. I think we have to be honest and admit that.

KALB: Social security?

BABBITT: Sure, and my contention is, What's unreasonable about saying we should subject social security benefits to taxation for those who can afford to pay it? Why should the Mellons and the du Ponts have tax-exempt benefits? Does that make sense? That's what a needs test is about. It's moral criteria, a liberal criterion about how you avoid this mindless kind of cutting, and say, in the progressive tradition, we can provide benefits to people who need them, and tanks that work, and defense systems that make sense.

KALB: Let's say if you applied this test across the board as you just indicated, within say two or three years of a Babbitt presidency, where would the budget deficit be by your projections?

BABBITT: My target would be to cut $100 billion out. I think that's a nice, manageable target.

KALB: You mean in your first term, over a four-year period?

BABBITT: I'd do that over two years.

KALB: You feel that you can? You've run the numbers through the computers and that's the way they come out?

BABBITT: I've run the numbers through by a young guy named Bart Gelman, who is my research assistant, and I've put them in a speech, and they're absolutely out there. You can go read them, you can look them up. They're there. It's not that hard. Now, the theory, I think, is that you have to do both. You have to have expenditure cuts over the next couple of years of about $40 billion, and then revenue increases of about $50 to $60 billion, which equals $100 billion. I think you can sell it by saying, "Look, our economic future depends on our ability to do it. If we're going to create jobs in this economy—in which the government is using a giant credit card and saying the due bills will be paid by these students in the form of a lowered standard of living, declining economy, and loss of leadership—we have to have the guts to step up." I think the way to solve it is to say it will be used for deficit reduction. A dollar down, a dollar up will cut expenditures and raise revenues. Have you heard any other candidate say that?

KALB: A couple who have come here have offered numbers and have talked in what they took to be specifics.

BABBITT: Yeah, oil import fees.

KALB: You have, in fact, stood up for this idea during the NBC debate.

BABBITT: Be careful or it will come again.

KALB: A number of people who find you an extremely attractive and very intelligent candidate are nevertheless disappointed by their inability to explain your feeling that you had to stand up, why you felt the need to go on to a skit on the "Saturday Night Live" program. In other words, I guess the question is related to the way in which the political process takes place.

BABBITT: God, this is great. He's saying Bruce Babbitt is too frivolous. I haven't heard that for a long time.

KALB: I'm trying to ask this question: Did you feel yourself at this particular point in the campaign so frustrated by your inability to break out and become one of the acknowledged front-runners on the Democratic side that you felt the need to engage in this kind of television gimmickry, because I think, depending on your answer, that it may say something about the political process. And that's what I'd be interested in finding out your views.

BABBITT: Sure, I think that during 1987 there's been what I would call a politics of *People* magazine and *National Enquirer*. It hasn't exactly been focused on issues. And to some measure, I've kind of been out there in the wilderness making these points, always looking for a way to underline my point of contention. I began in the early debates by asking questions. You remember, I asked Governor Dukakis, "I'll give you a softball, give me two or three domestic cuts." Nothing happened, and I did it one-on-one. But what I was looking for was a way I could pose a question to all of them at once, and I figured that Tom Brokaw wasn't going to give me a chance to go down that whole list. How do I ask a question and put them all on the spot at once? And that gave rise to a challenge to stand up.

KALB: Is it in your view that the political process right now places such a low premium on intelligence? I mean one of the ironic accusations against Bruce Babbitt is that he's too intellectual. Does that mean the American people have such a short attention span, even when they're electing their own president, that they can't listen to substance over a period of more than 30 seconds?

BABBITT: The problem is not the American people. The problem is the leadership across the board in this country. What do you do when political candidates won't lead by talking honestly? What do you do when the corporate leaders of this country are saying, "We're going to compete and restore a sense of American leadership by impoverishing workers, by cutting wages, by going for a Hong Kong economy," instead of really leading and drawing the productivity out of people? What do you say about a White House in which Mike Deaver is selling access to the Oval Office for $150,000 a minute? When the attorney general is on the wrong side of the grand jury? Now, I think that's just a way of answering your question by saying it's hard to blame the American people, the problem is a failure of leadership.

KALB: Do you think part of the problem is the process that we all see you go through—not just you personally, but all of the presidential candidates? Another candidate had Uncle Sam on stilts precede him into a room in order to get somebody's attention.

BABBITT: God, I never thought of that.

KALB: Let's deal with a few more of the specific ideas you may have for governing this country, Governor. You've talked in the past about a workplace democracy, a way of getting workers actually involved in the ownership of the plant in which they work. I assume that to be a way of increasing the competitiveness of the American workplace. You've said that by 1996 you'd like to have two-thirds of the American workers participating to some degree, anyway, in the ownership of their plant. Two questions: As president how would you make that happen? How would it work?

BABBITT: I think it's an important concept, a big one. Rather than cutting wages and telling people you have to work longer and earn less to compete—the Hong Kong model—I think what we do is try to bring out the best, the initiative, in workers by listening to them, by asking for their cooperation, and by sharing the profits. Your question is, How am I going to do that? Obviously, much as I'd like to, as president of the United States, I'm not going to walk into the board room at General Motors and start handing out their stock to the employees. That's not my function. I think you use the bully pulpit. Instead of busting the air controllers union, sending a message that we ought to raise and exacerbate the tensions in the workplace, you start talking about these concepts. There are some economists, I must concede, at a neighboring university down the Charles River here—Martin Weitzman, some of those guys—who talk very compellingly about how to set up incentives in the tax code to give special preference to profit sharing, to employee stock ownership. The concept of sharing, of motivating people by saying you have a stake in the results.

KALB: I've seen a lot of this happen myself in Western Europe to some good effect. Are you using that as a model for your own proposal?

BABBITT: Sure, those are models, but there are better ones right here in the American economy. There's a company called Lincoln Electric in Cleveland, Ohio, which has been at it for 50 years. Procter & Gamble has had plans like this, and Ford Motor Company is moving in this direction. America is a huge, diverse laboratory full of really interesting examples. It seems to me that what the president does is from the bridge of the ship, looking at where we're going in the world, holds up the good examples and tries to put the moral authority of the office behind them. At the same time you point out the abuse. I was in Iowa last week saying that IBP is a corporate outlaw. People say that's pretty strong stuff. And I say, "Well, I'm running for president, and I think what they're doing is an outrage," and I think that's what campaigns are about: having the courage to say it.

KALB: Do you think as president, if you were elected, you'd be able to stand up before a national audience and just pick on a company and say that's a bad guy and that's a good one?

BABBITT: If they're really worthy, if they're bad enough to be worthy of that kind of attention, sure. That's what leadership is about—moral values. That's lacking in Washington now. That's why we have all these speculators running wild on Wall Street. Boesky and Deaver have kind of become symbols of the last seven or eight years. A quick killing, a speculative casino is what it's all about. Why don't we start honoring work and talking about the people who make things and produce things?

KALB: Governor, I'd like to move on to the time you were governor in the state of Arizona. You had to deal, obviously, with the problems of illegal immigration, and you had to deal with the constituency, a significant part of which is Hispanic. You speak Spanish. As president, how would you deal more effectively with the problems of illegal immigration?

BABBITT: Marvin, I'd start by trying to get at the root causes. I mean, suppose you were 20 years old living in the mountains somewhere in Mexico or Central America, trying to raise a family in an economy where the standard of living had dropped 50 percent in the last five years. What would you do? I know what I'd do: head for the border real fast. I met a kid in El Salvador at one of these return centers the Immigration Service sets up. He told me he was deported from the United States 17 times. I said, "That's a lot," and he said, "You'll never keep me out, because I don't have a chance here in my country." What that talks about, it seems to me, is dealing thoughtfully and decisively with the debt issues that are destroying those economies, redrawing the trading agreements to give them stronger access to American markets, working strongly on the economic issues. Obviously, you have to police the border, you have to do the best you can, but it's always a matter of a finger in the dike until we change the root conditions that are causing so much trouble in Central America and particularly in Mexico. Mexico is a tremendous problem. The President is obsessed with Nicaragua. I think he wakes up in the night with the ghosts of Nicaragua parading across the stage with this, "They're reading Marxist books down there," and that country has two million people. Mexico has 82 million people. Do you ever hear him say anything about that? That's both, I think, the problem and the opportunity.

KALB: In fairness to the President, I believe one of the first foreign leaders he met was the president of Mexico.

BABBITT: I remember that; they met and the President gave him a rifle as a present.

KALB: Governor, as far as the issue of the Spanish language, do you feel that, given the number of Hispanics in the United States now, that Spanish should become in effect—de facto, I suppose—the second official language of this country?

BABBITT: The word "official" is kind of a pejorative term.

KALB: That's why I tried to soften it. De facto.

BABBITT: We should be a country of many languages. We must, as we now move into this kind of unitary international world, stress the learning of languages.

KALB: But you know what I'm talking about. We're talking here about whether you would actually use Spanish along with English in many, many states in the Sun Belt to teach about American history and everything else.

BABBITT: English should be the language of instruction in commerce and daily intercourse in the United States. We should encourage the teaching of other languages and we should be aggressive about bilingual education. But do we want to be Quebec? No, definitely not. (Speaking Spanish) Enough.

KALB: You'll have to roll some slides for us. Governor, I'd like to ask you a few questions about your Catholicism, not as a personal matter, but how your religion might affect the way in which you would govern. You've described yourself as a "rigorous

Catholic." On the issue of abortion, do you see abortion as the killing of human life?

BABBITT: As a Catholic, yes. As a governor, I understand that there are many religious and ethical groups who come to a different conclusion, and that it is an ethical issue on which the very existence of so much diversity sends a message to public officials that it should be left outside the area of legislation—to the ethical conscience of individuals.

KALB: So that to be consistent from a Catholic point of view, you would favor a constitutional ban against abortion, but as a legislator—

BABBITT: As a Catholic, absolutely not. I am pro choice. It is an ethical issue that should remain outside of legislation, outside constitutional dictates.

KALB: On an issue such as revolutionary theology, which is widespread in Latin America, the Pope has taken a very strong position, even chastised a number of the priests who were part of the social upheaval, working out of the church in order to advance social needs, as they see it. The Catholic Church says no, officially. Do you support or oppose the Pope's position on this?

BABBITT: Well, look, if you become a priest or a bishop, I suppose, you acknowledge that the Pope tells you what to do. I happen to think the Catholic Church has been a tremendously progressive force in Latin America. That wasn't always the case. They used to automatically be palling around with all those guys wearing gold uniforms standing on balconies, resisting change. The wonderful story of Latin America is that more often than not, the Catholic Church is now on the side of the people, and liberation theology is just one manifestation of that. I think it's a tremendous change.

KALB: And a change for the good?

BABBITT: Oh, absolutely. Absolutely.

KALB: Governor, a little bit more, then, on foreign policy. You have said on the issue of America's nuclear deterrent, I quote, "We will never be the first to use nuclear weapons in any conflict." That sounds very much to me like the Soviet pledge of no first strike. It also seems to be a very radical change in the American nuclear deterrent position over the last 25 years led by both Republican and Democrats in the White House. Am I correct on both counts?

BABBITT: Marvin, no, that's not a complete sentence, that first quote.

KALB: Give me what your feeling is, please.

BABBITT: My feeling is this: We have to move as far as we can toward a posture of no first use.

KALB: That is not then a pledge of no first use?

BABBITT: No, because we simply aren't in a position to do that, particularly in Europe, and in a sense, an absolute pledge compromises deterrence. The problem is we've gone in the opposite direction in Europe. General Galvin over there says, "In the first week of a conventional war, I will be driven to the use of nuclear weapons." Now, my point, and it's one that somehow isn't being debated, how can the United States of America put itself in the position of a NATO strategy which says, "In the event, unlikely though it may be, of an outbreak of hostilities, we'll be firing nuclear weapons and escalating to Armageddon in the first week of a conventional war."

KALB: But you know why that's the case.

BABBITT: The reason it's the case is because we've become overreliant on cheap nuclear weapons. And we've abandoned our responsibility to think carefully about the conventional defense of Europe. How is it that we, for example, integrate the French back into NATO? How is it we have some modest increases in defense spending, build up the reserves, reconfigure the American support? We've gotten lazy. We've gotten lazy by relying on nuclear weapons. I'm saying we ought to try to reverse that as much as we can, by strengthening our conventional defenses.

KALB: Let us shift to the Middle East for a moment. There have been in recent weeks Palestinian riots and demonstrations on the Gaza Strip and the West Bank. In recent weeks as well the Reagan administration has chosen to abstain rather than to veto a U.N. condemnation of Israel for the deportation of a number of the Palestinians. As President, would you have vetoed or, like the Reagan administration, abstained on that issue?

BABBITT: Well, unaccustomed as I am to supporting the Reagan administration, I believe that their position on those two issues in the United Nations was correct. That's really not the issue. The issue is, What are we going to do about a situation which has become gridlocked? I think we're headed toward a tragedy in the Middle East if America continues to acquiesce in a psychology which says the problem is insoluble and therefore we'll quit trying—in Jerusalem there's a gridlock. The Israeli process is beginning to look like American politics. There's no consensus for anything, and there's drift. And we all know that that's ultimately going to threaten Israel, it's going to threaten our interests, and that it's up to the United States to have some active diplomacy in the Middle East. After all, a guy named Jimmy Carter pulled off an extraordinary success.

KALB: Specifically, you're president and you address that problem. What specifically would you do?

BABBITT: Well, I would go to the Israelis and remind them that America is now supporting their economy and their military forces at unprecedented levels, that our commitment to Israel is correct, properly placed, and I would reaffirm it. But I would say, "The best thing a friend can do for another friend is to speak the truth. And the truth is you must take stronger initiatives and be more creative about how it is you move toward forms of autonomy for the residents of Gaza and the West Bank." I would then go to the Arabs and say, "You guys better wake up. I've got the United States Navy in the Persian Gulf defending all of you, and I'd like something in return, and it consists of a little more creativity and a little more emotion." I'd go to the Egyptians and say, "You were the pioneers, we can bring you back in the process." I'd like to stiffen King Hussein's spine a little bit. I'd try to isolate Assad. I think the events in the Arab world are moving him off to the periphery. Have you heard him saying anything in Washington? That's the problem, we've checked out of the process. I don't know what the ultimate result is. I know what the principles are. The principles are written in the Camp David Accords: motion toward autonomy for the Arabs, security for Israel. And we have to start searching for it.

KALB: So I'm clear on what you just said, you would, as far as the Israelis are concerned, go there with a threat of a cutback in U.S. economic and military support unless they did something?

BABBITT: You don't threaten your friends. You just remind them of the facts.

KALB: And assume they would pursue it?

BABBITT: Sure. The Israelis are on dead center because of some very complex problems in their own society, but also because they're not feeling any pressure from us.

KALB: As a leverage, the pressure you would apply, for example, on the Egyptians, who also receive a significant amount of American money, is the same? The threat of a cutback in order to—

BABBITT: I'd remind them of the friendship and the value of the aid, and suggest they should begin reciprocating by getting back into the game.

KALB: And would you also feel that you would actually cut back on both sides if they didn't come through?

BABBITT: That's the question you don't answer in advance among friends.

KALB: Let me just ask you a few more questions about politics, and then we'll go to the audience. When Gary Hart reentered the race, you said we'd know in a few days whether he'd be the front-runner again or whether he'd be a ghost of Christmas past. Christmas has come and gone.

BABBITT: And my crystal ball has been shattered to bits.

KALB: The specific question is, Has Hart's reemergence helped or hurt Bruce Babbitt in Iowa?

BABBITT: Well, Senator Hart entered the race saying, "These other guys have nothing to say. I have a universe of big, bold new ideas," and we ought to hold him to that test. The first debate of 1988 is tomorrow night in Sioux City, Iowa. Senator Hart is not going to be there. What kind of campaign is that? If he has all these great ideas, I think he ought to show up and start talking about them. I thought of something. Maybe he doesn't have the price of a plane ticket. That's a problem in this campaign, too. And I'd be happy to buy him a ticket if he needs it.

KALB: Does it help or hurt Bruce Babbitt in Iowa? You've looked at the numbers. What do they say to you?

BABBITT: I think it's potentially an opportunity, because he comes in claiming to be the harbinger, if not the anointed agent, of new ideas—and that's a turf that I have some interest in. Therefore, I think potentially it's a big help, because if I can kind of flush him out of the woods and actually get him into one of these debates and say, "Okay, you say there are new ideas, but most of them are old, and a lot of them aren't very good." We'll see if we can get a discussion going. That's the opportunity. Obviously, in the short run, he's hurt all of us in the Iowa polls—cut Senator Simon's support in one of those polls in half, and mine in more than half. But in the long run, it's an opportunity.

KALB: Governor, I want to thank you. We're at the point in the program where I stop asking the questions and go out to the audience. Our first questioner is Dean Patricia Graham, who knows a good deal about education here at Harvard University.

GRAHAM: Governor Babbitt, I'd like to ask you a question about how you'd see your role differently as president of the

United States than as governor in the field of education, particularly about the federal government's role in education and what your priorities would be to meet what I believe you call the needs test for federal expenditures, the moral criteria to be used. The current administration has escalated the rhetoric about education to a considerable effect. I wonder what you would do about programs for children of low-income families in the schools, for preschool programs, and for educational research.

BABBITT: I think you covered in the last sentence the real priorities. Early childhood is the source of the greatest opportunity in American education. I'll tell you, I learned one thing as a parent and as an educational reformer in Arizona. After seeing all the delinquency, the dropouts, the drug abuse, I rediscovered something that we all know as parents. And that is, that you can spot the dropouts in the first and second grade. Our failures are coming in early childhood. First grade is too late in a changing society that we all understand the implications of. I think the absolute first priority is universal headstart for four-year-olds and a strong, strong program of subsidized day care in voucher form for working parents. We simply have to get these kids started earlier. Now, the other important education issue is at the university level. It comes in two forms, and one is student aid. I don't think it's realistic to say, and I don't think we should say to students, "You're entitled to a free grant." We should say to every student, "You're entitled to low-interest loans if you want to pursue education." We can forgive them on the back end for public service for teaching, for that kind of thing. We must step up dramatically our aid for research, particularly laboratories and instrumentation.

QUESTION: There's a growing concern from parents and teachers about the increasing use of the abusive drug Ritalin in our school systems, which is considered the most destructive element to the quality of our failing school systems. What would you do about this as president?

BABBITT: There's no silver bullet on drugs. Obviously, eradication at the source, coordination of prosecution efforts. I have to tell you, we're never going to solve the drug problem until we deal with the demand side. Until we change the culture of the demand for drugs.

QUESTION: I want to clarify this, sir. This is actually a psychiatric drug that's used abusively on children for curing a fictitious hyperactivity.

BABBITT: I'm sorry, I'll have to learn a little more about it. I don't know the drug and I don't know the problem. Invite me back.

QUESTION: Governor Babbitt, *The New Republic* named you as a very effective governor of Arizona dealing with a Republican legislature in a very conservative state. I'd be interested to know how you accomplish pushing through progressive legislation in a conservative state, and as president, how you would deal with the legislature, whether you think it's comparable to the Federal legislature, how you deal with Senators Dole and Simon as president.

BABBITT: Senators Dole and Simon? Well, Dole will still be a senator, and so will Simon. Now, let me see if I can translate that question. I think what you're really saying is, Can a governor really deal with the United States Congress? I'll tell you, after nine years of dealing with a wall-to-wall Republican legislature, the United States Congress isn't going to be that difficult. How do you deal with them? You use the veto power, you use the bully pulpit to weigh out an agenda, and you use carrots and sticks. You remember that everybody in Congress needs recognition. Half of them want a new traffic signal in some district or a new school grant program. And you keep a little book; you reward your friends. People who don't cooperate never get the traffic light or the school district. But most of all, you appeal to a sense of common decency and expectations and deal with them as people and recognize them and work with them. It's been done in the past. And it's not that complicated. You have to have some human juice in it, of course.

QUESTION: Mr. Babbitt, in two different newspaper articles, you were described as one who is a master of the art of the impossible in politics, and another one described you as a Catholic who believes in miracles. And I want to know which of those things holds true as far as your chances are concerned to wind up at the other side of the Democratic pack, as you're obviously now?

BABBITT: Wow. Anybody else got a question? I'm a practitioner of the possible. I believe in miracles in this world. How am I going to win in Iowa? Is that what you're really asking? Look, I believe that people out there are sick and tired of candidates who reflect this moral deficit that I talked about, who believe that America really has a future, who understand intuitively that America is winning all over this world, that our ideals are in the ascendency, that we've created a new world economy, that Marxism is dead meat. What we need here are leaders at home who will explain to us candidly how we make a few changes to reach that new world, who will have the guts to say, "There's a ticket to that destination and voyage, and it's not free." We need to deal with that deficit. We need to make these changes in the American workplace. My wager is real simple: that in the Iowa caucuses on February eighth, there's going to be a surprising number of people who will say, "Yeah, that's right, that's what America is about. This guy doesn't have the most money, not the best known, but he's saying something, and he ought to be president." The pollsters are saying who will be president. I think they're going to ask who ought to be president.

KALB: I'd like to call to Mike Labson, a member of the student advisory committee of the Institute of Politics.

LABSON: Governor, my question is about Central America. I read that you would not send aid to the Contras and that you do support the Arias peace plan. Do you think that plan has produced any progress towards peace in Central America, and what do you think the United States role should be in the region?

BABBITT: Look, I think we all understand that the Arias peace plan is having tough sledding. One reason it's been so slow is because the Reagan administration, by its rhetoric and by its deeds, and in the person of Elliott Abrams, is trying to sabotage the Arias peace plan. They're doing everything they can to fulfill their prophecy that it will not work. What should we do? Terminate Contra aid. We should listen to our friends in those countries, back up that peace plan, and try to take a broader view to understand it's the other 97 percent of Central America that's at risk and at issue and it is the opportunity—all the way from Mexico to Panama. The meeting in Guatemala City, I think, began to illustrate the power those presidents have when they come together. And we ought to try to raise the ante economically with trade, with movement back toward a Central American common market with a systematic plan for debt reduction. We should try to get a wave going in the opposite direction.

QUESTION: Governor, in the hearing of Irangate, Ollie North revealed that there is a plan under which, in an emergency situation, all our constitutional liberties can be suspended. Neither the press, newspapers, television, nor the Congress chose to discuss it. Do you know about this plan? Can you explain the need of the press and the Congress not to discuss it? There is a very dangerous precedent: a plan in Germany in 1933. What do you know about it? What can you tell us?

BABBITT: I don't know anything about the plan. If you elect me president, and if I discover it, I will apply a match to it immediately.

QUESTION: Governor, when working-class Americans, particularly those who belong to unions, hear the name Bruce Babbitt, many think immediately of your role as the governor of the state of Arizona and a bitter strike by copper miners against the Phillips Dodge Company. There you mobilized the resources of the state, including the National Guard, to intervene on behalf of the company, escorting strikebreakers across the picket line. As a result, the strike was broken, the union was broken, and thousands of copper miners permanently lost their jobs. My question is, Do you still feel you did the right thing, and can working Americans expect the same treatment at the hands of President Babbitt as the copper miners received under the hands of Governor Babbitt?

BABBITT: That guy is not a Babbitt supporter, I suspect. There were actually two copper strikes, one in 1983. It got bitter, the violence began to escalate, and one night in a small town named Aho, Arizona, there was a lot of random gunfire in the street, and a three-year-old girl named Chandra Terrano woke up in her bed in the middle of the night screaming with blood gushing out of her head. A .22 bullet had gone right through her forehead—just off the street through the head of this child. We airvacked her out to Phoenix, she had emergency surgery, and miraculously she recovered. I went up a couple days later to visit this child, and I walked into this room, and here's this kid sitting in a bed recovered, playing with a teddy bear. The mother picks the kid up—we're all kind of yucking it up—and puts the child in my arms and looks at me, and I'll never forget what she said. She said, "Governor, what are you doing to make sure this doesn't happen to somebody else's three-year-old kid?" About a month later the violence broke out again in another town called Morency—the rocking, the arson, the gunfire. And I did what I had to do as governor: I simply said there isn't going to be anymore violence, I'm going to protect everybody, strikers, scabs, but most of all, innocent people. There was no more violence, and no one else was killed. The union was decertified, and obviously, there wasn't a lot of celebrating about what I had to do as governor. But three years later there was another copper strike—Do you know about that one? Do you know how that one ended up, the 1986 copper strike? What happened? It was settled, they won a contract, right. Went up to a strike deadline, didn't it? There was a long, intense mediation. Do you know who was called in as the mediator in that copper strike? The Governor of Arizona, Bruce Babbitt— because the unions understand that I've supported their efforts across the years. And when they came up to the edge the second time around—I got a call from Pittsburgh, Pennsylvania from the United Steelworkers saying, "We can't find an appropriate mediator. Will you do it?" And I did it: I took them behind closed doors, and I won a settlement. What does that add up to? Bruce Babbitt is a friend of labor. We've had our differences, but I'm a friend of labor.

QUESTION: Governor Babbitt, in recent weeks, national attention has been focused on the racially motivated murders in Howard Beach, New York. Furthermore, in your home state, Governor Mecham has a shaky history, relative to racial relations, and has even abolished the Martin Luther King birthday, among other things.

BABBITT: Established by whom?

KALB: Yourself, sir. Ask the question, please.

QUESTION: In light of Dr. King's upcoming birthday, to what extent do you see racism as a problem in modern America, and as president, what steps would you take to alleviate such problems?

BABBITT: It's a real problem. It kind of reminds me of climbing a mountain. In the last 30 years in this country we've come an extraordinary way—made a lot of progress. I was in the streets of Selma, Alabama in 1965; I spent two years in the civil rights movement. And I watched as we made enormous progress in eliminating the legal barriers, but we've only gone halfway because the economic barriers are still there. The reason tensions are rising is because there's no perception of progress. What would I do as president? First of all, I'd do an extraordinary thing. I'd hire an attorney general who believed in law enforcement. I would then try to deal honestly with the economic issues—kids with no jobs roaming the streets of cities because there aren't any jobs, high school dropouts, continuing discrimination in the workplace. I'd say, "Come on, we can do a better job." We can find the resources to keep those kids in school, to provide public work to help them make the transition and then to get the economy going, and make certain there are jobs for everyone who needs them.

QUESTION: Mr. Governor, Bhopal, India, has witnessed a chemical holocaust. What programs do you have to prevent a multinational corporation from using Third World countries as a dumping ground for solid and hazardous waste, and in case of nuclear and chemical emergency in America, what programs do you have to protect our life?

BABBITT: Look, we haven't had any environmental enforcement in this country. We need to deal with the toxic problem by eliminating the use of toxics, by setting higher toxic standards, by having a national ground water law, by having an acid rain law, and by recognizing that we live in a global commons and what we prohibit at home, we cannot tolerate abroad. We simply have to say we're not only going to provide an example here at home, but we will adopt the same standards abroad, and even go to summit meetings and say the environmental issues ought to be dealt with in the context of international treaty making.

QUESTION: Governor Babbitt, as an Arizonan, welcome. We are besieged in Arizona with the contamination of ground water, here, with the shores and sea and other types of contaminants, including air, of course. As president of the United States, what programs or policies do you have to clean up our environment?

BABBITT: I think the priority is water, because, obviously, it's not just an environmental problem, it's a health problem. Too much lead in water results in mentally retarded infants, too many nitrates, in the blue baby syndrome. We need a law enforcement officer at EPA. We do need a national ground water law. We need to start setting standards for toxics, and they're not doing it. And we need to get on. They've identified 20,000 hazardous waste dumps; they've cleaned up 13. At that rate they'll have the job done in the year 3,000. We need to understand that it's a priority, it must be done.

QUESTION: Governor Babbitt, you've spoken to us about your view on increased worker participation and control in American businesses. My question is a bit more general. What do you perceive as the ideal relationship between American government and private business in this country, and to the extent that your view differs from the relationship as it exists now, what would you as president in 1988 begin to do to change that relationship?

BABBITT: Well, I've talked already about the need for government to set an example, to use the tax system, the regulatory system, the securities and exchange commission, all of those tools, to make a statement, to say we're headed the wrong way when we try to compete by saying to businesses, "You can cut wages, you can exploit workers, and we'll compete by impoverishing workers on the Hong Kong model." It's the wrong way to go. We must turn back instead and encourage participation, equity, and speak out about the abuses of golden parachutes and outrageous employee bonuses—the General Motors model, where you cut workers' wages and then give the managers $170 million in bonuses. But above all, we must deal honestly with this issue of the deficit, because there won't be any jobs, there won't be futures, there won't be money for higher education, for health care for our parents, for education. Marvin, I told you I'd come to it, this issue of the deficit. People aren't being honest about it. What I did in that debate back in December was say to the other candidates, "Let's get honest. Won't you, by standing up, agree with one simple proposition? That in order to assure our future, we will all acknowledge that we have to tell the truth, that we must deal with that deficit, we must cut expenditures and raise taxes." Now, let me ask you, are you willing to stand up and acknowledge that that's the beginning of truth in the political process? Are you willing? Are you willing to stand up?

KALB: We have one more questioner, and that is Kurt Campbell, a lecturer in public policy here at the Kennedy School of Government.

CAMPBELL: I'd like to draw you out a little bit on U.S.-Soviet relations. In the wake of the recent so-called Gorbomania which swept the United States, some have suggested that in fact we've perhaps concentrated too narrowly on his style rather than his substance. In the realm of foreign policy Gorbachev has surrounded himself with a coterie of shrewd and sophisticated foreign policy associates, some with decades of experience. Our own administration has depended on perhaps a less experienced group of advisers. My question to you, Governor, is this: As president, where would you look—in commerce, in business, in academia—for our own foreign service, and to what kind of individuals will you look to help shape American foreign policy, particularly vis-á-vis the Soviet Union?

BABBITT: Of course, I'd start at the Kennedy School of Government.

CAMPBELL: I have a resumé upstairs.

BABBITT: And let me just take that question quickly in two different directions. We've demoralized the foreign service in this country by bringing in amateurs and ideologues rather than relying on talent. There are people right here—Graham Allison, Al Carnesale, Joe Nye. They are all over the United States waiting to be called into service. Now, the fundamental fact of our relationship with the Soviet Union is that it's undergoing a dramatic change. It's a change that's being driven by the fact that American economic ideals are taking root all over this world. The cold war is over. We've won. Marxism is dead. Gorbachev knows that. I don't know whether he's reading my memos or listening to my speeches, but he's ready to sign the death warrant for Marxism. That's the explanation of why it is he's now out seeking accommodation and change. And above all, America must respond. We're not. We're remaining silent, as if we're on the defensive. It's time to recognize the cold war is over, that we're winning, and that together, we can remake the world.

KALB: Governor, finally, in about 15 seconds, what would be the one question you'd like to ask Gorbachev if you sat down with him?

BABBITT: Whether or not Raisa is really running the show.

KALB: Do you think she is?

BABBITT: She's an impressive woman. And so is my wife.

A CONVERSATION WITH
BOB DOLE

Photo by Martha Stewart

About the Candidate

Senator Bob Dole, 64, was the most interesting of the Republican candidates for president, the most like a character in a good novel. The two sides of his body seemed to represent the two sides of his personality. When he spoke, his left arm was in constant motion, making gestures of expansiveness or emphasis, generosity or determination. His right arm, as if in silent reproach to all that animation, stayed still and crooked, the small, wrinkled hand always twisted around the pen he clutched to warn off any unwelcome touch.

That maimed right arm was not only the symbol but also the source of the bitterness—the word was one he often used himself—that had touched his life. In 1945 he was a young officer serving in the elite 10th Mountain Division in Italy when a shell shattered his shoulder. The wound paralyzed him from the neck down for a year, put him in the hospital for 39 months, and left him reluctant to this day to look in the mirror. It also launched his political career. He often quoted the Kansas Republican pol who urged him to run for the state legislature: "You got shot, we can get you elected." The story is typical of Dole's justly celebrated humor: laconic, somewhat bleak, lethal to cant.

Elected to Congress in 1960 and to the Senate in 1968, Dole moved swiftly into the leadership. As President Ford's running mate in 1976, he cost the ticket votes by saying, in his vice presidential debate with Walter Mondale, that all the U.S. conflicts of this century were "Democrat wars." But as majority leader of the Senate during the first Reagan term, he won nearly universal respect as a brilliant and knowledgeable legislative maneuverer. His Goldwaterite views moderated over the years, and although a slashing partisan he was also a master of bipartisan compromise. On the stump in 1988, he often pointed to his support of civil rights legislation and his key role in hammering out the 1981 deal that made social security solvent.

Dole's candidacy presented the most serious threat to that of Vice President George Bush. Dole ran as a can-do senator who had "a record, not a resume." "I've made a difference," he liked to say. His wife, Elizabeth, former secretary of transportation in President Reagan's cabinet, was among his strongest assets. At the time of his appearance on "Candidates '88," he was on the roll that would carry him to victory in the Iowa caucuses. But his campaign was as poorly organized as it was well financed. He would lose in New Hampshire, where most reporters expected (and hoped—he was popular with the press) him to win, and Bush would shut him out on Super Tuesday. After that, his withdrawal would be only a matter of time.

H.H.

The Interview

KALB: Senator, you are now obviously in a graduate school of government, and many of the students here are probably going to choose a career in public service. You've been in politics, which some people say is a form of public service, for more than 20 years, and I wonder on the plus side what you can tell them about the kind of things they can look forward to in public service.

DOLE: They can't look forward to making any money, so you start off on that basis. That's not important anyway, really. But I think if you're interested in public service, and I know many here are, that there are a lot of opportunities to not only help other people, to play pivotal roles in our relationships with other countries around the world. So it depends on whether you're looking for foreign service, something in the domestic field, maybe even politics. That's good public service. And I find a lot of outstanding men and women in politics in both parties.

KALB: What about the down side? What can you warn them about?

DOLE: Well, you have to have a fairly thick skin, particularly if you get on the political side. My mother could never understand those nasty letters to the editor that people wrote about me, or the ones I wrote about others.

KALB: You've just released to the public your tax records for the last 21 years. A lot of people would say that's a very private matter and really not the public's business, but yet you felt the need to do it. Why?

DOLE: Well, George Bush suggested we do that out in Iowa a couple of weeks ago or about ten days ago. I didn't know it was just aimed at me, but apparently it was. So I called him and raised him. He wanted 10 years, and I said let's go for 21. So I want to see his next 11 years because I think it is important. If anybody has any question about what we've done, what we may have, any investments we may have made or anything of that kind, they can take a look at my tax return since 1965. And I think that gives you a pretty good cross-section. They're all out there for people to see.

KALB: Do you think, Senator, the public is demanding too much of its public officials?

DOLE: I don't think so. Once we step into the arena, I don't say we lose all our rights of privacy, but we're going to be closely scrutinized—everything we've ever done, any transaction, if you're in the Congress and you're running for president, your voting record, as it should be. I think sometimes the media struggles with it, too. They don't know just how far to go. We certainly have some rights of privacy, but I don't see it going over the line yet.

KALB: Well, I think on that basis I'm free to ask you virtually any question.

DOLE: And I'm free not to answer.

KALB: I'd like to recall for you a conversation that the two of us had during a taping of "Meet the Press" a year or two ago. I said at that time that it was my impression there are two Bob Doles almost at war in the same person. There is the Bob Dole we see today who talks about compassionate issues and about the poor and the disadvantaged, and broadening the base of the Republican party, and there is the Bob Dole who, at least some of us remember from 1976, accused the Democrats of instigating, in effect, three wars. A million and a half Americans were killed in those Democrat wars. The question is a simple one, Senator: Which is the real Bob Dole?

DOLE: I think I know, but I hope everyone else understands. You have to play a role, whatever you are, Democrat or Republican. In 1976, I was on the ticket with Gerald Ford. We were, depending on what polls you looked at, 10 points, 20 points, 35 points behind when we left Kansas City. We had a very short time, nine weeks, to catch up, and I was sent out into the brier patch and, obviously, my role, as Gerry Ford says in his book, was to go into the brier patch and keep Carter and Mondale on their toes. And I think I did a pretty good job of that. I was the heavy, and I didn't shrink from it, but I didn't think that was the real Bob Dole. I really believe now that I can set the tone. I'm the candidate for president, I'm not the running mate. I'm the candidate, and what I say and what I do, in my view, is the real Bob Dole. Where I am on the issues, what my record is, certainly would underscore that.

KALB: And you did not feel at the time that the Democrats were responsible for the last three wars and the deaths of a million and a half Americans were their responsibility and fault?

DOLE: I don't know if it came out quite that way. That's a pretty shorthand way. But we've been the party of poverty, according to the Democrats; Herbert Hoover is still running in the eyes of some Democrats. And we were the party that caused people depressions and things like that. And we were always the party of peace and "poverty," and they were something else. But I guess, having a little experience in war myself, I didn't know what I was when I was in Italy. I wasn't anything; I wasn't a Democrat or a Republican. I got into politics by accident. Democrats asked me first to run. I said, "I don't know anything about politics." And they said, "You don't need to, you've got a shot. I think we can get you elected." But I became a Republican when I learned there were twice as many Republicans in the county as Democrats. There wasn't any great philosophical judgment on my part.

KALB: Let's talk about the word and the issue of compassion. And there is no question going through your record that you have demonstrated compassion on a number of issues. I'd like to talk about your voting record from one point of view. The *National Journal* has looked through those records of every senator in 1985 and broke the results down into three categories: economic, social, and foreign policy. You were rated as more conservative on economic issues than 86 percent of your colleagues, in the same category as Senator Helms of North Carolina, and on social issues more conservative than 83 percent of your colleagues, and again Senator Helms, and Garn, were in the same high ranking. Isn't there a clear inconsistency between your frequent appeals for compassion and a voting record that is so conservative on the very issues that would help people who are underprivileged?

DOLE: Well, again, I'd have to check those votes. But I was the majority leader then, too, and of course we had a party position, a president's position we had to maintain. Tomorrow, for example, we celebrate Martin Luther King's birthday. I remember that when that bill came to the floor, I managed it—Republican senator from the state of Kansas—we'd been trying for years to get a national holiday, and it fell to me to get the bill passed. I did it. I didn't get Senator Helms's vote and a lot of other votes. We had the genocide convention hanging around for 38 years to get it passed. I said, "We're going to do it next year," and we did it. I'd have to go through issue by issue. The one chairmanship I kept when I was majority leader was the nutrition committee dealing with food stamps and the school lunch program because I understand those programs and I understand the need for those programs. I think it depends; I think my record is fairly consistent. Those may be abortion votes, maybe prayer and school votes.

KALB: These are all of the votes. They went through every vote you cast in 1985.

DOLE: I am conservative. I don't want to suggest otherwise. But I think you can be conservative and still be sensitive and compassionate. And if we're going to build the Republican party as I want to build the Republican party, then we're going to reach out and bring more people in. I don't want to be hide-bound. I don't want to be inflexible.

KALB: Let's talk about that issue of leadership, which is probably the most overused word in this particular campaign from every candidate.

DOLE: Not many leaders.

KALB: Your point is that you have demonstrated leadership in the Congress, and you would now like to demonstrate leadership in the White House, but is the leadership that you demonstrate in the legislative branch a transferable leadership to the White House in your view?

DOLE: I think to some extent it is, because the bottom line is you have to deal with Congress. And presidents don't like congresses. Governors don't like state legislatures, but they're going to be there. And I think if I have any strength—and you can go to any Democrat in either body—it's getting along and dealing with other members. Sometimes we can't agree, sometimes we just say we can't agree. You don't try and work out something you can't work out. So I think it's an advantage I would have. In '76 the pendulum swung, we went to outsiders and got Jimmy Carter. He was an outsider. Four years later we got another outsider, Ronald Reagan. And now the pendulum is swinging back. The American people are saying give me someone who understands a Congress and can make it work—less confrontation, more production—and I believe I may be the right person for the time.

KALB: Senator, I ask the question because in the White House in addition to the art of building coalitions, which is so central on the legislative side, you are also asked as a president to inspire the American people and to set forth the vision for them, for their future. On that issue of vision, could you just very briefly tell us what yours is?

DOLE: I can tell you, but I think you need more than just saying what it is. Everyone wants a better America, more security, education, whatever it may be. But I think you have to go back and look at my past, my legislative record. I think you're going to find in that record a consistent effort to make it a little better for some people, whether it's the tax code, creating more jobs and more opportunities, or whether it's food stamps, working with McGovern—which I'm criticized for by some of my conservative friends—and you find the character of the person. What would this person do if he had the authority? What would he outline for America? What would he want to be in the year 2000 with his foreign policy and his domestic policy? Like everybody else, I want to make the world better. I want America to be stronger. I want more opportunities for young people, more jobs, better education. I want to bring in the disabled and others who have been left out in the cold. So my vision is to look back after a couple of terms and say, "Well, Bob Dole has left a better country. We're stronger. We've handled the deficit, we've dealt with some of the problems dealing with the hungry and the homeless and done it all with a conservative Republican president."

KALB: Senator, I think I ask the question because a lot of people who follow you believe you have a "problem" on this vision issue. The *Wall Street Journal,* for example, ran the following headline over a profile last fall, which you probably remember: "Ferocious Ambition Drives Political Junkie Dole, But Candidate Lacks Carefully Fixed Philosophy."

DOLE: Otherwise it's a very objective piece.

KALB: Now, in terms of a political junkie, I don't think that anybody would particularly argue that, and many of us in this room are as well. But it has to be more than ferocious ambition.

DOLE: If you're driven to be president, you're not going to be very good. I have a lot of stamina, a lot of drive, and I love politics. And you've got to be ambitious. Show me somebody who's not ambitious, and I'll show you somebody who's not going anywhere. I don't care if it's in education or wherever. So I plead guilty to all of those. But I think sometimes you can't let the press set the pace. And they were looking for a vision a year ago, and if I'd had one, they'd say it was no good. And we thought about the "vision of the month club," so I'd have one for spring and one for the fall just for the media.

KALB: But they would point out the inconsistency.

DOLE: That's right. They'd say, "That's the wrong one." So I'd say, "I have another one."

KALB: Senator, if you were president, could you delegate responsibility? I ask it, again because people say you keep things terribly close to the vest. And people who have worked with you say it's tough sometimes with Dole because he can be very quick and sharp.

DOLE: That's right. I wouldn't turn it over to some colonel. I'm one of these who believes that if you're the boss, you ought to have all the information. I'm the one running for office, not Colonel North or Admiral Poindexter. They don't have the right to say what they're going to withhold from me if I'm elected president. I don't have a right to tell the American people, "I can deny this because nobody told me what was supposed to be." And Ronald Reagan accepted that responsibility. So yes, I want to delegate, but I'm not going to be Jimmy Carter and check people in and out on the tennis court. But I'm going to know what's going on in the White House whether down in the basement or upstairs.

KALB: You mentioned North and Poindexter, so I would like to ask if you agree with the vice president; are they national heroes, certainly North?

DOLE: I've said before, I think we toss the word *hero* around pretty loosely these days. I haven't known many heroes in my lifetime. I thought General Eisenhower was a hero. And I can name a lot of individuals who are not in politics who are heroes who saved somebody's life or done something that ought to be recognized. I think Colonel North may have been a patriot, but certainly not a hero. He didn't serve his president well; he didn't serve his commander in chief well. In my books, he's not a hero, and hero is something I feel strongly about. It's a small group of men or women who have made an outstanding contribution. This man almost pulled down his president or could have pulled down his president. To me, you don't get an award of excellence for that.

KALB: Senator, let's talk about foreign policy for a little while. There's a fairly widespread impression that you may be developing your views of foreign policy issues from the standpoint of either the Republican party or specific partisan domestic interests rather than a very broad historical conceptual vision of America's place in the world. In other words, if it's good for the Republicans, it may be good for the United States and Bob Dole. Is that unfair?

DOLE: I don't know if I'd put it quite that way, but obviously when you're in the Senate you've got one role to play. You're a legislator, you're dealing with what the president sends to you. My president, Ronald Reagan, I think he's done a good job. So from that standpoint, maybe it's not what's good for Republicans is good for everybody else. But if it's Contra policy or Persian Gulf policy, then as a Republican leader, I either carry the ball or give the ball to somebody else. Sometimes you carry the ball when you don't want the ball. That's the way it works.

KALB: What issues were like that?

DOLE: I had a few reservations. Let's take the Persian Gulf. We were told by some that we were going to make $5 million off of each ship we were going to reflag. That didn't make much sense. We were talking about foreign policy, about getting into a treacherous area, exposing young Americans to danger. I thought we had a right to be in the gulf; we've been there 40 years. I don't quarrel with that. And now we have a little more burden sharing with our allies. The policy seems to be working. But I voiced some reservations up front. I voiced reservations even about the Contra policy. I get a little troubled by the people living in plush hotels in Miami saying we ought to send more money so these 18- and 19-year-olds can go out and fight. I believe in the freedom fighters, I support the policy, but I still have reservations and I would like to see a settlement there. And maybe what Ortega has done recently may tend to go in that direction, but I doubt it. I don't think he's very credible. So I would guess that in a number of areas we have had some reservations, but in the final analysis you can only have one president. And I may get a question on apartheid and South Africa—I saw a few people carrying little signs out there. I'm not so certain sanctions are the best policy. I think apartheid is repugnant. But I also think it's good for the Americans to speak with one voice, not the Congress speaking and the president speaking. In this particular case the President is willing to do everything except one thing the Congress wanted, and so Congress said we can't do that, and we'll just override his veto. It seems to me that I understand foreign policy in a broad sense.

KALB: Senator, let's try to tick off, if we can, a couple of these issues, starting with U.S.-Soviet relations. You have described Gorbachev as the fit, truly modern Soviet leader. But at the same time you went on to say he's selling the same worn-out solutions. If he is selling the same worn-out solutions, do you then feel this is not a particularly propitious moment for improving U.S.-Soviet relations?

DOLE: I think he's selling the same solutions, but he's saying that he's not. He's selling glasnost and he's restructuring and all those things. He's young, he's articulate, he's dynamic. He even had a favorable poll rating versus Reagan when he was shaking hands with Bush up and down the street there. So my view is he's for real and he's going to be there for a while. I don't think the issue is whether or not we trust Gorbachev. The issue is that we have to continue dialogue with the Soviet Union. We ought to have a meeting every year, not have a summit every three or four years. We ought to have a lot of expectations—and say, okay, every March 1, we're going to meet and sit down and talk about our problems. We want arms reduction. We also want to make certain we protect our interests. So anything I do with Mr. Gorbachev, the bottom line is going to be whether it is in our national interests, not whether or not I trust him. He's there, they're for real, and they're a Super Power.

KALB: Do you feel you made a political mistake by not endorsing the medium-range missile treaty more quickly than you did?

DOLE: Before I read it? That's what Bush was asking me to do, George Bush that is. It seems to me it took Ronald Reagan three years to negotiate the treaty, so I should have three weeks to look at it. I wanted to check with people I had confidence in and people who are experts in nuclear weapons—I'm not—and make a judgment. So I have a lot of visits with a lot of people. As I said last night in Hanover, I even called Margaret Thatcher. I didn't know whether she'd take my phone call or not, but she had seen the Iowa polls and took my call. I wanted to make certain that they were really on board, because we were being told by some very good people in the country that we twisted allies' arms. But she was strongly on board. I met with the prime minister of Italy. I talked to Helmut Kohl. I talked to Richard Nixon, I talked to Gerald Ford, I talked to General Rogers—a lot of people who have had a lot more experience than I have. And I told the President I'm ready to support the treaty. And I think we're going to have 90 votes for ratification.

KALB: I want to ask you about a possible reservation. At the Dartmouth forum, you said that the points raised by Alexander Haig were very valid. And if I understood Haig, he was saying after a year and a half, or half way into the implementation phase, we would check and see what the Russians were doing on conventional forces, what they were doing on strategic forces, and if we thought that they weren't reforming as we thought they should, then we would stop the implementation of that missile treaty. Is that the kind of reservation you would like to see added to the treaty during the debate in the Senate?

DOLE: You don't have to do that. There's already a clause in there: six months' notice, either side can terminate—sort of boiler-plate treaties. So it's there.

KALB: I'm talking about the year-and-a-half to look at it at that particular time.

DOLE: Well, there's a three-year phase-in on removing the missiles. And I hope it's going to fall to me. I hope I'm the next president, because not much is going to be done in Reagan's last year. But, if I'm the one, I'll have to make certain it's being verified—verify what the Soviets are doing and they're going to verify what we've done. And if we find it's not happening, then yes, you terminate it. But I don't think we're going to add any reservation that would take care of Mr. Haig's problem. That may come in the next treaty. If we get a START agreement, then we have to worry about Soviets in Afghanistan, about emigration policy, about conventional weapons in Europe. There are a whole host of things.

KALB: Let's move on to SDI, the strategic defense initiative. You said last summer, "We can't just give it away or bargain it away or legislate it away. There is no higher priority than preserving the promise or prospect of SDI." What do you mean "no higher priority"? You have already ticked off very high priorities.

DOLE: That day.

KALB: That day is top priority?

DOLE: I was talking about defense. I was talking in that context.

KALB: Would you go for deployment of SDI as quickly as you possibly could as president of the United States?

DOLE: As quickly as there's something to deploy. Jack Kemp is saying deploy now. As far as I know, there's nothing there. I have periodic meetings with General Abrahamson, who I think is pretty reliable. He's a pretty good source. We're not going to be looking at that until the mid-90s. But I would be willing to deploy if there's something to do.

KALB: On the Middle East, particularly right now, the Israeli-Palestinian problem, would you have done what President Reagan did, namely to go along with the Security Council condemnation of Israel for the deportation of Palestinians?

DOLE: I would have done it very reluctantly. I think they're excessive force there.

KALB: As president, what specific steps would you take to use American influence to promote a settlement between the Israelis and the Palestinians?

DOLE: Obviously, everything you could do. But if we look back at the Camp David Accords, it probably wasn't so much one of the finest hours that President Carter had, but we had Anwar Sadat and Begin—they made the difference—leaders in Egypt and Israel who were willing to come together and reach an agreement. I'm not certain we have that now. As I said last night also in the debate, every time there's a down side maybe there's an up side. With all these problems in Gaza and the West Bank and the Israelis being taunted by the radicals and the Israelis probably using too much force, maybe there's an opportunity for the United States.

KALB: Any specific ideas you have?

DOLE: As Al Haig says, there're already some things going on. I don't know what they are. But if we can bring the parties together and start the process, let's just start a process. And I don't think we need to include the Soviets in it, either.

KALB: What would happen if you were president, on the domestic side? You have said one of the first things you would do is bring together the leaders of the Congress and hammer out a settlement that would bring some kind of resolution on the budget deficit question. Could you share with us what specific steps? What would be your vision of that kind of domestic settlement?

DOLE: I think I know one thing we can agree on, knowing the members of Congress like I do—and I think that's a big advantage. I think I know precisely what they would tell me. I think we'd agree on a freeze.

KALB: For a year, two, three?

DOLE: That depends. If you want to freeze budget authority, you'd need more than a one-year freeze. A one-year freeze would save you about $50 billion the first year, $150 billion over three years. And I think that's something we can work out. They might not want to go for a freeze on outlays—that means how much is actually spent. There is room for compromise there because even as we were talking about deficit reduction last year in late December, I think there were 28 senators who took to the Senate floor and said they'd support a one-year freeze. And these were people like Joe Biden on the Democratic side, Nancy Kassebaum, my colleague, and very credible Republicans and Democrats.

KALB: Is this the major element in a Dole package?

DOLE: That's fairly major. I'd like a lot of other things—line-item veto and a balanced budget. But Congress has to start. I think we can start and reach some agreement on some option of a freeze. Maybe it's a freeze plus 1 percent, maybe everybody gets a 2 percent raise, but that's saving real money.

KALB: Now let me get to that taxes issue. George Bush says no tax increases under any circumstances. Jack Kemp says essentially the same thing. You seem to be saying under some circumstances possibly—

DOLE: I hope not.

KALB: I said you seem to be saying maybe some increase in taxes. If I'm wrong in that, just tell me. Under no circumstances no tax increases?

DOLE: I said as specifically as I could, we don't need to raise tax rates. We had tax reform in '86—took a lot of things away from a lot of people. We said we were going to lower the rates. And then we said we ought to freeze the rates, raise the rates. Let's let the rates trigger in at the lowest possible rate. We can still do a lot of things to get revenue if we have to have revenue. Don't change the rates on individuals or businesses. They can't operate that way.

KALB: But an oil import tax is something you could support?

DOLE: I could support, under certain conditions, rebates on heating oil—use the extra money to increase the petroleum reserve.

KALB: Let me ask you one thing on this also which I was curious about in the Dartmouth debate. Kemp spoke about "morning in America," and you quickly said, "high noon in America." What is the distinction you were trying to draw there?

DOLE: Well, I'm from out west; Dodge City is in my state. And we use the term "high noon." That's the time to get ready and do something. It takes a while to get up in the morning. We need to deal with the deficit now. It's high noon in America. It's time we sat down together and said we're going to hammer out the deficit reduction package. We'll stay here all week or two weeks. We're not being fair to our children and grandchildren. People in this school, people viewing us, expect more from us.

KALB: Senator, for a minute or two, you have had an off-again, on-again spat with the vice president for the last couple of weeks in the campaign, and I'd like to ask whether there's anything personal between the two of you or if it's differences on issues?

DOLE: I think I have a feeling we both want the same office.

KALB: So what does that mean? What are the differences between you?

DOLE: It means the stakes are pretty high, and he was supposed to be the nominee. That was all laid out already, and there wasn't any alternative. And I've kept saying that I think there is an alternative, and I'm trying to be that alternative. I'm pushing very hard, but I've never said anything derogatory or critical of him as a person. I've said he doesn't have a record, and I'm talking about a voting record. He doesn't have a legislative record, but he's got a good resumé. And this is a national job application we've made and everybody has a chance to make recommendations. I think I'm a leader who could make a difference. So that's not personal.

KALB: On the issue of the Iran-Contra scandal, the vice president has said, "I believe nobody here is going to do anything but tear down the President, tear down the party, and further add to the Democratic fuel by continuing to debate this, the Iran-Contra scandal. The questions have been answered." Do you believe all the questions concerning the vice president's role in this scandal have, in fact, been raised and answered?

DOLE: Again, I think the vice president is right. I think the Iran-Contra thing died about six months ago. There isn't that much interest. A lot of people are concerned; they're concerned about the institution. They're concerned about the presidency. The President accepted responsibility. I said that it's an issue of credibility. How many positions can you have? First you're in the loop, then you're not in the loop, then you weren't at the meeting, and then Shultz, and somebody says you were in the meeting. All I said is that it would be in the vice president's interest to lay it all out.

KALB: Has he laid it all out?

DOLE: I don't know. I don't want to be critical of the vice president. It's not my nature.

KALB: Do you feel that he lacks credibility on this issue?

DOLE: Well, I think there is a question of credibility. Let's face it, you've already questioned me on some things where my credibility may be at stake, that I vote like Jesse Helms—you're questioning not very nicely.

KALB: Not very nicely?

DOLE: No, very nicely. You asked if I can be compassionate and be with Jesse Helms. My answer is yes. We're all going to be questioned on credibility. We've got to be credible. The American people want to believe in someone. They want to say, "I don't care how he voted, can he justify it?" The bottom line is the American people want somebody they can believe in, somebody who might even be an inspiration in some way.

KALB: Some of the American people are in the audience, so I'll stop asking questions and allow them to begin. Our first questioner is Ernest May, professor of history at Harvard, who knows a good deal about how the U.S. government works.

MAY: I wanted to ask a little bit more about your sense of how you would manage the executive branch. You've said that you would not delegate as much as President Reagan has, but you wouldn't micro-manage as President Carter did. And I wonder how you think about borrowing from other presidents, to the extent you might think your style of managing the executive branch might resemble Mr. Nixon's or some Democrat's?

DOLE: I look back over the presidents that I've known and the ones I've observed—I came in when John Kennedy was inaugurated and didn't have that much contact with President Kennedy, though he had a lot of bright people around him. I think right up front you have to bring people into the government who are really enthusiastic about giving of themselves. It's not the dollars involved. You need to pay people. Some people who are very able have to be paid. Others are willing to give two or three years of their life to public service. So you start by getting the very best people you can to serve in your cabinet. You're going to know pretty much who you're going to want as your chief of staff. And that's my premise. I don't have anybody out in Russell, Kansas, wanting to get in the cabinet. So we don't have a big cadre of people in Russell ready to move into the White House if I get elected. So there are no cronies out there that I know of, put it that way. So I would start on that premise. Second, it has to be understood right up front, nothing is withheld from the president. Harry Truman is right—the buck stops here. I think President Reagan used a sort of cabinet council approach. It was a pretty good approach, where different cabinet members, if they have any jurisdiction over any subject matter, get together and kick it around and make recommendations to the president. You have to use your cabinet. You want people you can rely on. I'm not an expert on everything, so I would want that. I think of management style; I watched Gerry Ford pretty closely. I think despite what happened to Richard Nixon, he brought a lot of good people into government. A lot of them weren't involved in Watergate. He had a very good management style. I think Ronald Reagan has a management style that's a little different than others. I'd tend to be more hands-on. I wouldn't want to hold on to everything, but I think the American people expect us to have a pretty good idea of what's going on, and if we see something happening in the Department of Transportation or the Defense Department that's an outrage, I ought to deal with it myself.

QUESTION: I represent a group here at the school concerned with disability issues. You mentioned your desire to address the needs of disabled people earlier. Given two-thirds of working-age disabled people are neither working nor looking for work, how would you plan, through programs, legislation, reform, et cetera, to change our current disability policies in the areas of employment, or education, et cetera?

DOLE: Well, I don't want to sound self-serving, but I think just having me in the White House would change the attitudes of a lot of people. I think you'd have a lot of private sector people willing to take a look at people with disabilities. Not that mine's that severe, but I've had one. I think I could help just from the standpoint of being in the bully pulpit and letting people know there are 35 million Americans out there with disabilities who are just like the rest of us. Maybe they can't talk or walk, but they can think and produce. So you start on that basis. I'd want to take a look at all the federal programs and make certain disabled Americans are being given opportunities in the federal government as far as hiring is concerned—every opportunity that everybody else has. So I'd try to set a standard myself and make people adhere to it.

QUESTION: Senator Dole, by all accounts you fought bravely in World War II, and you sustained a serious wound. Therefore, I ask you, having seen the horrors of war, how do you sleep at night given your active support of South African-backed insurgence in Mozambique that carried out numerous massacres, including one where over 400 men, women, and children were hacked to death?

DOLE: I don't know how this all got started. What I said a year ago in a letter was that we ought to use any structure to get food to the starving people. I haven't supported the "freedom fighters." I'm not sure there are "freedom fighters." That's not been one area I've been out on in front—the "freedom fighters" for Mozambique. I think that's been misconstrued because the nomination of Melissa Wells was held up for several months. But I voted for her nomination. Robert Byrd was the majority leader and could have called it up any time. We held it up thinking in this case Senator Helms and Secretary Shultz could work out their differences, but they couldn't do that. I think somebody misstated my position.

QUESTION: Senator Dole, what do you think we should do with our problematic nuclear power plants? We have Wolf Creek in your home state. On the East Coast we have the Shoreham and Seabrook nuclear power plants. Do you think these plants, which are completed but not yet operating, should operate? And secondly, do you think that the electric utility industry should be deregulated so we can avoid similar problems like this in the future?

DOLE: I think one thing we ought to do from now on, if we license another nuclear plant, we ought to have the evacuation plan agreed to before we grant the license, instead of the reverse. That's why we're in trouble in Seabrook. As far as Seabrook is concerned, there is a perception in this country that the Nuclear Regulatory Commission is in bed with the industry. That may or may not be right. I don't have any evidence to say it's right. But if it's a concern, then I suggest we bring in the National Academy of

Sciences. Look at the plan. They're nonpartisan, they're nongovernment, and they're experts. They've already agreed in a letter that they'd be happy to do that as far as Seabrook or Wolf Creek or anything else.

KALB: Our next questioner is John Bender, who is a member of the student advisory committee of the Institute of Politics.

BENDER: Senator Dole, I want to get back to the issue of a budget deficit. A budget freeze is still not going to reduce the budget deficit, because you still have the interest to worry about, and a lot of investors throughout the world are going to wonder if that's really going to restore confidence. Do you have any additional specific measures to tackle the budget deficit that will actually reduce it as opposed to prevent it from getting worse? Value added tax, corporation tax, cuts in social spending, anything else?

DOLE: Well, I agree that the freeze is not the best policy. If I could have my way for a couple of days as president, I could figure out a pretty good budget, if I didn't have to send it to Congress. And we could reduce spending and send the right signals around the world. But the budget freeze is fair. I find that most Americans, regardless of party—and I have a lot of support from Independents and Democrats—say this is fair and across the board, the only exception being low income, food stamps, Medicare, older Americans' programs, whatever. Then I think we send this signal. If we have $150 billion in real savings over a three-year period, we're sending a strong signal to markets and around the world. The best policy would be to kick out the bad programs and maybe increase the others. But the interest is not 14 percent of the budget. It's gone up from 7 to 14 percent in the last seven years. The debt is almost two and a half trillion dollars. We have to deal with it or we're robbing our children and our grandchildren from opportunities they should have in the future.

QUESTION: Senator, in last week's Iowa debate you said that S-2, the current campaign legislation to limit special interest PAC contributions, was not a PAC bill when, in fact, if S-2 would have been in effect in the 1986 election, it would have cut PAC contributions to all 1986 Senate candidates by two-thirds, from $45 million to $16 million—

KALB: Could you get to the question, please.

QUESTION: How can you say that you're for campaign reform when you have been blocking the effort with a filibuster?

DOLE: Well, it takes 40 people to carry out a filibuster, and

I'm only one. I see the pickets around, and I appreciate all the attention Common Cause has given me. But I think they overestimate my importance. I'm for campaign reform. When it costs 15 or 16 million dollars to run for the United States Senate in any state, then we've got to take a look at it. I'm not for public financing. I don't think we've reduced PACs enough in S-2. We think we're going to get a campaign reform bill in 1988. But there's one other thing about S-2 you should understand. I don't know your party affiliation. Hopefully, it's Republican. But if you live in the South, where you're outnumbered 4 or 5 to 1, S-2 says you can only spend X dollars. They put a cap on how much you can spend. You might as well tell the Republican party in the South, "You're never going to elect anybody." It's 5 to 1 registration against you. You can't go out and spend more money. You can't go out and create enthusiasm. In effect, S-2 is a perpetuity bill for the Democrats in this country. You give me a state where it's 50 percent Republican and 50 percent Democratic, then let's put a cap on it. But we want competition in politics. I think we can get a campaign reform bill that's not quite like S-2. And Barry Goldwater doesn't support S-2 anymore because of those problems.

QUESTION: Senator Dole, anti-Americanism is very much alive and well in Canada. It is being fed by the Polar Sea incident, the failure to deliver on acid rain legislation, and also the failure to recognize the culture sovereignty issue that is very important to Canadians. What will you do as president to shore up our relationship with the Canadians and avoid them being driven to be anti-American?

DOLE: I haven't thought much about that except in the acid rain area. We've had enough study of acid rain. It's time to get together on a program. I could go into some powerful forces in the United States Senate who won't let that legislation come up. But in Canada right now there's some positive things. The free trade is an excellent opportunity to build a better relationship with Canada. I support the free trade agreement. I think it's going to be adopted by the Congress and the parliament in Canada.

QUESTION: Senator Dole, as I understand it, the Senate Committee on Environment and Public Works recently suggested reauthorization of the Clean Air Act. Senator Byrd has come out against this bill. When it comes to the floor, what will be your position and what is your position on the environment in general?

DOLE: Senator Byrd opposes the bill because it ties into the last question. He feels strongly about acid rain. I can understand, he's from West Virginia. And he's fearful we're not going to have a balanced program, that we're going to close a lot of coal mining plants in his district or state. So he wants clean coal technology before we get into acid rain and how many tons are reduced in emission last year. What we did in the final days of the session last year is extend the Clean Air Act for eight months. It doesn't expire until August. I hope when that extension is over we can really get into all the issues. But let's face it, it's an election year. I have a feeling there's going to be another extension to 1989. And then I'll be in a position to send a program up to Congress.

QUESTION: Senator Dole, the Republican party, as you know, has had an image problem, regarding insensitivity toward the poor and disadvantaged. We hear people like Senator Paul Simon say things about going back to New Deal type programs, social spending, those kind of things. What would you do as president to help the poor and disadvantaged?

DOLE: I guess this gets back to the vision question Marvin asked me. You know what Bob Dole is going to do based on my record. I'm not going to let somebody go homeless or hungry in America. That's a tragedy that can't happen in America. If nobody is there to do it, the federal government is going to do it. I'm going to have a day care program. We've got a lot of low- and middle-income women with no place to take their children. I also want to encourage the private sector to get into more day care. We've got another problem; we have a long-term health care. We can pay for the day care thing by cutting out that nice little tax credit that goes up to $80,000. We can do a lot of things without spending more money, and we can do them in the Republican party. There is that perception that somehow we don't care about the people at the bottom—those who have been left out or the down and out—that we only care about those at the top. That's not an accurate perception. And again, I think someone like myself—and I don't have much and I've had a few bumps in my lifetime—I can set the tone for the administration and the party.

QUESTION: Senator Dole, you proposed a budget freeze across the board to deal with the deficit, yet at the same time the budget freeze does not really deal with the issue of priorities. The whole reason we elect people is to set priorities. Education, human services and even the state services have been cut under Reagan, while defense has skyrocketed. Do you honestly believe that a freeze is good public policy? Are we electing you to freeze the budget or set our priorities?

DOLE: As I said, it's not the best policy. But we have something to deal with. It's called the deficit. It's two and a half trillion dollars and it's going to go up to three trillion if we don't deal with it. Some say ten trillion before we get to deal with it. My policy would be to go through each program, kick out the bad and increase the good. You're never going to get that done in 1989. I think I've got about six or nine months as president in 1989 to start something. And I would start with a freeze. It is high noon in America. And then we can go back to what you suggest.

QUESTION: On the trade deficit issue, you've said you believe in opening markets, not closing them, and you've opposed some protectionist legislation. Presidents and congressmen have been saying this for years and the trade deficit has grown to huge proportions. What would you do specifically to open markets, and would this make a serious dent in the deficit?

DOLE: I believe in access and open markets. Where countries have competitive products they ought to come into our country, and we can get into their markets if we're competitive. If they're open and accessible—that's the big hang-up. So Senator Byrd and I put an amendment on the trade bill that says if there's a consistent pattern of fair trade practices, and the president won't act, Congress can act. So what we're looking for is something in the nature of reciprocity. We want the Japanese to know and friends in the European community to know it's a two-way street, and a lot of it is going to be sitting down at the next alliance summit and talking about we're not going to accept just another Japanese plan. We want concrete actions. We want the British and the Germans to stimulate their economy so they can buy more of our product.

QUESTION: Senator Dole, although many legislators have expressed interest in some form of national catastrophic health insurance that would include provisions for custodial care, have you any specific ideas how such a program might be administered and what provisions for funding might make such a program affordable for all Americans?

DOLE: Are you talking about long-term care?

QUESTION: Yes, sir.

DOLE: We don't want to limit it to just custodial care just because we get old.

QUESTION: I meant it would include custodial care.

DOLE: You might want adult day care. You might want home health care. When we get old, we ought to have options. It's not in the catastrophic bill that we passed in the Senate, that I think is going to be signed by the President later on, because of the costs.

We have to get these young people around—when they go to work, to set money into a payroll deduction plan for long-term health care. Medicare doesn't cover long-term health care. And a lot of older people are going to find out they have to spend down—go down to Medicaid or poverty to get any benefit. We've found in some states, people happily married for 50 years have to get a divorce to qualify for long-term health care. It shouldn't happen in America. So it's going to cost people money. We need to start working with the private sector, the insurance sector, to make certain young people are going to have it when they're 60 or 70 years of age.

QUESTION: Senator Dole, many people in the Republican party question your dedication to conservative goals. For example, in comparing you to Jack Kemp, one conservative leader said Jack Kemp is a conservative and Bob Dole is a politician.

DOLE: Who said that?

QUESTION: I believe it was Sandy Shoal. Do you see a problem trying to convince the conservative movement that you are one of them and at the same time retaining appeal to moderates?

DOLE: I'm trying to appeal to Americans, and I think most persons tend to be moderate to conservative. I don't have a quarrel with Jack Kemp, but somebody has to govern. I listen to Jack and Pete du Pont in the debate. They're against everything—we're not for this, we're not for this. What are they for? How are you going to send out social security checks if you didn't vote for the '83 Social Security Act? We live in a real world with real problems. I think my record is conservative. It's a good conservative record. I supported the President's tax reduction. I fought off efforts to repeal the third year of the tax cut. I closed a lot of loopholes and if I find a loophole where somebody is getting an unintended tax break, I'll close it. That's not raising taxes, that's equity. How are you going to get the American people to pay taxes if you find a big corporation getting millions and millions of tax dollar refunds through safe-harbor leasing which is a fraud?

KALB: Our last questioner is Marshall Goldman, a professor of economics at Wellesley College and associate director of the Russian Research Center here at Harvard.

GOLDMAN: Marvin, I want to thank you on behalf of all the viewers for having this idea. It's a wonderful idea. But my question is, Senator, Marvin mentioned that you initially were critical of the INF agreement. Yet I just came across a transcript of a press conference that took place during the summit just after you met with General Secretary Gorbachev. Senator Dole said, "The time-table is unrealistic and some Republican may want it to take longer. I congratulate you, Mr. Gorbachev, on the treaty. We'd like a big vote on the treaty." Then you became critical. Is that the way to conduct relations with the Soviets? Give them one signal, then publicly, give them another signal? Which is the real Senator Dole?

DOLE: I think there is more to it to that. In fact, there was an effort to get Bob Dole on board while Gorbachev was in town, and I told Mr. Gorbachev. I tried to arrange a private meeting with him, and I couldn't do it. But again, I think we told him how things were going in Iowa and we were able to see him for a few moments. But I told him I thought the treaty would be ratified. But before Bob Dole got on board as a Republican leader—because one thing as a leader, you have to convince your colleagues—I took 10 Republican senators down to see Ronald Reagan and I said, "Mr. President, here are 10 votes for you." I told Mr. Gorbachev it was going to be ratified whether Bob Dole is on board or not. But I wanted to check with Margaret Thatcher and other people I knew quite well. So the answer is, I think I did it right. I hope to see Gorbachev again. Next time he'll have breakfast with me.

GEORGE BUSH

About the Candidate

During the long run up to the 1988 presidential campaign, the smart money in that amorphous group of operatives, pollsters, journalists, and hangers-on known as "the political community" didn't think much of George Bush's chances. Too wimpy, these insiders would say. Also, they'd go on, Bush hadn't won an election on his own since he was a Congressman back in 1970; the conservatives didn't trust him; his c.v. was long on appointive jobs and short on real accomplishments; his mile-wide support was an inch deep; he was inept in debate; and he had absolutely nothing to say. He might have money and endorsements, but once the voters got into the act they would make short work of him. And anyway, the inside dopesters would add, driving what they imagined was the last nail into Bush's political coffin, what about the fact that no sitting vice president has been elected president for more than a century and a half?

Well, at least as of the spring of 1988, things didn't seem to be working out quite the way the insiders had predicted. Consider the last point first. It is true that the last veep to win the top job was Martin Van Buren, in 1836. But the notion that the vice presidency is some sort of political curse, blighting the careers of those unlucky enough to occupy it, is absurd. Of the nine vice presidents before Bush, four became president and six became their party's presidential nominee. And in seven of the last ten elections, the ticket of one or both parties has been headed by someone whose career had included a stint in the chair of Throttlebottom.

Bush certainly took his lumps for his down-the-line loyalty to Reagan. George Will called him a "lapdog." Garry Trudeau's "Doonesbury" comic strip had years of fun at Bush's expense, ridiculing him for putting his "manhood" in a "blind trust" and then depicting him as invisible. But Bush's loyalty also paid major dividends, winning him the support of many doubting conservatives and enabling him to ride Reagan's coattails—which, despite the Iran-Contra scandal, remained long among Republican primary voters. And Bush was able to use the clout and visibility of his job to build a superb, smoothly running organization and a gigantic campaign treasury.

In terms of experience in government, Bush at 63 was as well-prepared a candidate as the country had ever seen. His famous resume included two terms in the House of Representatives from the Houston area, two unsuccessful but presumably character-building races for senator from Texas, and a panoply of high government and political posts: ambassador to the United Nations; chairman of the Republican National Committee; ambassador to China; director of the Central Intelligence Agency; and of course the two terms as vice president. There was no doubt about his ability to find the men's room, no doubt about his proficiency at being what Washingtonians, addicted to sports metaphors, called a team player. The doubts—and there were plenty—centered mostly on two things: first, his ability to lead on his own, and second, his notions, if any, of where he wanted to take the country—what he sometimes referred to irritably as "the vision thing."

Yet Bush had been groomed for leadership, and he early showed a talent for it. A child of wealth and privilege, he grew up in Greenwich, Connecticut, and went to school at Andover, enlisted in the military, and at 18 became the youngest combat pilot in the U.S. Navy. He was a genuine war hero: 1228 hours in the air, 58 missions, 126 carrier landings, shot down in combat and rescued by a submarine—all before he was 21. After the war he completed Yale in two and a half years, captaining the baseball team and getting tapped for Skull & Bones, the most exclusive of the college's secret societies.

After graduation, by now married and a father, Bush struck out for Texas, where, with a bit of help from his banker father, Prescott Bush, he made a modest mark in the oil business. George Bush dabbled in the Eisenhower campaign against Robert A. Taft in 1952, the same year Prescott Bush won a Senate seat back in Connecticut. By the early 1960s George, too, was ready for full-time politics. In 1963 he became Houston's GOP chairman, saving the county party organization from a John Birch Society takeover. In 1964 he lost a bid for senator in the Johnson landslide, but in 1966 he won a seat in the House of Representatives, the first Republican congressman ever from Houston.

Bush compiled a generally moderate record during his three terms in the House. At President Nixon's urging, and against his father's advice, he gave up his safe seat to run for senator again, and was again defeated. Nixon rewarded him for his effort with the United Nations job, starting him on the ladder he has now climbed nearly to the top.

Bush has assiduously built ties to conservative groups, but it seems clear that he remains what he was bred to be: a mainstream Republican, as opposed to an ideological conservative. He is a man of the party, not of the movement. His most intimate advisers are moderates, a circumstance that presumably reflects his own under-lying inclinations. A Bush administration would probably bring a return to the kind of cautious, measured policies that marked the presidencies of Eisenhower, Nixon, and Ford. In this sense Bush is more truly "conservative" than Reagan and Reagan's ideological heirs.

After Bush lost to Bob Dole in the Iowa caucuses, it looked as if the smart money might be proved right after all. The Bush campaign teetered briefly on the lip of the abyss. But Dole's momentum stalled during the weekend before the New Hampshire primary, and after Bush's victory there and his Super Tuesday sweep it looked like clear sailing all the way to November. There were still some dangerous mines in those calm seas, however. The trials of the principals in the Iran-Contra scandal carried the potential for serious embarrassment; and so, less seriously, did the candidate's own penchant for fatuous remarks ("deep doo-doo," and the like). But by April, of the thirteen candidates who had set out on the long road to the White House only George Bush had a better than even chance of getting there. Maybe the key to political success in 1988 was avoiding an appearance on "Candidates '88."

H.H.

INDEX